The Thinking Muse

THE THINKING MUSE

Feminism and Modern French Philosophy

EDITED BY
JEFFNER ALLEN
AND IRIS MARION YOUNG

Indiana University Press
Bloomington and Indianapolis

Manufactured in the United States of America

Library of Congress Cataloging-in-Publication Data

The Thinking muse.

Bibliography: p.
Includes index.
1. Feminism.   2. Philosophy, French—20th century.
I. Allen, Jeffner.   II. Young, Iris Marion.
B2424.F45T47   1989   194'.088042   88–45388
ISBN 0–253–35980–5
ISBN 0–253–20502–6 (pbk.)

1 2 3 4 5 93 92 91 90 89

CONTENTS

ACKNOWLEDGMENTS

The editors would like to thank the following for permission to reproduce copyright material:

Feminist Studies, Inc., c/o Women's Studies Program, University of Maryland, College Park, MD 20742, for Jo-Ann Pilardi, "Female Eroticism in the Works of Simone de Beauvoir," revised and expanded from *Feminist Studies* 6, no. 2 (1980):304–13; the editor of *Human Studies* for Iris Marion Young, "Throwing Like a Girl: A Phenomenology of Feminine Body Comportment, Motility, and Spatiality," reprinted from *Human Studies* 3 (1980):137–56; the editor of *Philosophy and Social Criticism* for Jeffner Allen, "An Introduction to Patriarchal Existentialism: A Proposal for a Way Out of Existential Patriarchy," revised and expanded from *Philosophy and Social Criticism* 9 (1982):450–65; the editor of *Hypatia: A Journal of Feminist Philosophy* for Julien S. Murphy, "The Look in Sartre and Rich," reprinted from *Hypatia: A Journal of Feminist Philosophy* 2, no. 2 (1987):113–24; Columbia University Press for Domna C. Stanton, "Difference on Trial: A Critique of the Maternal Metaphor in Cixous, Irigaray, and Kristeva," from Nancy K. Miller, *The Poetics of Gender*, New York, Columbia University Press, 1986, 157–82; The University of Chicago Press for Namascar Shaktini, "Displacing the Phallic Subject: Wittig's Lesbian Writing," reprinted from *Signs: Journal of Women and Society in Culture* 8, no. 11 (Autumn):29–44.

INTRODUCTION

The Thinking Muse, which signifies at once "source of inspiration" and "thinker," marks a radical shift in the traditional philosophical separation between muse, female, and thinker, male. The muses, invoked by philosophers even prior to the time of Socrates as the source of philosophic inspiration, have been traditionally posited as the "other," forever outside the activity of philosophizing. Portrayed as muses but not as philosophers, women have been assumed by the Western tradition to be those who do not, or ought not, think. This has resulted in an arbitrary narrowing of the field of philosophy and of the styles of philosophic discourse, the exclusion of events and perceptions specific to women's lives, and the long-standing paucity of readily available philosophic texts written by women.

The Thinking Muse establishes, in contrast, a unity of inspiration and thought that moves within women's experience to the recognition and creation of more freeing modes of philosophizing. Beginning from women's perspective, philosophy need no longer get straight to the point, but consists in thoughtful wandering through the shadows of experience, not in order to bring them into light, but to reveal the ambiguous edges of things. No longer is "to muse" an amusement, a waste of time, a deception. The "musing" of feminist philosophers emerges, rather, as a thoughtful experience of wonder, profound meditation and inquiry, perplexity and uncertainty, genuine astonishment and surprise.

The authors in this book are all Americans who live within the context of the feminist movement in the United States and who interact with various aspects of modern French philosophy. The problematization of philosophy as the gatekeeper of rational authority, beginning with the writings of the late nineteenth-century German philosopher, Nietzsche, and continuing with Heidegger and Wittgenstein, took on a specific character in France during the 1940s. The philosophical concerns and social activism of that time, expressed in the philosophical and literary works of Sartre, Camus, Merleau-Ponty, and Beauvoir, especially in her *The Second Sex*, have been highly suggestive for feminist reflection. Indeed, many American feminist philosophers turned to existential phenomenology as a philosophy of liberation that recognizes the potential for change exercised by individual and collective action and the need for a philosophy of the body and lived experience. More recently, American feminist philosophers' involvement in French thought has included the post-structuralist discussions of language, power, and desire, both in the texts of Lacan, Foucault, and Derrida, and in the theories of "feminine writing" and "writing the body," which are addressed in the works of Kristeva, Irigaray, Cixous, and Wittig.

While all of the contributors to this volume find gaps, biases, and silences in modern French philosophy, they also seek to persuade American feminists that the thinkers discussed provide modes of discourse that offer unique opportunities for feminists, both for critique and for positive reflection. We have selected papers that we think represent the range and diversity of feminist engagement with the modern French thought which has been most widely read in the United States. French writers not treated here, but who merit attention by feminist philosophers, include Roland Barthes, Gilles Deleuze, Jean Lyotard, Annie Leclerc, Michèle Montrelay, and Nicole Brossard.

In this introduction we will discuss major features of the two French philosophical currents dealt with in this book, existential phenomenology and post-structuralism, with emphasis on the themes that have been of most interest to feminist philosophers in the United States. We will sketch the trans-Atlantic appropriations of these movements by American feminists. Finally, and most important, we will introduce some of the themes of the essays in *The Thinking Muse* and we will discuss the specifically feminist perspective that these essays bring to the texts of modern French thought.

Existential Phenomenology

"To the things themselves!" So resounded the slogan of the founder of the phenomenological method, Edmund Husserl. Phenomenology was to set aside all presuppositions and reflect on the relation of consciousness to things in order to discover their meaning. This Husserlian project hoped to break through the mechanistic, reductive worldview of modern science, which had come to dominate philosophical, psychological, and historical inquiry. Husserl proposed a return to the lifeworld by reflecting on how we know, and by a concern with issues of epistemology.

Existential phenomenology quickly affirmed Husserl's emphasis on the relationship of consciousness and things, and his return to the world of lived experience, but it expressed fundamental disagreement with his focus on the human being as primarily a knower. In opposition to Descartes's claim, "I think, therefore I am," which gave impetus to Husserl's philosophic work, existential phenomenologists such as Merleau-Ponty asserted, "I am what I do." The human subject was to be understood not primarily as an abstract knower, but as a living actor that makes itself what it is within a particular historical context. The existential analysis of the German philosopher Martin Heidegger, who made reflection on temporality central in his response to Husserl, influenced most of the philosophers treated in this volume.

Several essays in this collection transform basic tenets of existential phenomenologists such as Sartre, Beauvoir, Camus, and Merleau-Ponty, by setting forth contexts for philosophizing that have their locus in women's daily lives. In these essays, four themes emerge as central to French existential phenomenology: freedom, situation, the relation of self and others, and the lived body.

Critics of the existentialism of Jean-Paul Sartre and Albert Camus often seem to have misunderstood their focus on the freedom of the subject. Many writers have interpreted existential phenomenology's claim that the human subject is free to imply that the slave is as free as the master and the worker as free as the boss, that is, as implying a political quietism that denies the importance of oppression and domination. Nothing could be further from the intentions of these philosophers, who saw action against oppression as imperative. For the existentialists, human existence is free because it is not and cannot be determined, either by natural or by social laws. This means that there are always possibilities for the alteration of a state of affairs, that the future is always open. Far from counseling acceptance of one's slavery because deep down one is "really" free, this philosophy counsels revolution: The fact that one is a slave today determines nothing about one's being tomorrow.

Even the most apparently immutable human attributes are understood by the existentialists to be the product of human definition and thus subject to change. This position leads to a powerfully radical critique when used by feminists. As Simone de Beauvoir and Monique Wittig demonstrate, application of the existential principle of change to the issue of gender identity leads to a startling conclusion: One is not born a woman. Femininity and masculinity are socially defined forms of identity that need not, and according to Wittig, ought not, exist at all.

Human freedom is, for the existentialists, a freedom that is always situated. The subject is always already in a particular context with others, including diverse social groups, institutions, and historical events. The concept of the situatedness of human existence, which Heidegger calls "thrownness," stands in direct confrontation with the transcendental philosophical tradition from Descartes through Kant to Husserl, which conceives the subject as external to the object of its reflection. For existential phenomenology, the subject is irrevocably in the world. We find ourselves in a world structured by rules and institutions not of our own making, and which we must take up in order to shape our lives.

Existential phenomenology's insistence that we are always in an inter-subjective context emphasizes the unique possibility we collectively have to transform situations and to give them new meaning. The human subject in situation is not solitary, argues existential phenomenology, but is a being in the world with others. The anti-philosophical tendency in existential phenomenology denies priority to reason and gives careful attention to the role of the emotions in the generation of meaning. Thus, for Beauvoir, one's freedom is achieved by reaching out toward the freedom of others, by overcoming the separation of individual consciousnesses through acts of friendship and love. For Camus, whose work is concerned with the relation between solitary and solidary existence, the plagues of modern life are overcome by rebellion, which creates a communal "we" in which there are neither victims nor executioners. It is Sartre's account of the I-other relationship, however, which is the best known. His description of the I-other relationship may tend to absolutize Hegel's master-slave analysis. It nevertheless effectively brings to philosophical thinking the complexity and anxiety with which relations among persons may be fraught, especially insofar as I find that I define myself by the way others see me and that the gaze and evaluation of others is out of my control. By claiming that desire for a person is a quest for their desire, Sartre launched a social and dialectical conception of desire that has continued to be a subject of debate in recent French thought.

The existential themes of freedom, situation, and the relation of self and other, have been developed by Simone de Beauvoir to form the categorical foundation of the most comprehensive analysis of women's condition under patriarchy that has ever been written: *The Second Sex*. Women, according to Beauvoir, are objectified as the "other" when men set themselves up as the one, the subject. A woman's existence is situated by the daily actions, myths, and institutions, through which men constitute woman as the inessential, the other. Much of women's experience can be understood as an encounter with such oppression, whether in resistance to it, in complicity with it, or both. Beauvoir's account of women's situation, despite the limitations that writers in this volume identify, retains much of its intuitive and conceptual power and exercises deep influence on writings by later French feminists, as well as on virtually all the articles in this collection.

The human subject that existential phenomenologists assert as free and capable of transcending objectification retains a Cartesian mode, however,

which appears in Sartre and Beauvoir's frequent separation of consciousness, transcendent being-for-itself, and the body, immanent and inert
being-in-itself. Maurice Merleau-Ponty attempts to overcome the obstacles
such a dichotomy presents by locating consciousness in the body. With
the concept of the lived body, Merleau-Ponty uncovers the fluid spatiality
and orientation of the acting body, infused with meaning, understanding,
and expressiveness in gait and gesture. Since consciousness is bodily, such
a subject is thoroughly in the world, which always outruns her or him.
Beauvoir identifies ambiguity as integral to an ethics by which we might
grasp the genuine conditions of our lives. Merleau-Ponty defines ambiguity
as constitutive of the fleshy consciousness which inhabits a multi-dimen-
sional field where the senses intermingle, a field open to a multiplicity of
possible foci and interpretations. In Merleau-Ponty's understanding of the
ambiguity and overflowing of perceptual experience we find the portent
of the *différance* on which later French writers dwell.

Post-Structuralism

The term post-structuralism refers to currents of philosophy that have
prevailed in France since the early 1970s. Post-structuralism is a descriptive
term which characterizes theoretical reflection situated after the Saussurian
proposal that meaning resides not in a relationship between an utterance
and that to which it refers, but in the relationship of signs to one another.
Every form of subject-object epistemology, including the phenomenological
distinction between the constituting subject and the experience it constitutes, comes into question by this move of structural linguistics. Objects,
understood as entities existing apart from language, and consciousness,
posited as the origin of meaning and as that which has ideas of objects to
which signs refer, both disappear.

Although critical of structuralist pretensions to science, post-structuralists
elaborate the critique of the subject-object correlate that structuralism begins. Language is a central concern of post-structuralist writers, who, in
different ways, deconstruct the discourse of Western metaphysics to show
how it obscures and mystifies the constructed character of subjects and
truths. Although there is mutual influence among post-structuralist authors, such as Lacan, Foucault, Derrida, Kristeva, Irigaray, Cixous, and
Wittig, each has a distinctive style of writing, addresses specific theoretical
issues, and has grounds for some serious disagreement with the others.

In Jacques Lacan's psychoanalysis the subject shifts from a position as
the origin of speech and meaning to itself as a result of symbolic production.
To become a subject, Lacan maintains, is to be initiated into the symbolic,

into language as it embodies the laws and relations of culture. Once we are initiated into the symbolic, we speak it as autonomous subjects of our own production and we are spoken by it.

The self is identified by Lacan as that position in the process of speaking from which the speaker establishes a relation to an other. The other is an alter ego, a mirror in which the subject sees its image as likeness or distortion, and through which the self establishes its separate identity by fixing the other as the referent, the real. The self is necessarily split: the imaginary aspect of language enacts the repressed, playful, and fearful side of signification and threatens to undermine the orderliness of conscious reason. The symbolic aspect of language relates the subject to a reality other than itself and maintains the subject in the clear categories and rules of grammar and logic. Whereas the imaginary is the order of identity and presence that is linked to dyadic relationship with the mother, the symbolic is the ordering of our perceptions of difference and absence in which we become selves, and is linked to our acceptance of a third term, the father. The absolute signifier, the phallus, represents the name of the father. The phallus stands for that moment of rupture which comes to signify separation and loss to the child, but by which the child becomes a subject in society. Entry into the symbolic order is accompanied by the repression of the emotional nexus of the mother-child relation and the opening up of the unconscious.

For Michel Foucault the idea and experience of the subject, the unified self, is historically situated. The idea of the subject, Foucault argues, has been constructed by Enlightenment humanism, which took a self-reflective turn to construct "man" as an object of knowledge. Most of Foucault's writing turns on the assumption of an epistemological break in social discourse and cultural self-understanding, which he locates at the turn of the nineteenth century, during the emergence of biology, medicine, and the sciences of "man." These new disciplines not only articulated new forms of intellectual categorization and theories of experience and behavior, but structured and were structured by new liberal humanist practices of bureaucratic administration, institutional medicine, schooling, work regulation, and penal incarceration.

Foucault's later work concentrates on how discourses structure a modern form of subjection through disciplinary practices that constitute persons as isolatable individuals who enact their own self-controlling order. Power, in this modern form, has a particular locus in the body, not primarily limiting or restraining bodies, but through micro-processes of social interchange that direct the body's energies toward production, including the production of power. In his last work, the *History of Sexuality*, Foucault finds this individual subject, the agent of self-control and discipline, created in ancient Greek and Roman texts that report and recommend practices of sexual vigilance, diet, and exercise.

Deconstruction challenges not only the authority of various forms of discourse, but also the existence of the subject as the center of authority behind all discourse. Derrida, in particular, attempts to displace the autonomy and purity of the ego and its regulative role as the theoretical foundation of philosophical discourse. The notion of the subject as a unity, a point of origin that knows itself immediately and wills its desires in the world, is understood by Derrida as the product of a metaphysical hierarchy that privileges presence. The metaphysics of presence seeks to collapse time into a series of nows and to deny linguistic spacing by imagining meaning as there all at once. Metaphysics preserves the priority of the subject by generating hierarchical dualisms in which the orderly and rational rule and expel the deviant, the disparate, and all that resists classification: subject/object, self/other, mind/body, and identity/difference. Philosophical efforts to comprehend the whole in its unity undermine themselves by inevitably positing their own outside. The purity of any clearly defined category thereby depends on what it excludes, and the setting up of symmetries and complementary oppositions legislates an idealism that conceives the truth and being of things as lying outside time, space, and history.

With the term *différance*, Derrida offers an alternative mode of conceiving the movement of significance and meaning. The play of difference, erased by the metaphysics of presence, expresses the irreducible spatio-temporality of signification. The sign has meaning according to its place in a chain of signs, to how it differs from other signs. Any moment of signification defers, holds in abeyance, the completion of meaning. The signifying chain can be displaced by situating the sign in a different context, for signification takes place in a material and historical spacing process.

When women enter into philosophy in this era of post-structuralist challenge to the subject, they often advocate the destabilization of those gender-marked norms governing language and the subject which have been left in place by much of male post-structuralist theory. The reflections offered by these women drift away from the currently recognized conceptual terrain, and in so doing, undermine male-defined theory. The movement which brings phallogocentrism to an end is called, by Hélène Cixous, a starting on all sides at once, and by Monique Wittig, a fracturing and extension into space that is like Pascal's circle, whose center is everywhere and whose circumference is nowhere.

Beginning with Cixous's appeal for woman to write her body, intense controversy has developed both in France and in the United States concerning the project of feminine writing and its use to give expression to women's bodily and affective freedom. Only through some form of feminine writing, Cixous, Kristeva, and Irigaray claim, can we bring ourselves into symbolic systems that belong to us by choice and by right.

Julia Kristeva affirms a link between the feminine and language by transforming Lacan's distinction between the symbolic and the imaginary into a distinction between the symbolic and the semiotic. Kristeva understands the symbolic as the aspect of language that represents and defines, and through which the subject constitutes objects. In the semiotic, the body's drives and affects, carried from the movement of maternal *jouissance*, find their way into the material of language—in tonality, gesture, rhythm, rhyme, rhetoric, metaphor, and other figures of speech. Symbolic, rational, legalistic discourse rules in Western culture, Kristeva suggests, and the semiotic is repressed. Kristeva links the semiotic with femininity because its repression occurs through the establishment of phallic law, and because its repression includes repression of the infant's joy in relation to the maternal body. A renewed ethics must reclaim the repressed feminine, she contends, because of its potential for transforming both the speaking subject and language.

The work of Luce Irigaray begins from the standpoint of the deviant, the different. Irigaray describes phallogocentric culture as focused on a metaphysics of identity that begins by positing the one, the same, the essence that generates binary oppositions in which the first term defines the second as what it is not: in which woman is only not a man, a deficiency, a lack. In contrast to the phallogocentric preoccupation with the straight, the visible, the true, the proper, Irigaray proposes that women must find and speak the specificity of female desire, which has completely different values from those of phallic thinking. Women's eroticism is neither one nor two, but plural, as women's bodies themselves experience arousal and pleasure in a multiplicity of places that cannot all be identified. Touch, not sight, predominates, the touch of vaginal lips against clitoris, of intimate bodies touching. Feminine language displaces the sterility and oppressiveness of phallogocentric categorization by refusing to go straight to the point, by starting over again from different perspectives.

That woman must put herself into the text by her own movement is a guiding theme of feminine writing, or, as Cixous calls such textual action, a writing said to be feminine. Writing the body, Cixous suggests, is to write the language that speaks/is spoken by women when no one is listening to women to correct them. Unlike the language into which we are born, the language that speaks (to) us and that dictates its domestic, conjugal mode, a law of death, feminine languages are languages of life. They dissolve the logic of difference organized according to a hierarchy of opposition, male vs. female, the one vs. the many, and make of difference a cluster of new differences.

The feminine libidinal economy is neither identifiable by a man nor referable to the masculine economy. These economies, which are radically different for women than for men, are, Cixous claims, a product of history and culture. It would be inaccurate to interpret the feminine writing of Cixous, or that of Irigaray or Kristeva, in a narrow biologistic way. When Irigaray evokes the special pleasure of labia touching, or Kristeva the unique pleasures of the pregnant and nursing body, as the ground of a new language, they claim to be naming what is irreducible and specific in female experience. Appeals to the differences of women's bodily and sexual experience, to unique modes of feminine desire emerging from a plurality of erogenous regions, refer not to deterministically related physiological processes, but to the material movement of desire and pleasure. While the work of Kristeva, Irigaray, and Cixous may not be free of heterosexist ideology, especially concerning their prioritization of specific maternal experiences, such ideology need not be based on an appeal to an innate biologism.

Monique Wittig rejects the entire project of feminine writing on the grounds that it retains and essentializes the category "woman," rather than working to eliminate that category, both theoretically and practically. "Women," "gender," and "sex" are, Wittig writes, marks of oppression that must be removed if females are to be free. The separation of females from "woman," to be effected by breaking off the heterosexual contract in which, as Lacan affirms, man speaks and woman does not, is the only epistemological revolution that can undermine the authority of phallogocentrism. Wittig's work displaces the rigid hold of "straight thinking" over language and culture through the introduction of the lesbian body and lesbian writing.

Trans-Atlantic Appropriations

Since the early 1970s post-structuralist thought has predominated in French intellectual life and existential phenomenology has, to a large degree, been dormant as a living philosophical perspective. In the United States, in the early 1980s, some philosophers continued to engage in ex-

istential phenomenology, and the interest of philosophers in post-structuralism often lagged behind that of literary critics and film theorists. Despite, or perhaps because of, the strong affinity some philosophers felt
toward existential phenomenology, the relation between existential phenomenology and post-structuralism at first developed gradually, but then
rapidly gained momentum, as one of the most lively areas of philosophical
debate in the United States. The concepts of human existence that existential phenomenology sought to affirm, the primacy of experience and
the freedom of the subject, collided with post-structuralist emphasis on
language and its critique of the concept of the subject. Although today in
the United States most discussion of recent French philosophy centers on
post-structuralism, the issues under debate continue to be articulated by
an inter-continental reflection that borrows selectively from French
thought.

The appropriation of recent French thought by feminist philosophers in
the United States reflects these tendencies, as well as traits of its own.
Ambiguity that evidences sustained and nuanced reflection inhabits feminist philosophical discussion of the continuities and disjunctions between
modernism and post-modernism, in particular, between humanist philosophies that emphasize lived experience, engagement, and the empowerment of individuals and communities, and anti-humanist philosophies that
focus on the linguistic sign, structures of discourse, and the mechanisms
of power.

Much feminist philosophy, along with existentialism, is inclined to focus
on the freedom of the subject. Many feminists find the post-structuralist
injunction to relinquish the notion of the subject dangerous. A politics that
seeks to enact social change needs a concept of agency. Yet the encounter
between existential phenomenology and post-structuralism also brings forward the question of whether a notion of moral and political agency can
be retained without rarifying either the agent or its principles of action into
absolutes. While never claiming that the world has its being independently
of the meaning people confer on things and events, existentialism has a
conception of a world of material and social reality that agents work with
or against. Such a world view can be overly rigid and totalizing in the
absence of a critique that reveals the genealogy of worlds in discourse.
From the point of view of political action, however, post-structuralism can
appear to dissolve the world into a system of signs.

Yet American feminist philosophers often posit Western philosophy as
a tradition that is not quite our own, irrespective of whether it is interpreted
by existential phenomenology, by post-structuralism, or by a combination
of both. Feminist philosophers who study recent French thought are by
no means a homogeneous group. Nevertheless, these philosophers fre-

quently exhibit in their work a sense of distance from the tradition around which the conversations of modernism and post-modernism circulate. Not only has the Western philosophical tradition been written primarily by white men, but the contemporary interpretations of that tradition often echo the male perspectives that it exhibits. Male philosophers who discuss women, i.e., Merleau-Ponty in his phenomenological psychology and Sartre in his theory of the emotions, as well as Lacan, Derrida, and Foucault, rarely refer to texts written by women on women's situation, much less make such reference integral to their work. Thus discussion of women by modern French male philosophers tends to function as a discussion between men on men's views of women and the relation of women to male-defined thought. Feminists who seek the liberation of women through ideological critique and social change displace such a male-defined notion of woman as other, which still relates this other to a male tradition. Feminist philosophers often begin from women's specific experience and perspectives, in relation to which the male tradition may be addressed but is not central.

The distance of feminist philosophy in the United States from much post-modern debate manifests, as well, a circumspect attitude toward its assumptions concerning textuality. Post-structuralist prioritization of the text, its emphasis on intertextual interpretation and its claim that language and ideology develop in the conflicts, discrepancies, and gaps between texts, intrigues and concerns feminist philosophers. The conviction that "the personal is political," which has motivated much of the women's movement in the United States and most feminist scholarship, has some affinity with the emphasis that existential phenomenology has given to lived experience in an effort to circumvent the grasp of Western metaphysics. Feminist philosophy understands the slogan, "the personal is political," as valorizing individual and collective experience and showing why philosophy must engage in an unfolding of local narratives. In contrast, the post-modern focus on the text tends to leap over experience and to privilege a literacy that, by its racist and heterosexist presuppositions, ignores and misrepresents the lives, languages, and philosophizing, of many women. Here feminist philosophy seeks to dismantle the philosophical textuality of the West, which erects a truth or certainty cut off from history, and especially, from women's histories and experience.

The appropriation of recent French thought by American feminist philosophers effects a triple displacement: the displacement of existential phenomenology and post-structuralism to American grounds; the displacement of post-modern readings of philosophy by feminist grounds; and, as we will suggest, a friendly being displaced by, and displacement of, other forms of American feminist theory. The indigenous grounds of the feminist philosophy in this book are not one, but many, and it is in their interaction that there emerge new possibilities for philosophizing.

Feminist Philosophy

Feminism in the United States has developed from a wave of consciousness that some predicted would hit the shores and dissipate, to a sustained current of political and personal transformation giving rise to many, and more liberating, cultural formations. As feminist criticism and theory undermines more deeply and widely the foundations of received practice and knowledge, it surfaces with new streams of thought. The writings in this volume draw upon the authors' involvement in the women's movement and in women's studies in the United States. They share an explicit understanding of women as being in a condition of oppression in contemporary society and a commitment to eliminate that condition. The writings in *The Thinking Muse* appear not at the margins of Western philosophy, where woman is posited as the "other," but in the conversations of feminist theorists with feminist theorists. Several of the articles were formulated through discussion, consciousness raising, and presentation at the Society for Women in Philosophy, a professional group for empowerment and sisterhood.

The approaches to feminism represented by the authors in this volume cannot be reduced to any simple formula. In the past decade, what it means to be a feminist has become more problematic than it once seemed. In the early and mid 1970s it seemed clear that feminism named an analysis that identified the system of patriarchy as keeping all women in a common oppression, excluded from full human participation and forced to serve and depend on men. Female experience was defined primarily in terms of women's exclusion and victimization, and women's liberation was frequently defined as the elimination of gender difference along with male privilege.

This earlier feminist perspective has not vanished from feminist discussion in the United States, but it has come to appear more ambiguous and more complex. Partly because of the challenges by women of color and by Third World women to the white women's movement, and partly because of the critique lesbians have brought to heterosexist assumptions of the feminist movement, a critique of essentialism and a formulation of theories of difference have become integral to feminist discussion in the United States. Claims, frequently French inspired, that to define a common women's oppression is inappropriately essentialist, have motivated many American feminists to withdraw from the categorical claim that there is a single system of patriarchal expression. Reflection on the positive values of female experience of the body, female friendship, motherhood, and women's culture as expressed in feminist art, music, and poetry has brought feminists in the United States to develop varied understandings of women's liberation. The contributors to this volume express in their writings a thoughtful living through of many of these variations.

The essays in *The Thinking Muse* are committed to a feminism that seeks, by countless shifts of perspective, to overturn the foundations of Western philosophy and to evoke new grounds for philosophizing. Each essay engages in a critique of the writings of modern French philosophers and the limits they posit for feminist understanding. At the same time, the essays explore the creation of philosophical styles of reflection that give rise to positive accounts of women's experience. Critique as it appears in these papers does not take, primarily, the form of refutation, the dismantling of claims and arguments to reveal inconsistencies, invalidities, counter-examples, and absurd implications. Critique is exercised in the sense of showing the limits of a mode of thinking by forging an awareness of alternative, and more liberating, ideas, symbols, and discourse.

The work of Simone de Beauvoir, who has been an inspirational figure for all the contributors to this volume, is studied in the first two essays of *The Thinking Muse*. In "Female Eroticism in the Works of Simone de Beauvoir," Jo-Ann Pilardi examines the development of Beauvoir's thought on female eroticism, from her early novels to *The Second Sex* and several of her later writings. Pilardi approaches eroticism from an existential phenomenological perspective, as that dimension of human existence that has to do with the sexual, a situation and a lived experience, not a collection of genital facts. Pilardi explores the possibilities and limits that Beauvoir's work offers for an intellectual reclaiming of our bodies through its involvement in the difficult creation an "other" to patriarchal ideology, a creation of descriptions that inform the silences surrounding a female erotic.

Eléanor H. Kuykendall, in "Simone de Beauvoir and Two Kinds of Ambivalence in Action," proposes that women's power to reach one another is circumscribed by our use of a language that we perceive as damaging to ourselves. By study of Beauvoir's references to women's collectivity, she shows how women may resolve such linguistic ambivalence. Feminist deconstruction of language, Kuykendall claims, shapes a feminist ethics of linguistics which offers as an imperative that speaking and writing promote mutuality and reciprocity, rather than dominance and control, among the people whose social relationships are thereby constituted.

Iris Marion Young, in her essay "Throwing Like a Girl: A Phenomenology of Feminine Body Comportment, Motility, and Spatiality," analyzes how we as women are conditioned by sexist oppression to live our bodies as object as well as subject. Her existential phenomenological study focuses on the situation of women in contemporary advanced-industrial, urban society, and on those movements which involve the body as a whole and which aim at the accomplishment of a definite purpose or task. Young maintains that patriarchal definition of women as mere body, and not in-born "womanly" traits, conditions us not to use our full bodily capacities in free and open engagement with the world.

In "An Introduction to Patriarchal Existentialism: A Proposal for a Way Out of Existential Patriarchy," Jeffner Allen argues that the possibilities for freedom that existentialism portends are impossible to realize in the context in which existentialism has established itself. Retaining only the existential emphasis on the importance of change, and its claim that philosophy is a sustained reflection on lived experience, Allen traces the movement of sinuosity: a paradigm for women's lives which emerges in the turning of women to one another, a dynamic structure that enables the emergence of a positive women-identified sensibility and feminist experience.

Judith Butler, in "Sexual Ideology and Phenomenological Description: A Feminist Critique of Merleau-Ponty's *Phenomenology of Perception*," finds that Merleau-Ponty's view of sexuality seems to restore the historical and volitional components of sexual experience, and to open the way for a fuller description of sexuality and sexual diversity. Yet the potential open-ness of Merleau-Ponty's theory of sexuality is deceptive, for it presupposes heterosexual relations as normative, and misogyny as an intrinsic structure of perception. Philosophical feminism must still discover a theory in which sexuality is to be understood as a scene of cultural struggle, improvisation, and innovation.

A phenomenological approach to sexist oppression reveals the lived situation of oppressive kinds of seeing, claims Julien S. Murphy in "The Look in Sartre and Rich." Murphy asks, How can we look back with fresh eyes when even our backward glance is shaped by the look of the op-pressor? Her reading of the poetry of Adrienne Rich shows how we women discover, in the look of feminist vision, that our eyes need be neither those of victim nor of oppressor. The boldness and freedom of feminist vision enable us to take a fresh look at ourselves and our situation and to move beyond the distance, desire, and destruction described by Sartre in his analysis of the look.

Derrida's positing of woman as textual enigma leaves no room for self-defined female subjectivity or for space in history for women as agents, argues Linda Kintz, in "In-different Criticism: The Deconstructive Parole." Using the metaphor of theater as a heuristic device to investigate decon-struction's denial of the reference of text to context, Kintz argues that just as we can never prove reference, neither can we completely disprove it.

Kintz proposes a redefinition of referentiality in its cultural context, focusing on the gender of the subject doing the reading and writing.

Linda Singer, in "True Confessions: Cixous and Foucault on Sexuality and Power," examines whether the discursive representation of women's sexuality is, as Cixous asserts, still a vital liberatory practice, or whether, as Foucault implies, such discourse contributes to the proliferation of the mechanisms of social control. Rather than accept Foucault's position, which Singer reads as a prolongation of a patriarchal logic, she asks that we formulate feminist imaginaries and symbolics, writing new sexual stories in ways that do not repeat old endings.

Any inscription of difference is overdetermined by the indifferent dominant discourse, maintains Domna C. Stanton, in "Difference on Trial: A Critique of the Maternal Metaphor in Cixous, Irigaray, and Kristeva." Woman exists in the real and the symbolic neither by nor for herself, from which there has emerged in feminist methodology the idea of the female as principal metaphor for difference. Yet when the female is understood within the strands of the extended metaphor, woman as/is mother, feminist methodology remains within sameness. Stanton proposes that women must articulate, instead, the supplement that is multiple, women in the plural.

In "Questions for Julia Kristeva's Ethics of Linguistics," Eléanor H. Kuykendall asks whether Kristeva's notion of the speaking subject is masculine, gender neutral, or feminine. Kristeva attempts to render a gender neutral reading of Freudian and Lacanian accounts of the child's acquisition of symbolic capacity. Yet, Kuykendall argues, because Kristeva endorses the notion that the capacity for speech occurs under the threat of castration, she retains an understanding of the speaking subject as masculine. The positive place that Kristeva purposes for the feminine, in her theorization of the semiotic aspect of language, is outside ethics and rationality. Kuykendall finds that Kristeva cannot be called feminist, for neither her linguistics nor her heretical ethics provides a place for female agency.

Namascar Shaktini, in "Displacing the Phallic Subject: Wittig's Lesbian Writing," demonstrates how lesbian writing brings about an epistemological revolution through a fundamental reorganization of metaphor, from its traditional center in the phallus to the constantly changing relations of the lesbian body. She reads Wittig as turning deconstruction inside out, bringing its method out of the center and into the island-like origins of culture, creating a rupture between phallic existence and the self-moving, free, and lesbian text.

All of the essays in *The Thinking Muse* are dedicated to the discovery of sites of reflection in which feminist philosophizing can flourish. The assumption of human universality implicit in existential phenomenology is thereby challenged. As Judith Butler states in regard to Merleau-Ponty's assumptions about the sexual subject, the assumption of the neutrality and universality of the subject devalues gender. Because this allegedly universal subject nearly always resembles the concrete characteristics of men, moreover, such universality devalues women. The resulting gender oppression objectifies, marginalizes, and silences women.

Several of the authors in this volume argue that although post-structuralists reject the universal humanism typical of existential phenomenology, they, too, leave women no place to stand. Derrida, Foucault, and Kristeva do not deny gender difference, but they explicitly argue against a focus on gender difference and a specificity of women's situation and oppression. Kintz, Singer, and Kuykendall suggest that post-structuralist gender indifference has consequences akin to the more naive indifference of existentialism.

Not to dismiss the condition of objectification women have had to live out in patriarchal society, but to find ways to speak that oppression, is a primary task for feminist philosophy. Beauvoir's thesis in *The Second Sex* is that women in patriarchy are located as the object complementary to male subjectivity. Pilardi shows, however, that in Beauvoir's discourse on sexuality she does not free herself from this conception, but describes male sexuality as active and female sexuality as passive. The larger existentialist project of replacing God as creator of the universe with man as the creator of meaning and value, Allen argues, excludes women from creative subjectivity and situates us as objects in relation to that activity. Crucial to the articulation of oppression is a bringing to expression of the experience of being a subject objectified and marginalized by the institutions and language of the society in which a woman lives. Young and Murphy, in different ways, describe this experience of objectification and marginalization from the perspective of those who live it and are constrained by it.

Some post-structuralist writers reflect on the dichotomy between the masculine, active subject, and the feminine passive object, seeking to subvert that dichotomy and revalue the "feminine" position. These writers maintain that representation and symbolization assume the expulsion of the feminine as unrepresentable, as non-being dependent on being for its representation. Kuykendall and Stanton propose, nevertheless, that the association of the unrepresentable with the feminine, set forth by Lacan and Kristeva, as well as by others, retains a distinction that necessarily marginalizes the feminine. Kintz suggests that Derrida's indifference to the association of Woman, a position in signification, with women, the concrete people, betokens an indifference not only to those concrete people called women, but to the question of how gender structures writing and reading.

The assertion of gender indifference by Derrida and Foucault fails to attend to the specificity of author and audience. Women and men in patriarchal society have different and unequal relations to texts. Thus, Kintz and Singer claim, a writing that does not make explicit the historically situated position from which it speaks and that does not address the specificities of its audience continues the tradition of false authorial neutrality.

If feminist philosophy thrives neither in the domain of the human universal, nor in a position of marginalization, from where can women's lives be spoken? Several essays in *The Thinking Muse* endorse the claim that women should speak the specificity of female difference. Domna Stanton points out that attention to difference has its dangers for feminists. If we name female difference, we risk becoming entrapped in the patriarchal structures we are challenging, because they already have a position for the "feminine." If we decline to name this difference, we reinforce and accede to the continued marginalization of women in a gender indifferent discourse. Kuykendall, in her discussion of Beauvoir's effort to appropriate the traditional language of liberation and equality for women, identifies this dilemma as one of linguistic ambiguity and offers as one resolution the naming of community as sisterhood. Murphy traces a way out of this dilemma when she poses the project of seeing women's experience with fresh eyes while still situated within the experience of women's objectification.

None of the women in this volume think that the way out of these dilemmas and ambivalences is to get things straight. Each author shapes, rather, a conceptual environment in which a feminist discussion can unfold. Shaktini suggests that the power of Monique Wittig's poetic language resides in exploiting linguistic ambivalence by constructing gender neutral nouns and pronouns in a female mode. Allen's notion of a sinuous female writing evokes winding, flowing ways in which women get around the demands of male dominated culture. Singer invites us to deal with feminist ambiguities and ambivalences by joining in sisterly laughter.

The feminist engagement with modern French philosophy that emerges in these essays is a contribution to a burgeoning and exciting discussion taking place among feminists and philosophers in the United States today. The essays offer us diverse, overlapping, and far-reaching thoughts on which to muse.

FEMALE EROTICISM IN THE WORKS OF SIMONE DE BEAUVOIR

Jo-Ann Pilardi

The canon of Western literature is filled with lectures by men about female sexuality, from Ovid to Diderot to Freud. To create and maintain the myth of male superiority, patriarchy has required that the "other" voices on eroticism be silent, or be reduced to silence through ridicule and omission. Yet that is hardly surprising. Erotic experience is an important dimension of human life. Indeed, some would argue that it is a dimension more fundamental than any other. It is, thus, inevitable that women's erotic experience, like every other dimension of women's lives, has been structured—constrained—by patriarchal society.

Simone de Beauvoir's is the sole female voice to be heard among the first generation of existentialists and phenomenologists of twentieth-century France. In *The Second Sex*, Beauvoir struggled to create a theory of women's oppression from an existentialist philosophy of subjectivity and freedom. Her analysis of female eroticism in that book was constrained by patriarchal conceptualizations as much as it was by the limits of existentialism. The problems she met with in that work provide a good example of how difficult it is to create an "other" to the patriarchal ideology. Yet it is critical that women do so. The effort of women to reclaim our bodies must include an intellectual reclaiming as well as direct physical control. It must include women's own descriptions and analyses of our own sexuality.

In this essay I trace the development of Simone de Beauvoir's thought on female eroticism from her early novels, through *The Second Sex*, to two later essays, "Must We Burn Sade?" and "Brigitte Bardot and the Lolita Syndrome." In such a study, *The Second Sex* will remain of central importance, however, because there she directly presents her analysis of eroticism. Yet the directness of Beauvoir's analytical method in *The Second Sex* is offset by a certain indirectness, since the analysis of eroticism appears scattered throughout the work. Beauvoir's analysis of eroticism is at base existentialist and phenomenological, although she makes use of the work of other contemporary French thinkers and, of course, adds to this her own unique vision and sensitivity about woman's situation.

Although Beauvoir claimed more than once that an analysis of women's eroticism was necessary, it remains unfinished in *The Second Sex*.[1] In that work Beauvoir adopts a position that remains problematic in two ways: (1) it is an analysis of female eroticism that is traditional and phallocentric in that it describes women's experience as passive and men's experience as active, and (2) it "betrays" the existentialist analysis that is the work's announced philosophical foundation in that it focuses on, indeed describes, the determining factors that limit women. In spite of Beauvoir's occasional calling women to task for not insisting on our freedom, freedom is overshadowed by limitation, determination, or in Sartrian language, "facticity." Women's situation is spelled out, from prehistory to mid-twentieth century, as one of confinement and oppression within a patriarchal world.

Eroticism

Following the existential-phenomenological tradition, Beauvoir maintains that eroticism is that dimension of human existence that has to do with the sexual, but always insofar as it denotes a situation and a lived experience, not a collection of genital facts. "The body is not a thing, it is a situation," she says, acknowledging a debt to Heidegger, Sartre, and Merleau-Ponty.[2] Eroticism cannot be reduced to mere energy, or reflex, but should be understood as a form of *desire*, which is the choice of a human consciousness.[3] The essential character of eroticism, for Beauvoir, is a movement toward the other.[4] What will be discovered in this movement is not only that I am flesh, but that I am an active consciousness as well—in short, I discover the "ambiguity" of the human condition.[5]

The concept of "ambiguity" had already been discussed by Beauvoir in *The Ethics of Ambiguity*, published in 1947. The term "ambiguity," functioning on two levels, first carries the existentialist claim that human life is ambiguous, not ever fixed, i.e., human existence has no nature, neither participating in a universal human nature nor having an individual but fixed nature. It is "ambiguous"—uncertain and undefined. Second, ambiguity besets those "truths" of the human condition which have a contradictory nature: freedom and servitude, solitude and the bond with others, life and death, and the insignificance as well as importance of the human being. Thus understood in an existential and ethical sense, ambiguity is the mark and the tension of the human condition within the self-other configuration:

> . . . each is bound to all; but that is precisely the ambiguity of one's condition: in one's surpassing toward others, each one exists absolutely as for one's self; each is interested in the liberation of all, but as a separate existence engaged in one's own projects.[6]

Because our existence is lived out in relation to our being flesh so differently than men's, an understanding of women's eroticism is central to an existential-phenomenological understanding of women.

The erotic may include, but certainly need not include, love. In Beauvoir's novels, the emotion of love is a favorite topic, most often in the form of the dependency relationship of a woman upon a man. Although some claim that Beauvoir is a didactic writer, Merleau-Ponty's assertion that she is not morally but metaphysically or ontologically didactic is more precise.[7] A lesson that Beauvoir teaches well—particularly in her novels—is the evil of the dependency of women and, relatedly, how perfect a medium the emotion of love is for this. She finds a woman in love a necessarily conflicted human being, first because of the nature of love itself, and second because of the ease with which love entraps a woman, to the extent that it provides her with a reason for being satisfied with less than freedom. So "love represents in its most touching form the curse that lies heavily upon woman confined in the feminine universe, woman mutilated, insufficient unto herself."[8]

The Novels

Beauvoir's first novel, *She Came to Stay* (*L'Invitée*), investigates love, but not eroticism, in the relationship of a romantic triangle that is based on the hope of the development of "a real trio, a well-balanced life for three, in which no one was sacrificed."[9] The main character, Françoise, experiences greater and greater anxiety as the important distinction blurs between essential and contingent love, and her primacy to her lover Pierre weakens. As Françoise becomes convinced that her own existence is threatened, coexistence with the other woman seems impossible and she is driven at the end to kill her. In so doing, we are told, she "had chosen at last. She had chosen herself."[10] This woman in love had no other alternative but to destroy the other woman, an end to the primacy she enjoyed with her lover being unbearable in that it would involve her "suicide," for her own existence was so marked by her dependence on him. Thus the Hegelian malediction Beauvoir uses as epigraph for this novel is realized: "Each consciousness seeks the death of the other." In *Les Belles Images*, a much later work, we find a similar theme: women living unsatisfactory and unsatisfied lives not only because they are members of a degenerate bourgeoisie, but also because they are mere reflections, mere dependencies, of the men through whom they live.[11]

In *The Blood of Others*, an early novel set in the period of the French Resistance, we find described not only love but eroticism. Beauvoir metaphorically renders one woman's erotic experience as a gradual metamorphosis from woman, to plant, to spongy moss, to jellyfish, enveloped always in darkness and vapors, becoming less and less capable of voluntary movement. The female erotic subject she describes becomes more uncomfortable as she finds herself becoming like an object in the natural world, a status particularly threatening to a woman, and consequently she fights against this "naturizing" process.[12] To continue her metaphors, we could say that the woman seeks to retain the stark light of subjectivity against the dark and spongy forest world of the female flesh. For this woman, carnality and subjectivity at once will be no easy task. The hardest fight, clearly, involves her subjectivity.

Eroticism in *The Second Sex*

The Second Sex contains extensive comments on female eroticism, primarily in the chapters on psychoanalysis (chapter 2), and sexual initiation (chapter 14). Beauvoir relies heavily on the existential categories of transcendence and immanence to define the relationship of female to male sexuality. Her analysis of female eroticism focuses on heterosexuality, except in one chapter on lesbianism.

Transcendence, the forward movement into the future of a willing subject, struggles with the urge toward immanence that also tempts the subject, the urge toward passivity, toward the being of a thing. This struggle Beauvoir had analyzed in *The Ethics of Ambiguity*. In *The Second Sex*, she writes: "Every subject plays his part as such specifically through exploits or projects that serve as a mode of transcendence; he achieves liberty only through a continual reaching out toward other liberties. . . . Every time transcendence falls back into immanence, stagnation, there is a degradation of existence."[13]

Beauvoir's description of women carries out the existentialist approach mentioned earlier in regard to her notion of eroticism. A woman is defined as "a human being in quest of values in a world of values, a world of which it is indispensable to know the economic and social structure."[14] The body itself is described as a situation, that particular situation which makes possible our grasp on the world.[15] A person is a sexual body, better, a "sexuate" body, because sexuality is not a part of the person, is not "appended" to a human being. The human being is, rather, a totality, and sexuality is one dimension of that totality.

The constraint which women suffer due to social and cultural oppression is a denial of choice—i.e., our own projects, through which the self transcends itself. To be a woman is to be "other," but also still to be a subject, even given the subjection under which that particular subjectivity usually functions, for subjection is never total enough to force the for-itself to give up transcendence.[16] The result is immanence, rather than transcendence, the being of the *en-soi* (in-itself, the thing), and not the *pour-soi* (for-itself, human consciousness). Such is a woman's "drama," her conflict. And if she manages to overcome external male-imposed constraints, she is caught in internal conflict, in that insofar as she succeeds, she defeats her *feminine* self as a subject-self.[17] An autonomous existence for women conflicts with women's "objective self," i.e., self as "other," for to be feminine is to be nonautonomous, passive.[18]

This conflict between being "other" and being a subject is incarnated in the body. Within the existential phenomenological perspective of *The Second Sex*, the body which the subject "is" is not a thing; its existence is never merely factual: " . . . if the body is not a *thing*, it is a situation, as viewed in the perspective I am adopting—that of Heidegger, Sartre and Merleau-Ponty: it is the instrument of our grasp upon the world."[19] Directly related to the for-itself's existence-as-body is the body as sexual, erotic existence. The general condition which, as we saw, meets a female self, in that her success as self means the realization of transcendence, or subjectivity, and at the same time means her failure as a female (other/object), also meets the female self in sexual experience, but doubly so. According to Beauvoir, erotic experience itself intensely reveals the ambiguity of the for-itself, both as subject and as object for another. But the female self begins by feeling itself as object. Hence its subject status is twice in question in sexuality, or rather, its message of its own immanence is intensified, doubled.

From the point of view of a strict existentialist, one might be tempted to say that Beauvoir's notion of the self in *The Second Sex* is philosophically flawed, because it places too much emphasis on the constraints on freedom in "situation." In Sartrian existentialism, the subject's situation is constituted from two moments, freedom and facticity. The existentialist philosophy in Beauvoir's early work, *The Ethics of Ambiguity*, stresses the use of one's freedom and the respect for the freedom of others as the core of morality. The philosophy of *The Second Sex*, on the other hand, stresses facticity. Due to its stress on the individual subject, the Sartrian existentialism of *Being and Nothingness* neglects consideration of the long-term historical situation of a group. In *The Second Sex*, Beauvoir suggests that the "situation" of a certain group, women, is so impressed upon the individual as to hamper or prevent the use of freedom, that is, the individual's transcendence of her facticity. In the "Introduction to Book II" of *The Second Sex* Beauvoir says, "It is not our concern here to proclaim eternal verities, but rather to describe the common basis that underlies every individual feminine existence." Such a statement not only radically undercuts the notion of freedom relative to "every individual feminine existence," since through that common basis a woman is "confined,"[20] it also radically changes the focus of the analysis of existence that existentialist philosophy had made from Kierkegaard to Sartre.

A general analysis of the commonalities of any *group* of individual existents does not make the use of existentialist categories impossible by any means, though it changes the emphasis of the analysis. Each individual human being experiences facticity, according to Sartre in *Being and Nothingness*, whether or not we would call this being "confined." The innovation represented by Beauvoir in *The Second Sex* is twofold: not only is the analysis focused on facticity but individual facticity does not remain individual; it is generalized—genderized—since Beauvoir describes the common basis of the lives of all women, a basis provided by education and custom.

The chapter on psychoanalysis in *The Second Sex* reflects the tension between these twin elements of Sartrian existentialism, freedom and facticity, and displays the shift toward facticity that Beauvoir's thinking was taking (a shift Sartre's thinking made later as well). In this chapter Beauvoir claims that psychoanalysis lacks the existential perspective of the human being as a totality, a perspective that disallows the notion of sheer fact. Beauvoir claims that for psychoanalysis, sexuality is an irreducible datum, and human existence is mistakenly understood in terms of this irreducible datum rather than in terms of the transcendence that can be accomplished by a human being which is a totality, that is, in terms of an existential choice.

But Beauvoir's rejection of Freudianism is hardly complete. In order to retain some of its notions concerning sexuality in women, she uses the idea of the "constant," that is, "certain factors of undeniable generality and repetition,"[21] which can be found in every individual case. These "constants" are not "eternals." They last as long as any particular epoch, according to Beauvoir. We might call them "epochal," not eternal, truths. Thus within the patriarchal epoch, it is a "truth" that the phallus is a symbol of transcendence.[22] It is in keeping with the power of men within a patriarchal society that the male sexual organ "means" liberty, and symbolizes the flight from facticity, from immanence, which is the human enterprise.

Within patriarchal society, men are not unique in engaging in transcendence, but because they are the sex in power, they become the sex in which the properly human—transcendence—and the genital symbolically merge. Woman, a transcendent being also in that she is human, is continually denied access to subjecthood through her life situation in general. For a woman, then, transcendence will be seen as a personal *and* cultural triumph.

Further, for Beauvoir this sexist oppression has turned woman into an "imperfect being," to use Thomas Aquinas's phrase, and this means sexual as well as intellectual, metaphysical, and psychological imperfection. A woman within patriarchal society is a creature "intermediate between male and eunuch," Beauvoir says, not a fully but only a partially sexed being, because she is not a phallic creature.[23]

Beauvoir claims that it is to Freud's credit that he maintains that for women, unlike men, there are two distinct erotic systems at work: the clitoral and the vaginal. With this fact, a woman's erotic history, as well as her erotic problems, commence. Before a woman reaches sexual maturity, she must not only pass through the narcissistic phase (at puberty) but she must also go through a second transition, from the clitoral to the vaginal. Beauvoir's notion of "constant" is at work here again, in her acceptance of the Freudian analysis of a general path of psychogenital development for women—for all women.

The phallocentrism of Freudian thinking is destructive to a thorough analysis of women, but not simply because it is modeled on male sexuality. It has, according to Beauvoir, prevented the study of female eroticism in its own right. The male libido has become not only the model of sexuality; it has also acted as the *mask* over the female libido.

Within the pages of *The Second Sex*, Beauvoir indeed attempts a description of female eroticism. The starting point for her analysis, an existential-via-Hegel one,[24] is the idea that eroticism is, in its essential character, "a movement toward the Other."[25] But this creates a problem for a woman, because she is continually made, or making herself, object, not subject.[26] In a striking statement of this fact, Beauvoir tells us, "Woman, like man, is her body; but her body is something other than herself."[27] Yet as an erotic creature she will have to extend herself to the Other. This amounts to a kind of "aggressiveness"—a will to be more than passive flesh, more than immanence. A woman still has an ability to be aggressive erotically, because she is never reduced finally and forever to the status of object, yet her eroticism becomes, and can remain, a source of ontological confusion to her, due to her being-made-object and not being-made-subject. She is required to *be* passively, but must at the same time *be* actively, in an erotic experience. Carnality and subjectivity simultaneously will be no easy task for woman. The hardest fight, clearly, involves her subjectivity.

A woman's erotic experience, Beauvoir maintains, is nearly always the experience of passivity. The strength of Beauvoir's assertion of women's passivity cannot be underestimated. It is extreme. A woman feels the "shame of her flesh," when gazed at, more than a man, and she "feels trespassed upon in her flesh."[28] "She always feels passive; she *is* caressed, penetrated; she undergoes coition, whereas the man exerts himself actively," Beauvoir says.[29] A woman requires a man to reveal to her her own body; she is therefore more reliant on him than he on her. She is from the beginning not her own sexual being, but becomes her own through being his—to the extent that she ever becomes her own.

We can understand easily enough the source of Beauvoir's assertion that the phallus is a symbolic organ of transcendence, and, for woman, of domination as well, but she is not careful enough, so that occasionally it seems she wants to claim that the phallus is both a symbolic and a *real* organ of domination, both a symbolic and a *real* organ of transcendence. The contrast continues. We read elsewhere: "The sex organ of a man is simple and neat as a finger; it is readily visible . . . but the feminine sex organ is mysterious even to the woman herself, concealed, mucous, and humid as it is. . . . Woman does not recognize herself in it."[30]

Beauvoir provides a striking metaphor to carry her theory. "Feminine sex desire is the soft throbbing of a mollusk,"[31] thus it is similar to an animal that lacks a backbone, and with a soft and unsegmented body. I discovered that Sartre had said, six years earlier in *Being and Nothingness*, "I desire a human being, not an insect or a mollusk."[32] Beauvoir seems to be replying, "What one receives, however, is a mollusk!" A woman's erotic experience is thus characterized by Beauvoir as primarily vaginal—for the "soft throbbing of a mollusk" is a clear reference to the vulva, and it is from this that all female eroticism is claimed to emanate. *The Blood of Others*, as mentioned earlier, contains a fascinating and similarly biological description of one woman's erotic experience.[33]

It is disappointing that Beauvoir never acknowledges, to any extent, the other erotic areas of a woman's body. The dependence on the "mollusk" metaphor is what leads her to the cliché that a woman's sexuality is inward, mysterious, and unlocalized. By calling attention to the more inward and "invisible" nature of a woman's genitalia, Beauvoir claims that, sexually, a woman is something she can neither see nor understand. Her "wetness" and her bleeding—both signs of her sexuality, erotic and non-erotic (or reproductive)—are dismissed as alienations from, not realizations of, her sexuality.

Woman lies in wait like the carnivorous plant, the bog, in which insects and children are swallowed up. She is absorption, suction, humus, pitch and glue, a passive influx, insinuating and viscous; thus, at least, she vaguely feels herself to be. Hence it is that there is in her not only resistance to the subjugating intentions of the male, but also conflict within herself.[34]

And this conflict within herself will bring about, on more than one occasion, considerable disgust, even physical disgust, both at her own erotic being and at sex in general, Beauvoir claims.

But we need to call Beauvoir's descriptions into question. If woman's eroticism is "unsegmented" in quality, like a mollusk, it is because it has not been "segmented" intellectually, and verbally, by a culture that treats female sexuality as, precisely, mystery. And this is exactly the way Beauvoir herself treats it.[35] Because Beauvoir fails to go beyond cultural stereotypes of woman's eroticism, she leaves us no richer on this topic than we were prior to reading *The Second Sex*. Stopping at the wall of mystery that has been built around woman's sexuality, she articulates for us only the message of a patriarchal culture: passivity, immanence, oppression lived in the erotic night, as well as in the day.

The generalized, unlocalized sexuality and consequent passivity that a woman is forced into leads Beauvoir, dialectically, to assert that a woman's general erotic experience is characterized by its stronger intensity than a man's. She says that, in lovemaking, a woman "loses her mind." Because the very goal of eroticism for a woman is in itself uncertain, according to Beauvoir, so too her enjoyment as it occurs "radiates throughout her whole body,"[36] that is, her enjoyment is not localized, nor is a woman conscious that her genital organs are the center of this experience.

Because female eroticism is distinctively a general, totalized body state, unlike men's, Beauvoir says that women are often repulsed by the too obvious attempts to help women achieve orgasm. Due to a woman's own special form of eroticism, she wants the achievement of a spell: "She would abolish all surroundings, abolish the singularity of the moment, of herself, and of her lover, she would fain be lost in a carnal night."[37] In Beauvoir's novel, *The Mandarins*, one can find described such a generalized, unlocalized female eroticism, and the corresponding desire for the creation and maintaining of a "spell."[38] Sexuality becomes a form of mindlessness.

Although early in *The Second Sex* Beauvoir denies that anything human is totally innate or totally "natural," she comes dangerously close, in her descriptions of female eroticism, to affirming what she should be denying by her own standards. At a point where we would expect Beauvoir to suggest social, historical, or cultural explanations for behavior, we find she avoids them.

Clearly, there are a variety of ways in which an individual may *actively* object to societal oppression—whether it is the oppression of a particular system of morality, as Beauvoir shows in her essay "Must We Burn Sade?" or the political oppression felt by a proletariat that eventually revolts, or the oppression of women, whose oppression/situation is unique within human history.[39] We need to understand if women's erotic passivity, suitable behavior for a patriarchal culture, is not also a protest—a political action—similar to the actions American slaves took, through their listless movements and pretended incompetencies. Is women's erotic passivity a dimension of women's political rebellion? Beauvoir does not ask the question in *The Second Sex*. Further, one might place the body and sexuality in a cultural context, taking account of historical changes and political movements, like feminism, which have had tremendous effects on how a woman lives her body, and consequently, her sexuality.

According to Beauvoir, a woman may overcome the erotic passivity that men and culture require of her in two ways. The first way is by rejecting men permanently, by a woman living out her erotic life with women, thus satisfying her sexuality as well as her ontological need to exercise her subjectivity, for she will be engaging her eroticism within an experience in which the roles are not always, already, determined according to gender. Beauvoir claims that all women are *naturally* homosexual. Women experience the female body as desirable largely because it is the locus of their first experience of sensuality—the mother—and because the culture has made of it the erotic object par excellence.[40] In addition, lesbianism is the form which an active eroticism may take because:

> Woman is an existent who is called upon to make herself object; as subject she has an aggressive element in her sensuality which is not satisfied on the male body; hence the conflicts that her eroticism must somehow overcome. . . . Woman's homosexuality is one attempt among others to reconcile her autonomy with the passivity of her flesh.[41]

The second way a woman may overcome the erotic passivity she experiences within patriarchal culture is through the creation, within heterosexual couples, of a *reciprocal* relationship between female and male, in order that a woman's subjectivity be permitted and acknowledged, as her body is desired.[42] Beauvoir displays too cavalier an attitude about the ease of achieving this state. Its content is also unclear. She provides a simplistic answer through her evocation of existentialist categories, which seem to operate merely as rhetoric. We must ask: How can one become an erotic subject if one is not a genuine subject already, that is, within the culture? And how does one escape the fear of cultural male domination, even in order to allow for the production of generosity and reciprocity in sexual intercourse?

Nonetheless, Beauvoir provides for the possibility of our thinking through human sexuality as one species differentiated into two "subsets"—female and male—rather than into two separate species. She asserts: "As a matter of fact, man, like woman, is flesh, therefore passive, the plaything of his hormones and of the species, the restless prey of his desires. And she, like him, in the midst of the carnal fever, is a consenting, a voluntary gift, an activity; they live out in their several fashions the strange ambiguity of existence made body."[43]

Focusing as it does on the mutuality of the difficulties and pleasures of human sexuality, this passage beautifully and succinctly demystifies heterosexual sexuality. But it is, of course, only comprehensible as a utopian description of heterosexuality because it requires a state of equality between the sexes which does not yet exist, although among "verbal" political acts no work has done more than *The Second Sex* to bring about such a state.

Sade and Bardot: Beyond *The Second Sex*

In her essay "Must We Burn Sade?" Beauvoir contends that insofar as Sade's sexual aberrations were acts of cruelty directed at individuals, they are to be condemned, but insofar as his fundamental enterprise was to challenge some of his society's most basic values, he should be understood and appreciated as a type of social and moral critic, one who chose to work out his argument with society through erotic experience. (The extent to which he differs from the "ordinary" sex criminal in this is an important question, though not to be taken up here.) "It is not the object of debauchery that excites us, but rather the idea of evil," he said, his design being (in a kind of pre-Nietzschean spirit) to oppose evil to good, to will evil in his actions as well as in his writings, as a form of active objection to the societal oppression embodied in a particular system of morality.[44]

The Marquis de Sade did not simply torture, and thereby produce his pleasure; he dramatized his eros within the framework of a play. Beauvoir asserts that fundamental to Sade's delight in the screams of his victims, the desire for the play, really only a desire for control, was entrenched. By creating a spectacle within which the erotic can happen, the classic sadist seeks control of the other, but more important, of himself. To maintain the sovereignty of the erotic subject, too easily lost in the ecstasy of the erotic moment, that moment is mapped out in advance, scripted to protect the still un(self)mastered master.[45] Nietzsche had said that the true man loves woman as "the most dangerous plaything," but for Sade it was not woman but erotic ecstasy which was loved, desired, as the most dangerous plaything, and for that reason he sought control over it.[46]

For the reader of *The Second Sex*, two related questions arise from Beauvoir's analysis of sadistic eroticism. First, does woman's eroticism as understood by Beauvoir carry out woman's argument with society, as Sade's carried out his, and if so, how? Second, can we discover a reason for Beauvoir's interest in Sade, one related to the development of a female erotic?

First, in *The Second Sex* and elsewhere, a woman is described by Beauvoir as so totally merged with her erotic experience that her own body seldom appears to her as anything but a fevered "receiving machine." She is "there" carnally, like a bog, like a mollusk, darkly and slowly feeling her own sensuality, waiting not only for a man but for herself, to be overtaken by her own sensuality—hardly the "lived body" that Merleau-Ponty, another French existential-phenomenologist whom Beauvoir cites, had described.

Unquestionably, we need to advance from this standpoint, an overgeneralized, simplistic assertion of female erotic passivity. The particular erotic behavior Beauvoir is describing, passive female behavior, must be seen as only one possible form of a woman's erotic life, a Beauvoirian "bog," or Freudian "dark continent," only for those who choose to limit their own sight—and insights—of it. Such behavior is only one way in which a woman's sexuality can and has been lived out—even within the patriarchal epoch, though it may indeed be, or have been, the most common. Further, and with reference to Beauvoir's analysis of Sade, it can be claimed that this passive sexuality may indeed carry out, for women at least, their argument with society, as Sade's did his. Although in one sense this passive behavior hinders the development of a woman's subjectivity and active sense of self, in another sense, i.e., if it is a *choice* in response to patriarchy, it *is* the exercise of subjectivity within an unjust world, a response of protest or rebellion in the same sense that certain actions of black American slaves were indirect forms of protest. Perhaps in "the passive form" of erotic behavior, as Beauvoir says in another context, a woman "refuses to play the game because she knows the dice are loaded."[47]

Second, what led Beauvoir to study Sade? If the foregoing is correct, this becomes clearer. The Sade essay may have been derived from her will to study how a connection may be made between subjectivity and eroticism. Sade had combined a will to evil with a will to mastery and carried these out within a totally controlled erotic experience. A woman's erotic enterprise must be nearly the reverse. For a woman there can be no pretense of mastery, since she is always cast in the role of erotic object, Beauvoir says, and denied the state necessary to mastery, that of subject. But things are not always what they seem, she reminds us, for "there is in her . . . resistance to the subjugating intentions of the male."[48]

Beauvoir's analysis leads me to suggest that women's will to be something more than erotic object has led women to develop a control system of passivity within erotic experience. That is, we need to question whether erotic passivity, to the extent it does exist in women, has been developed as a survival tactic. But ultimately, erotic passivity is useless, just as the sadist's tactics for control are useless. The moment of erotic ecstasy, if attained, is precisely the moment in which women are uncontrolled. Moreover, erotic passivity in women is inadequate as a response to cultural domination.

The spectacular achievement of an eroticism not founded in domination will not be easy. It presupposes societal changes, as well as changes made directly by a woman upon her own eroticism. In *Brigitte Bardot and the Lolita Syndrome*, published in 1960, Beauvoir claims that the real basis for Bardot's appeal lies in the new quality of female eroticism she displays: an aggressiveness.[49] Bardot, in film after film, is every bit as much the erotic hunter as the male—a self-conscious being, innocent of tricks and, in fact, oblivious to the opinions of others. Her eroticism is intimidating to men, particularly French men, because it is so unconventionally aggressive. Bardot—the ingenue with a woman's body and a sexual appetite we supposedly find only in men. The result of Bardot's presence on the screen in this role of erotic hunter is a "debunking of love and eroticism," according to Beauvoir, which has tremendous implications for the demystification and humanization of women's eroticism.

The age of Bardot has passed, and Beauvoir's analysis seems problematic. The sixties brought a sexual revolution via the increased practice of free love. The availability of sex outside the strictures of marriage certainly increased for women. Whether the quality of a woman's sexual experience also increased, and her erotic "passivity" decreased, is questionable. In any case, if there was a lessening of female erotic "passivity," the women's movement of the late sixties and seventies would, I think, have to be granted more than a little responsibility for this.

In the conclusion to *The Second Sex*, Beauvoir tells us that "there will always be certain differences between man and woman; her eroticism, and therefore her sexual world, have a special form of their own and therefore cannot fail to engender a sensuality, a sensitivity, of a special nature. This means that her relations to her own body, to that of the male, to the child, will never be identical with those [of] the male."[50] It is at this point, the last full page of the book, that Beauvoir is on the verge of concretely connecting for us a woman's body/form and a woman's eroticism.

In her novels after *The Second Sex*, Beauvoir continues to dwell on female characters, but she never gives more than a fleeting look at the peculiarly female erotic experience which she claims in *The Second Sex* needs a spokeswoman. She continues in her novels, as she had done earlier, to pay great attention to love, in particular to women in love and problems resulting from that experience, but nowhere will one find the descriptions of female eroticism she implied should be made. It was not via existential phenomenological description, but through autobiographical narration, the telling of the story of her own life, that she intended to concretize the analysis of woman that she had begun earlier. In an interview with Alice Schwarzer in 1978, Beauvoir expressed dissatisfaction with her memoirs, specifically on this point:

> I would have liked to have given a frank and balanced account of my own sexuality. A truly sincere one, from a feminist point of view; I would like to tell women about my life in terms of my own sexuality because it is not just a personal matter, but a political one, too.[51]

It is important to keep in mind that Beauvoir's descriptions of the passivity of "carnal fever" into which a woman submerges are meant to be descriptions of a *specific historical* woman—i.e., patriarchalized woman, rather than some "*eternal* woman," doomed in an "innate" or "determined" sexuality of passivity. Beauvoir ends not with female passivity, in *The Second Sex*, but with *difference*: "There always will be certain differences between men and women; woman's eroticism and therefore her sexual world have a specific form and therefore a special sensuality."[52]

Thus we need to begin at the point to which Beauvoir led us, and where she unfortunately leaves off: with a description of a female erotic, a description of a woman's "special sensuality," and with a comprehension of the relationship to this of human consciousness and human history. The specific task confronting feminist thinkers now is a comprehension of women's lived body, which might include: (1) the sensory systems of the clitoral and vaginal areas, (2) the breasts, for women, as zones of erotic pleasure in themselves and as instruments within an erotic drama in which men participate, and are manipulated, (3) female experience of the male body, (4) female experience of the female body, and (5) women's "unlimited" sexuality, as well as whether and how this is diminished through the controls and regularization of marriage, as Beauvoir has claimed.[53] Some of this has been addressed already in feminist poetry and novels, but more needs to be done.[54]

Women's victimization within a patriarchal society includes an elaborate intellectual system of silences constructed against the simple fact of our existence, which ignores women's manner of being and invalidates our experience. We need to create, and it is a political act to do so, precise descriptions to "inform" the silences surrounding all aspects of female human existence. In particular, discovering what in women's eroticism derives directly from situations of oppression, what is derived from and determined by our bodily structures, and what dimensions women's eroticism can hope to take on in a nonsexist world, become basic issues of a feminist theory of eroticism.

NOTES

The first version of this essay was presented to the Society for Phenomenology and Existential Philosophy at its 1978 meeting at Duquesne University, Pittsburgh, Pennsylvania. A second version was presented at The Second Sex Conference, sponsored by the New York Institute for the Humanities, at New York University, in September 1979. A third, shorter version was published in *Feminist Studies* 6(Summer 1980) under the name Jo-Ann P. Fuchs. I would like to thank the Faculty Development Committee of Towson State University for support in the preparation of the final manuscript of this essay.

1. Simone de Beauvoir, *The Second Sex*, trans. H. M. Parshley (New York: Alfred A. Knopf, 1952, Bantam, 1970), 44–45, 133.

2. Beauvoir, *The Second Sex*, 30.

3. Jean-Paul Sartre, *Being and Nothingness*, trans. Hazel E. Barnes (New York: Philosophical Library, 1956), 379–412.

4. Beauvoir, *The Second Sex*, 420.

5. In some cases, Beauvoir uses "sexuality" to refer simply to the reproductive function, as in the chapter "The Data of Biology," but in most cases, "sexuality" is used interchangeably with "eroticism." I will make use of this same interchange.

6. Simone de Beauvoir, *The Ethics of Ambiguity*, trans. Bernard Frechtman (New York: Citadel Press, 1970), 112. I have changed Frechtman's translation of "he" to "one," for the French "*chacun.*"

7. Maurice Merleau-Ponty, "Metaphysics and the Novel," in *Sense and Nonsense*, trans., with a Preface, by Hubert L. Dreyfus and Patricia Allen Dreyfus (Evanston: Northwestern University Press, 1964), 28.

8. Beauvoir, *The Second Sex*, 629.

9. Simone de Beauvoir, *She Came to Stay*, trans. anonymous (Cleveland: The World Publishing Co., 1954), 294.

10. Beauvoir, *She Came to Stay*, 404.

11. Simone de Beauvoir, *Les Belles Images*, trans. Patrick O'Brian (New York: G. P. Putnam's Sons, 1968), 143: "A woman without a man is entirely alone."

12. Simone de Beauvoir, *The Blood of Others*, trans. Roger Senhouse and Yvonne Moyse (New York: Alfred A. Knopf, Bantam, 1974), 86.

13. Beauvoir, *The Second Sex*, xxviii.

14. Ibid., 47.

15. Ibid., 29.

16. Ibid., 57.

17. Ibid., 376.

18. Ibid., 316.

19. Ibid., 38.

20. Ibid., p. xxiv. I am not the first to make this claim. In "Simone de Beauvoir and Existentialism," *Feminist Studies* 6(Summer 1980), Michèle Le Doeuff claims that

in order to use existentialism in *The Second Sex*, Beauvoir had to overcome certain aspects of it that were limitations to her project.

21. Ibid., 42.

22. Ibid., 43.

23. Ibid., 249.

24. An important discussion of the Hegel-via-Kojève influence on Beauvoir's thinking in *The Second Sex* was presented in Carol Craig's excellent paper at the workshop on "The Philosophical Writings of Simone de Beauvoir" at The Second Sex Conference, sponsored by the New York Institute for the Humanities, September 1979.

25. Beauvoir, *The Second Sex*, 420.

26. Ibid., 381.

27. Ibid., 26.

28. Ibid., 357, 366.

29. Ibid., 361.

30. Ibid., 362.

31. Ibid., 362.

32. Sartre, *Being and Nothingness*, 384.

33. Beauvoir, *The Blood of Others*, 86: "She felt enveloped in some pale, sickly vapor: she closed her eyes. She abandoned herself unresistingly to the charm that was slowly metamorphosing her into a plant; now she was a tree, a great silver poplar whose downy leaves were shaken by the summer breeze. A warm mouth clung to her mouth; under her blouse a hand caressed her shoulder, her breasts; warm vapors increased about her; she felt her bones and muscles melt, her flesh became a human and spongy moss . . . fingers wove a burning tunic about her belly; her breath came in quick gasps; . . . paralyzed by that net of burning silk . . . enclosed in that viscid darkness, forever an obscure and flabby jellyfish lying on a bed of magic sea-anemones. She pushed Paul away with both hands and sat up."

34. Beauvoir, *The Second Sex*, 362.

35. Beauvoir had little to go on; the Kinsey Report (on female sexuality) was not published until 1953, and it in fact footnotes *The Second Sex* a number of times.

36. Beauvoir, *The Second Sex*, 371.

37. Ibid., 372.

38. Simone de Beauvoir, *The Mandarins*, trans. Leonard M. Friedman (Cleveland: The World Publishing Co., Meridian Books, 1960), 81–82: "I closed my eyes and stepped into a dream as lifelike as reality itself, a dream from which I felt I would awaken at dawn, carefree and lighthearted . . . I abandoned myself to the black swell of desire. Carried away, tossed about, submerged, aroused, dashed headlong; there were moments when I felt as if I were plummeting through empty space, were about to be stranded in oblivion, in the blackness of night . . . .Becoming aware of my flesh, seeing his unfamiliar face, and under his gaze losing myself within myself—I looked at him and was halted midway in my inner turmoil, in a region without light and without darkness, where I was neither body nor spirit . . . I delivered to his curiosity a slough which was neither cold nor warm."

39. Simone de Beauvoir, "Must We Burn Sade?" trans. Annette Michelson, *The Marquis de Sade: An Essay by Simone de Beauvoir, with Selections from His Writings Chosen by Paul Dinnage* (New York: Grove Press, Inc., Evergreen, 1954), 40.

40. Beauvior, *The Second Sex*, 382.

41. Ibid., 381.

42. Ibid., 377.

43. Ibid., 685.

44. Beauvoir, *The Marquis de Sade*, 40.

45. Ibid., 43.

46. Friedrich Nietzsche, *Thus Spake Zarathustra*, trans. Thomas Common (New York: The Modern Library, 1927), 69.

47. Beauvoir, *The Second Sex*, 577.

48. Ibid., 362.

49. Simone de Beauvoir, *Brigitte Bardot and the Lolita Syndrome*, trans. Bernard Frechtman (New York: Arno Press and *The New York Times*, 1972), 37.

50. Beauvoir, *The Second Sex*, 688.

51. Alice Schwarzer, *After THE SECOND SEX: Conversations with Simone de Beauvoir*, trans. Marianne Howarth (New York: Pantheon Books, 1984), 84.

52. Beauvoir, *The Second Sex*, 688.

53. Ibid., 410, 418.

54. The descriptive task I mention here, a feminist phenomenology of eroticism, needs to be clearly differentiated from pornography. The distinctions could be the subject of another paper.

SIMONE DE BEAUVOIR AND TWO KINDS OF AMBIVALENCE IN ACTION

Eléanor H. Kuykendall

Simone de Beauvoir has shown that the presupposition of male dominance as a natural phenomenon mystifies women's experience. When this presupposition is created and sustained by the conventions of language, women's use of that language to represent thought and to communicate becomes a problem for ethics. I shall call this problem linguistic ambivalence.[1]

In the following remarks I characterize linguistic ambivalence as implicitly recognized in Beauvoir's early existential ethics, as exemplified in her writings in a manner overlooked by standard conceptions of linguistic ambiguity, as eluding theoretical conceptions of linguistics offered by Saussure and Chomsky, and finally as manifesting Beauvoir's continuing concern with women's access to language.

I

The solitary existential heroine of Simone de Beauvoir's early novels and memoirs vacillates among multiple choices, manifesting that paralysis of consciousness which Søren Kierkegaard had earlier characterized as "double-mindedness" and "inner psychical disagreement."[2] This oscillation arises from within and engages the subject in the uncertain repetition of all of her intentions to act. I will call this state, in which the subject risks failure to act at all, primary or psychological ambivalence.

The socially attuned antiheroine of Simone de Beauvoir's later writings finds her intentions blocked through circumstance or through material scarcity. The ambivalence perhaps resolvable through individual efforts of courage, as Beauvoir had first supposed, here appears as an opposition from without, not so to be resolved. Such an opposition can nonetheless be known. The subject's reinterpretation of her psychological inability to act rather as an adverse social definition of her acts as alien and of her as Other enables her to revalue the opposition that she lives through, or at times simply lives. This state I will refer to as secondary or social ambivalence.

Primary ambivalence—the repetition of intention—and secondary ambivalence—the revaluation of that repetition—are manifest in linguistic ambivalence, which is at one and the same time a third level of ambivalence and a representation of the first two levels of ambivalence. At times linguistic ambivalence is manifest as a phonological, semantic, or syntactic ambiguity which clouds the understanding of speaker or hearer, author or audience, until the ambiguity can be resolved. But at times linguistic ambivalence is masked, since it escapes standard linguistic definitions of ambiguity. The unmasking of linguistic ambivalence—as of Kierkegaardian "double-mindedness" or of the schizophrenic's double bind—can help to bring about its resolution.

To advocate unmasking linguistic ambivalence in order to promote its resolution is, of course, to advocate a feminist ethic. Such an ethic might offer as a categorical imperative that speaking and writing promote mutuality and reciprocity, rather than dominance and control, among the people whose social relationships are thereby constituted. This ethic would be compatible both with Julia Kristeva's proposal that an "ethic of linguistics" supports the subject's access to the phonological origins of the unconscious[3] and with Jürgen Habermas's proposal that a conception of "communicative competence" supports the subject's access to discourse.[4] The ethic which I am proposing, however, attempts a project at once more general and more specific than those proposed by Kristeva and by Habermas. The project is more general, in that it considers linguistic ambivalence as both individual and social. Yet the project is also more specific than those proposed by Kristeva and by Habermas, in that it considers, particularly, differences of gender expressed as clashing psychological and social presuppositions.

There is an ethics of linguistics, though not of feminist linguistics, to be drawn from Beauvoir's early writings. For example, in *The Ethics of Ambiguity* she wrote, "To declare that existence is absurd is to deny that it can ever be given a meaning; to say that it is ambiguous is to assert that its meaning is never fixed, that it must be constantly won."[5] The existential challenge to win meaning from existence can be interpreted linguistically as the subject's challenge to win an understanding of the ambiguous sign— to attach a meaning to a word. Again, in *The Ethics of Ambiguity* Beauvoir compares oppression to the flow of air through which the soaring dove (in homage to Kant's image of perception through the senses in *The Critique of Pure Reason*) finds support in the very resistance which would appear to impede its flight.[6] Winning altitude by transforming the very material which would appear to impede one's ascent can be interpreted linguistically as the subject's transcending the social definition of the very sign whose presuppositions would appear to block her discourse.

Three years before *The Ethics of Ambiguity*, Beauvoir had specified that a linguistic interpretation of such existential efforts of will as winning meaning from existence and transcending its material limitations by transforming them, cannot remain solitary. In *Pyrrhus et Cinéas*, as the German occupation of Paris ended, Beauvoir observed that although in speaking or writing one certainly must know what one wishes to communicate, one must also know with whom one can so engage.[7] In the same work she also wrote, "One speaks only to men; language is an appeal to the liberty of the other since the sign is a sign only through a consciousness which takes possession of it."[8] This passage, in which 'homme' or 'man' must be interpreted gender-neutrally, as was standard in French in 1944, exemplifies in English translation nearly forty years later the source of a linguistic ambivalence to be located in a changing understanding of presuppositions of gender in both French and English.

In *The Second Sex*, five years after *Pyrrhus et Cinéas*, Beauvoir was by no means speaking to men only. In writings that have succeeded *The Second Sex* Beauvoir has increasingly recognized that women's access to one another through the sign is blocked as women lack access to the sign itself—in that women must communicate with one another in men's language. The sign—as it is used to presuppose distinctions of gender to differing effect, as it is available to women and men to differing effect, and as it can be transformed—is the material of an ethic of feminist linguistics whose outline I now pursue through a number of examples.

II

A standard test for semantic ambiguity is the truth of the sentence in which the sign is used. If a sentence is true under one interpretation of that sign, but false under another interpretation, then the sign itself is ambiguous. But if different interpretations of the sign do not affect the truth of the sentence in which it is used, then the sign is merely nonspecific in reference and its interpretation is only a question of the speaker's understanding of the larger context within which the sentence is used.[9] This conception of semantic ambiguity appears different from Beauvoir's characterization of existence as ambiguous, in that its meaning must be constantly won. But semantic and existential ambiguity coalesce when the analysis of a sign as ambiguous, or not, becomes controversial, as it does for a feminist ethics of linguistics.

According to a standard linguistic conception of ambiguity, 'He saw her duck' is ambiguous because the sign 'duck' may be interpreted either as a noun or as a verb and both interpretations of the sentence cannot be true together. 'He cooked her goose' can similarly be counted as ambiguous, according to the linguists who proposed this definition of semantic ambiguity, because the sentence may be interpreted as literally true and as metaphorically false, or vice versa, and the two interpretations cannot both be true together. On the other hand, according to the same linguists, marking a sign for gender, as in substituting the male-marked 'gander' for 'goose' in 'He cooked her goose', cannot affect the truth of the sentence in which it is used. Therefore gender is not part of the meaning of the sign and presuppositions of gender do not count as contributing to its ambiguity.[10]

I take exception to this semantic test for ambiguity as excluding gender even though I believe that what's sauce for the goose is sauce for the gander. Literally, 'He cooked her goose' can be changed to 'He cooked her gander' without affecting the truth of the sentence. Metaphorically, though, only geese are cooked, ganders are not; what's sauce for the goose is not sauce for the gander after all. Metaphors often are said to be neither true nor false; but the literal truth or falsity of a sentence is what is frequently under dispute for gender-marked signs used in these sentences. For example, 'chairman' formerly interpreted conventionally as gender-neutral, now is increasingly interpreted as gender-specific only. The interpretation that 'chairman' cannot truly refer to a female is implicit in the use of 'chairwoman' to refer to her, as well as in the American Philosophical Association's gender-neutral 'chairperson' ("Association of Department Chairpersons") and 'chair' (as in the programs of divisional meetings). At times, however, speakers and writers insist upon the use of 'chairman' to refer to themselves gender-specifically, as did a male philosophy professor who changed catalogue copy referring to him from 'chairperson' to 'chairman'. These examples appear to meet the linguistic test for ambiguity outlined above in that for many speakers and writers a gender-specific interpretation of the sign determines the truth or falsity of its reference.

However, to complicate the analysis, gender-neutral and gender-specific uses of nouns are not symmetrical in English and French. In French there is no gender-neutral noun to refer to a person who must be referred to in English as the director of an international exchange program and professor of philosophy. The person who holds such a position in France will be referred to as 'un professeur' and 'un directeur' if male. Such a person may be referred to either as 'un professeur' and 'un directeur' or, more conservatively, as 'un professeur' and 'une directrice' if female. A native speaker of English so referred to in French experiences no dissonance if he is male; she cannot help but experience dissonance if female.

Native speakers of French deal with such dissonance in a variety of ways. If a woman is referred to as 'un professeur' and 'un directeur'—in the masculine—she may also be referred to in the same sentence as specifically female through such idiomatic, though ungrammatical, structures as 'Elle est belle, le professeur'.[11] If, on the other hand, a woman is referred to as 'un professeur'—in the masculine—but as 'une directrice'—in the feminine—the second reference marks the referent as specifically female. Yet the referent is not marked as specifically female when the feminine 'la personne' is used, as it is regularly, to refer to a man.

Thus to refer to a woman in French as 'une directrice' or to refer to a woman in English as 'a directress' is to carry out an act whose ethical interpretation differs in the two languages. The use of 'la directrice' bespeaks a certain conservatism, the use of a hyper-correct construction—a construction "un peu classique" for some, but certainly correct. On the other hand the use of 'directress' to refer to a woman in English raises eyebrows. A French tutor who knew English and accepted 'la directrice' as the title of an American administrator expressed shock upon reading a report referring three times in English to that administrator as a 'directress'. Native speakers of English express similar responses to the use of 'directress'.

These differences between interpretations of female-marking in French and English might, however, be interpreted simply as differences of degree, since native speakers of both languages consider that dropping the female-marked form of a word like 'director' is a more contemporary use of the sign. The question for a feminist ethic of linguistics is whether marking the use of a sign for the female gender, as is done with 'directress' and 'une directrice', carries with it ethical consequences which are different from those of marking the term for the male gender, as is done with 'gander'. And again, a feminist ethic of linguistics must continue to question the consequences of using the same form, like 'chairman', 'director', and 'un directeur', to refer both gender-neutrally and gender-specifically. We may attempt to make progress with an answer to this question by examining an apparent asymmetry in reference by gender in Beauvoir's *The Second Sex*. I will use this example to show how a new word must evolve to express what the existing words could not.

Beauvoir opens the last chapter of *The Second Sex* with a citation from a male writer, Jules Laforge: "No, woman is not our brother."[12] Yet she ends the chapter, and with it the book, with an assertion that appears to contradict the first: "To gain the supreme victory, it is necessary, for one thing, that by and through their natural differentiation men and women unequivocally affirm their brotherhood."[13] The translation from French to English is complicated by the fact that in French the word 'le frère' or 'brother' has, of course, a counterpart in 'la soeur' or 'sister'. But 'la fraternité', a feminine noun, had no counterpart in French in 1949 when the passage was published; and moreover, its translation into English might more appropriately be rendered as 'fraternity'. 'Fraternity', which was used to translate 'la fraternité' in Sartre's *Critique of Dialectical Reason*, captures the close association of the French sign with the motto of the French Revolution, 'Liberté, égalité, fraternité,' which appears on all French coins and public buildings, to evoke a political event completely passed by in the English translation of 'la fraternité' as 'brotherhood'.

The English word 'sisterhood' is not symmetrical, either, with the newly coined 'la sororité'. The English word means both a relationship of kinship and of community—as of a religious community—specific to women and standardly referred to as such. The French word means primarily a political relationship and it is so experimental as not yet to be accepted by dictionaries. As recently as 1977 Beauvoir herself did not accept the term 'la sororité', although she did recognize the political interpretation then being given to the English word 'sisterhood'.[14] Further, the coinage 'la sororité' is rejected by some native speakers of French as reflecting an excessive American influence on the language. Consequently the apparent asymmetry of reference by gender in the two passages from the 1949 *Second Sex* cited above is more complicated than it might first appear.

We may pursue an analysis of this complication by examining successive revisions of the previously cited ending of *The Second Sex*:

(1) To gain the supreme victory, it is necessary, for one thing, that by and through their natural differentiation men and women unequivocally affirm their brotherhood.

Eliminating the hedges and intensifiers, we obtain:

(2) To gain the supreme victory, it is necessary that by and through their natural differentiation men and women affirm their brotherhood.

But making a substitution for 'brotherhood' in English we obtain an ungrammatical sentence:

(3) To gain the supreme victory, it is necessary that by and through their natural differentiation men and women affirm their sisterhood.

This result leads us to suspect that, in English at least, 'brotherhood' exhibits an alternation between gender-neutral and gender-specific interpretations similar to that of 'goose', which may refer either gender-neutrally or gender-specifically to females of the species; or to the now controversial 'chairman', which previously was said to refer either gender-neutrally or gender-specifically to males. For some speakers of English the closer translation of 'la fraternité' as 'fraternity' may not exhibit this alternation; for example, the female president of a local chapter of the United University Professors signs her letters "Fraternally yours."

For some speakers both of English and of French, the absence of a specifically feminine translation in French of the English 'sisterhood' is objectionable on ethical grounds. Beauvoir's passage ending *The Second Sex* can be rewritten grammatically in English to incorporate a feminine noun only by changing its meaning:

(4) To gain the supreme victory, it is necessary that by and through their natural differentiation from men, women affirm their sisterhood.

It is unlikely, however, that Beauvoir herself would have accepted such a revision. For example, in 1976, questioned about separatism, which she opposed, in the women's movement, Beauvoir offered the example of the many men who had supported women in the struggle to legalize abortion in France. Of these women only Beauvoir then said, "They make a reality of fraternity, without their relationships' depending on lesbian sexuality."[15]

In contrast to the English sign 'sisterhood', the experimental French coinage 'la sororité' does not mean a family relationship. For example, in a 1981 article entitled "Liberté, égalité, sororité: le troisième mot" ("Liberty, Equality, Sorority: The Third Word"), Cathy Bernheim and Geneviève Brisac observe:

If Fraternity permits men to reinforce their own identity and to meet one another under the same banner, that of Human Being, Sorority for us is a weapon which deconstructs *the* woman, that obscene gawk in the name of which we are oppressed, and puts our identity as women into question. Sorority helps us confront the universal legitimacy of the hatred of women in this male world.[16]

Clearly, the experimental coinage "la sororité", which appears to have arisen spontaneously, has ethical consequences. These are the result of making women's felt psychological ambivalence explicit as linguistic ambivalence, as much when such ambivalence is felt by women among one another as when ambivalence is felt by women among men. As Bernheim and Brisac conclude, "And then sorority is also what permits us to write this text in two voices."[17]

The question remains whether a sign which permits the writing of a text in two voices is ambiguous, in that a change in its interpretation affects the truth value of the sentence in which the sign is used; or whether such a sign is but indefinite in its reference, in that the speaker's or hearer's understanding alone is affected by a change in the interpretation of the sentence. I would suggest that it is precisely in raising this question that, at the same time, one raises as ethical the question of classifying a linguistic sign as ambiguous. Speakers of English differ as to whether 'chairman' can be used truly to refer to women; speakers of French differ as to whether 'la fraternité' can be used truly to characterize relationships among women; but speakers of both languages agree that neither 'la sororité' nor 'sisterhood' can be used truly to characterize mixed or male relationships. Perhaps it is 'la solidarité' that is sought for both languages, for gender-neutral political relationships at least. In the meantime, the differences that speakers evince in assessing the truth-values of sentences using purportedly gender-neutral signs to refer in a variety of ways cannot be resolved simply, as differences in belief must be resolved, through recourse to the facts. It is rather an attitude toward the facts—an attitude manifest as the acceptance or rejection of linguistic change—which remains to be resolved.

III

English-speaking male philosophers reject the authority of the American Philosophical Association in continuing to use 'chairman' to refer to a woman, or in using 'chair' or 'chairperson' with ironic intonation. French-speaking feminists continue to use 'la fraternité', with political connotations special to the language, to characterize relationships among women. Given this apparently incoherent ethical situation some feminist speakers of English, and especially of French, have begun to raise the question whether women can speak to one another at all in men's language. This question raises the specific issue of psychological ambivalence in language—the effect on the consciousness of the speaker of speaking in two voices—to another plane. Speaking and writing in two voices is an activity which appears to be imposed upon the author from without. Yet this imposition may arise from the alternation of solitary reflection with social engagement common to writers of both sexes, through their very choice of their project. In either case, conceptions of language which perpetuate the theoretical separation of the psychological from the social elements of the speaker's or writer's knowledge of language mystify the process in which an author uses language both to represent her thoughts and to communicate them.

The politically engaged writer, like all writers, cannot but engage in writing as an alternation between the solitary reflection which makes writing possible both as the representation of thought and as the social engagement through which such reflections may be made to move the audience to action. As Julia Kristeva has observed, the committed intellectual who would use writing to act discovers in her own consciousness an internal dissidence requiring both detachment from the circumstances reflected upon and engagement with the reader.[18] Writing on intellectual power in France, Régis Debray observed of his own project, "I am alone when I write a book, I am alone in being able to write it; it is a matter between me and myself."[19] Yet in the same passage Debray also points out that even in the very selling of the resulting work, the author establishes a relationship with the audience.

One may question, of course, whether such terms of social engagement are explicitly linguistic. In a deeper sense they must be, in that philosophy is practiced by using language to impel an audience to revalue its own presuppositions. The linguistic nature of this process of revaluation may be masked by its being done indirectly, forcing the reader to make an inference which the author evokes rather than describes. Such was the "indirect communication" described by Søren Kierkegaard as having an "entire essential content" which was "essentially secret";[20] such is the project of the feminist novelist and poet Marge Piercy, as she has described it to me in conversation; and such is the "deconstruction" of the French feminists Cathy Bernheim and Geneviève Brisac, cited above, when they use 'la sororité' to "speak in two voices." Speaking or writing so as to evoke in the audience the consciousness of the voices of reflection and communication through which the author confronts conflicting individual and social presuppositions locates these conflicting presuppositions in language. When these conflicting presuppositions are of gender, the feminist writer, through language, turns upon itself the very material by which these conflicting presuppositions of gender are created and sustained.

Conceptions of language influential both in France and in the United States, however, mask that alternation. For example, the Swiss linguist Ferdinand de Saussure distinguished between language as *la langue*—the structures of language, as socially recognized at a given time—and *la parole*—the uses of language in individual acts of speaking and writing. *Le langage*, for Saussure, was but an accidental and individual product—the style of the speaker or writer.[21] Saussure's terms conform to nontechnical uses of them in French. It was 'le langage' that Beauvoir used in asserting, in the passage from *Pyrrhus et Cinéas* cited earlier, that language is an appeal to the liberty of the Other. When the individual subject speaks up, as at a public meeting, that action is referred to commonly as a 'prise de parole'.

For Saussure, these exercises of individual style or eloquence are not proper to linguistics, which studies a code reached, in effect, by consensus—a social entity—as it exists at a given time. Yet it is in transformations of living languages over time that linguistic ambivalence reveals itself in the dissidence which such transformations bring about—as in the introduction of 'chair' and 'chairperson' into English and 'la sororité' experimentally into French. Each change, challenging the gender-neutrality of a noun in English and the gender-specificity of a noun in French, shocks speakers and writers into recognition of their previously unacknowledged presuppositions of gender in either language.

A conception of syntactic transformation unknown to Saussure, together with a Cartesian conception of knowledge of language as cognitive, abstract, and separate from its practice in communication, distinguishes Noam Chomsky's conception of linguistic competence from Saussure's conception of *la langue*. Like Saussure, Chomsky would restrict linguistics to the study of language as spoken at a given time; unlike Saussure, Chomsky considers the speaker's knowledge of the language to be solitary, rather than social.[22] Chomsky's conception of competence is very powerful in its capacity to explain individual departures from syntax as a cognitive structure, as Saussure's conception of *la langue* cannot do. For example, Luce Irigaray has demonstrated the usefulness of a Chomskyan conception of competence to explain deformations of French syntax by schizophrenics.[23] Neither Saussure's nor Chomsky's conception of language, however, is adequate to account for the ethical consequences to speakers and writers of the dissonance occasioned by clashing individual and social presuppositions of gender. For both linguists, and for Chomsky especially, the two functions of reflection and communication are to be studied separately; in that separation, the clash is muffled.

Given linguistic ambivalence as an ethical problem escaping the explanatory limits of Saussurian and Chomskyan linguistics, since it is manifest and lived through a process of language change, we are led to consider language change itself as a possible source of resolution for the very problem its conflicting presuppositions of gender present. But proposing language change self-consciously, by introducing a new literary style, and participating in language change, self-consciously or not, through speech, are two different projects, as Simone de Beauvoir pointed out. The first project, practiced by some French feminists as *l'écriture féminine*, or women's writing, can be done by a few. The second project, evidenced in the introductions of such signs as 'chair' and 'chairperson' into English and of 'la sororité' into French, is an effort of many. To choose the type of language change attempted in creating a literary style is for Beauvoir an act of elitism, of creation accessible to only a few. By contrast, to participate in language change through speech is to participate in an act of creation with no individual authorship, accessible to all; for "a language is not something which is created, it is something which is inherited, of which one can never say that it is an individual who made it. . . . It is necessary to make use of the language of the oppressor to combat the oppressor."[24] We must now turn directly to the question of women's access to the language itself, that women may create the resolution of linguistic ambivalence from the very material through which ambivalence is imposed.

IV

In a work comparing the views of Cartesian phenomenologists and Cartesian linguists, James M. Edie remarks: "I want to leave in suspense here the question of whether language is essentially a question of communication. Certainly we use language for other purposes, as in philosophical writing, for instance, to clarify and bring to consciousness the articulation of experience."[25] This remark succinctly captures a metatheoretical dilemma for an ethic of linguistic. Beauvoir had recognized the ethical consequences of a Cartesian psychology as early as *The Ethics of Ambiguity*: "After Descartes how can we ignore the fact that subjectivity radically signifies separation?"[26] But writing itself, she later observed, is "a complex activity: it means a simultaneous preference for the imaginary and a desire to communicate. And in these choices there appear very different and at first sight contradictory tendencies."[27]

Beauvoir, however, has not drawn the Cartesian linguist's conclusion that theoretical explanations of the use of language to represent thought and to communicate must be separated. Rather, her observations concerning the ethical problem of women's access to language flow directly from her conception of the subjectivity both of self-reflection and of communication—a conception present as early as *The Second Sex*:

> It is on the level of communication that the word has its true meaning: it implies a stammering presence that fails to make itself manifest and clear. To say that woman is mystery is to say, not that she is silent, but that her language is not understood; she is there, but hidden behind veils; she exists beyond these uncertain appearances.[28]

In this passage, in contrast to Jacques Derrida's much later proposal of a conception of woman as mysterious in style, veiled and inaccessible in intent,[29] Beauvoir was already proposing women's purported inaccessibility through language rather as a moral problem to be unmasked than as an aesthetic phenomenon to be celebrated.

The problem of linguistic ambivalence is masked by conceptions of language which offer separate descriptions of its psychological and social function, as I have already suggested. The problem of linguistic ambivalence is also masked as merely one of social circumstance. "In France, if you are a writer, to be a woman is to provide a stick to be beaten with,"[30] Beauvoir offers as an example of such a circumstance. Reversing Beauvoir's observation we obtain, 'In France, if you are a woman, to be a writer is to provide a stick to be beaten with'. That, of course, is the experience of any woman whose language is not understood, for her own lack of access to it, as Beauvoir had proposed. In this way linguistic ambivalence is created by social circumstance.

As Beauvoir also suggested in a novel translated into English twenty years after *The Second Sex*, men and women do differ in their access to language and in their own perception of that access. In *Les Belles Images* she makes a male lawyer say, "Man is a talking animal and he will always let himself be swayed by the power of the word."[31]But a few pages earlier in the same novel Beauvoir makes a mother speak of her powerlessness to communicate with her daughter:

> I don't think she distrusts me: it's rather that we lack a common language. I've let her run very free and at the same time I've treated her as a baby; I've not tried to talk to her: so I think words intimidate her, at least when I am there. I can't hit upon a point of contact—can't get through.[32]

As in Adrienne Rich's "Power," from *The Dream of a Common Language*, Beauvoir had already proposed the ethical problem of women's access to language as that of women's power to reach one another by using a language which its female speakers and writers also perceive as damaging to them.

Finally, the question of clashing psychological and social presuppositions of gender in language presents itself as the ethical problem of the speaker's and writer's access to language change, thereby to control and to change the presuppositions which the use of language imposes upon consciousness. Linguistic ambivalence manifests itself as the speaker's or writer's dilemma of having access only to a form of words whose presuppositions must distort the very results of the reflection, including moral reflection, which she would seek to communicate. As Beauvoir observed very clearly in a 1976 interview:

It is evident that woman wishes to take up the instrument. That is to say that for her language is a universal which she wants to appropriate. But this language, at the same time that it is universal, is nevertheless a universal which has been marked and forged by men and there are a number of words which are specifically masculine, which carry masculine values and of which it is absolutely necessary to beware because, if one is caught in the trap of these words, one ends up thinking, writing, like men; that is, thinking exactly like them. That must be avoided.[33]

This passage, translated from spoken rather than from literary French, exemplifies its argument. In it Beauvoir uses 'language' to refer to the "universal which is marked and forged by men"; but the word that she uses in French is 'langage', which, by Saussure's definition, can count merely as stylistic variation. To characterize a male-defined universality thereby as particular is to begin to offer a feminist critique of it; to offer that critique is to deconstruct or dismantle its pretense to universality. Through such deconstruction linguistic ambivalence is resolved and language made accessible to its disenfranchised speakers and writers.

Simone de Beauvoir observed that the political struggle in which feminists engage is as much psychic as social, and to that observation she added that the psychic confrontation that an examination of language provokes will surely disturb us. Yet this confrontation will also break some of our bonds and open us to new truths.[34] The speaker's or writer's struggle with the semantic or syntactic definitions of her language, varying the forms of words prescribed for it, constitutes a struggle to seize meaning from existence first characterized as individual in *The Ethics of Ambiguity*, and now conceived as social as well. An ethic of feminist linguistics construes this process as ongoing, like language change itself. A further development of such an ethic might specify the ways in which, through acceding to the control of the presuppositions of gender to which her use of language commits her, a woman comes to exercise a power of speech or *prise de parole* founded on some principle other than that of control.[35]

NOTES

1. Candace Watson suggested this term to me in conversation.

2. Søren Kierkegaard, *Purity of Heart*, trans. Douglas V. Steere (New York: Harper Torchbooks, 1956), 117: "So the double-minded person may have had a will to the Good, for the one who is betrayed into double-mindedness by feeling, or by that distant recognition, he too has a will; but it received no power, and the germ of double-mindedness lay in the inner psychical disagreement."

3. Julia Kristeva, "The Ethics of Linguistics," in *Desire in Language*, ed. Leon S.

Roudiez, trans. Thomas Gora, Alice Jardin, and Leon S. Roudiez (New York: Columbia University Press, 1980), 23–35.

4. Jürgen Habermas, "What is Universal Pragmatics?" *Communication and the Evolution of Society* (Boston: Beacon Press, 1979), 1–68. See also Thomas McCarthy, *The Critical Theory of Jürgen Habermas* (Cambridge: MIT Press, 1981), chap. 4.

5. Simone de Beauvoir, *The Ethics of Ambiguity*, trans. Bernard Frechtman (New York: Citadel Press, 1964), 129.

6. Ibid., 105.

7. Simone de Beauvoir, *Pour une morale de l'ambiguité, suivi de Pyrrhus et Cinéas* (Paris: Gallimard, 1944), 342.

8. Ibid., 348: "On ne parle qu'à des hommes; le langage est un appel à la liberté de l'autre puisque le signe n'est signe que par une conscience qui le ressaisit."

9. Arnold M. Zwicky and Jerrold M. Sadock, "Ambiguity Tests and How to Fail Them," in *Syntax and Semantics*, John M. Kimball, ed., vol. 4 (New York: Academic Press, 1975), 4–10.

10. Ibid.

11. Francine Wattman Frank, "Sexism, Grammatical Gender, and Social Change," paper delivered at the Ninth World Congress of Sociology, Uppsala, Sweden, August 1978.

12. Simone de Beauvoir, *The Second Sex*, trans. H. M. Parshley (New York: Vintage Press, 1974 [1952]), 796. See also Beauvoir, *Le Deuxième Sexe* (Paris: Gallimard, 1949), 483.

13. Ibid., 504 [*Le Deuxième Sexe*, 504]: "On ne saurait mieux dire. C'est au sein du monde donné qu'il appartient à l'homme de faire triompher le règne de la liberté; pour remporter cette suprême victoire il est entre autres nécessaire que par-delà leurs différenciations naturelles hommes et femmes affirment sans équivoque leur fraternité."

14. In an interview given to Dorothy Tennov in English on New York Public Television January 17, 1977, Beauvoir said, "It is not possible to use the term 'sororité'. There is no word to say 'Sisterhood,' which is a very beautiful word. But there is sisterhood among a lot of women I know. They are very friendly and they help each other. They really work in Sisterhood. But not all. Not all women are Sister to all other women." The text of the interview was printed in *Spokeswoman* (January, 1977).

15. "Le Deuxième Sexe vingt-cinq ans après," interview by John Gerassi, *Society* (January-February 1976), trans. Claude Francis and Fernande Gontier. The interview was reprinted in Beauvior, *Les Ecrits de Simone de Beauvoir*, ed. Claude Francis and Fernande Gontier (Paris: Gallimard, 1979), 555: "A présent, surtout comme résultat de ces prises de conscience, les femmes sont non seulement capables d'être de véritables amies, mais elles ont appris à être chaleureuses, sincères, profondement affectueuses les unes avec les autres; elles font une réalité de la fraternité sans que ces rapports dépendent de la sexualité lesbienne. Bien entendu, il y a beaucoup de luttes, même des luttes strictement féministes avec des conséquences sociales; les femmes comptent que les hommes y participeront, et beaucoup l'ont fait. . . . "

16. Cathy Bernheim and Geneviève Brisac, "Liberté, égalité, sororité: le troisième mot," *La revue d'en face*, 11(fourth trimester 1981):5: "Remarquons aussi que, si la Fraternité permet aux hommes de renforcer leur propre identité et de se rapprocher sous une même bannière, celle de l'Être humain, la Sororité est pour nous une arme qui déconstruit *la* Femme, ce carcan au nom duquel on nous opprime, et remet en question notre identité de femmes. Contre la légitimité universelle de la haine des femmes dans ce monde mâle, la Sororité nous aide a faire front."

17. Ibid., 10: "Et puis la sororité, c'est aussi ce qui nous permet d'écrire ce texte a deux voix."

18. Julia Kristeva, "Un nouveau type d'intellectuel: le dissident," *Tel Quel*, 74(Winter 1977):3–8.

19. Régis Debray, *Le pouvoir intellectuel en France* (Paris: Ramsay, 1979), 233–34: "Je suis seul quand j'écris un livre, je suis seul à pouvoir l'écrire, c'est une affaire entre moi et moi."

20. Søren Kierkegaard, *Concluding Unscientific Postscript*, trans. David F. Swenson and Walter Lowrie (Princeton: Princeton University Press, 1941), 73.

21. Ferdinand de Saussure, *Course in General Linguistics*, trans. Wade Baskin (New York: Philosophical Library, 1959), chap. 1. See also Ferdinand de Saussure, *Cours de linguistique générale*, ed. Tullio de Mauro (Paris: Payot, 1980), chap. 1.

22. Noam Chomsky, *Aspects of the Theory of Syntax* (Cambridge: MIT Press, 1965), 3–17; Chomsky, *Reflections on Language* (New York: Pantheon Books, 1975), 24; Chomsky, *Language and Responsibility*, based on conversations with Mitsou Ronat, trans. John Viertel (New York: Pantheon Books, 1979), 48–51. On the other hand, in *Lectures in Government and Bindings: The Pisa Lectures* (Dordrecht, Holland: Foris Publications, 1982), 18, Chomsky refers to "the interface of grammatical competence, one mentally represented system, and other systems: the conceptual system, systems of belief, of pragmatic competence, of speech production and analysis and so on."

23. Luce Irigaray, "Le schizophrène et la question du signe," *Semiotexte*, 2(Spring 1975):31–42, *Le Langage des déments* (The Hague: Mouton, 1973), and "Production de Phrases chez les déments et les schizophrènes," *Parler N'Est Jamais Neutre* (Paris: Les Editions de Minuit, 1985), 105–116.

24. "Sur quelques problèmes actuels du féminisme: entretien avec Simone de Beauvoir," interview conducted by Geneviève Brisac, Marie-Jo Dharernas, and Irène Théry, *La revue d'en face*, 9-10(first trimester 1981):11: "Un langage n'est pas quelque chose qui se crée, c'est quelque chose dont on hérite, dont on ne peut jamais dire que c'est un certain individu qui l'a fait. . . . Il faut se servir du langage des oppresseurs pour combattre les oppresseurs."

25. James M. Edie, *Speaking and Meaning: The Phenomenology of Language* (Bloomington: Indiana University Press, 1976), 201.

26. Beauvoir, *The Ethics of Ambiguity*, 105.

27. Simone de Beauvoir, *The Coming of Age*, trans. André Deutsch (New York: Putnam, 1972), 400.

28. Beauvoir, *The Second Sex*, 290.

29. Jacques Derrida, *Spurs/Eperons*, trans. Barbara Harlow (Chicago: University of Chicago Press, 1978), 46–47, 54–55.

30. Simone de Beauvoir, *Force of Circumstance*, trans. André Deutsch (New York: Putnam, 1964), 645.

31. Simone de Beauvoir, *Les Belles Images*, trans. Patrick O'Brian (London: Fontana Books, 1969), 79.

32. Ibid., 65–66.

33. "Entretien avec Claude Francis," in *Les Ecrits de Simone de Beauvoir*, ed. Francis and Gontier, 571: "Il est évident que la femme souhaite s'emparer de l'instrument, c'est-à-dire que le langage pour elle c'est un universel qu'elle veut s'approprier. Mais ce langage en même temps qu'universel, c'est quand même un universel qui a été marqué et forgé par les hommes et il y a une quantité de mots qui sont spécifiquement masculins, qui transportent des valeurs masculines et dont il faut enormement se méfier parce que, si on est pris au piège de ces mots, on finit par penser, par écrire comme des hommes et, c'est-à-dire, par penser exactement comme eux. Ça il faut l'éviter."

34. Simone de Beauvoir, "Présentation," *Les Temps modernes*, 29(April-May 1974): 1719–20. This issue was reprinted as *Les femmes s'entêtent* (Paris: Gallimard, 1975).

Beauvoir's introduction was also reprinted in *Les Ecrits de Simone de Beauvoir*, ed. Francis and Gontier, 519–21.

35. Previous versions of this essay were presented at The Society for Phenomenology and Existential Philosophy, Duquesne University, November 1978; at Hamilton College and Union College, January 1979; and at the American Philosophical Association, Central Division, April 1983. Thanks to members of those audiences for comments, and to Phyllis Sutton Morris.

THROWING LIKE A GIRL

A PHENOMENOLOGY
OF FEMININE BODY COMPORTMENT,
MOTILITY, AND SPATIALITY

Iris Marion Young

In discussing the fundamental significance of lateral space, which is one of the unique spatial dimensions generated by the human upright posture, Erwin Straus pauses at "the remarkable difference in the manner of throwing of the two sexes"[1] (p. 157). Citing a study and photographs of young boys and girls, he describes the difference as follows:

> The girl of five does not make any use of lateral space. She does not stretch her arm sideward; she does not twist her trunk; she does not move her legs, which remain side by side. All she does in preparation for throwing is to lift her right arm forward to the horizontal and to bend the forearm backward in a pronate position. . . . The ball is released without force, speed, or accurate aim. . . . A boy of the same age, when preparing to throw, stretches his right arm sideward and backward; supinates the forearm; twists, turns and bends his trunk; and moves his right foot backward. From this stance, he can support his throwing almost with the full strength of his total motorium. . . . The ball leaves the hand with considerable acceleration; it moves toward its goal in a long flat curve (p. 157–160).[2]

Though he does not stop to trouble himself with the problem for long, Straus makes a few remarks in the attempt to explain this "remarkable difference." Since the difference is observed at such an early age, he says, it seems to be "the manifestation of a biological, not an acquired, difference" (p. 157). He is somewhat at a loss, however, to specify the source of the difference. Since the feminine style of throwing is observed in young children, it cannot result from the development of the breast. Straus provides further evidence against the breast by pointing out that "it seems certain" that the Amazons, who cut off their right breast, "threw a ball just like our Betty's, Mary's and Susan's" (p. 158). Having thus dismissed the breast, Straus considers the weaker muscle power of the girl as an explanation of the difference, but concludes that the girl should be expected to compensate for such relative weakness with the added preparation of reaching around and back. Straus explains the difference in style of throwing by referring to a "feminine attitude" in relation to the world and to space. The difference for him is biologically based, but he denies that it is specifically anatomical. Girls throw in a way different from boys because girls are "feminine."

What is even more amazing than this "explanation" is the fact that a perspective which takes body comportment and movement as definitive for the structure and meaning of human lived experience devotes no more than an incidental page to such a "remarkable difference" between masculine and feminine body comportment and style of movement. For throwing is by no means the only activity in which such a difference can be observed. If there are indeed typically "feminine" styles of body comportment and movement, then this should generate for the existential phenomenologist a concern to specify such a differentiation of the modalities of the lived body. Yet Straus is by no means alone in his failure to describe the modalities, meaning, and implications of the difference between "masculine" and "feminine" body comportment and movement.

A virtue of Straus's account of the typical difference of the sexes in throwing is that he does not explain this difference on the basis of physical attributes. Straus is convinced, however, that the early age at which the difference appears shows that it is not an acquired difference, and thus he is forced back onto a mysterious feminine essence in order to explain it. The feminist denial that the real differences in behavior and psychology between men and woman can be attributed to some natural and eternal "feminine essence" is perhaps most thoroughly and systematically expressed by de Beauvoir. Every human existence is defined by its *situation*; the particular existence of the female person is no less defined by the historical, cultural, social, and economic limits of her situation. We reduce women's condition simply to unintelligibility if we "explain" it by appeal to some natural and ahistorical feminine essence. In denying such a feminine essence, however, we should not fall into that "nominalism" which denies the real differences in the behavior and experiences of men and women. Even though there is no eternal feminine essence, there is "a common basis which underlies every individual female existence in the present state of education and custom."[3] The situation of women within a given socio-historical set of circumstances, despite the individual variation in each woman's experience, opportunities, and possibilities, has a unity which can be described and made intelligible. It should be emphasized, however, that this unity is specific to a particular social formation during a particular historical epoch.

De Beauvoir proceeds to give such an account of the situation of women with remarkable depth, clarity, and ingenuity. Yet she also, to a large extent, fails to give a place to the status and orientation of the woman's body as relating to its surroundings in living action. When de Beauvoir does talk about the woman's bodily being and her physical relation to her surroundings, she tends to focus on the more evident facts of a woman's physiology. She discusses how women experience the body as a burden, how the hormonal and physiological changes the body undergoes at puberty, during menstruation and pregnancy, are felt to be fearful and mysterious, and claims that these phenomena weigh down the woman's existence by tying her to nature, immanence, and the requirements of the species at the expense of her own individuality.[4] By largely ignoring the situatedness of the woman's actual bodily movement and orientation to its surroundings and its world, de Beauvoir tends to create the impression that it is woman's anatomy and physiology *as such* which are at least in part determinative of her unfree status.[5]

This essay seeks to begin to fill a gap that thus exists both in existential phenomenology and feminist theory. It traces in a provisional way some of the basic modalities of feminine body comportment, manner of moving, and relation in space. It brings intelligibility and significance to certain observable and rather ordinary ways in which women in our society typically comport themselves and move differently from the ways that men do. In accordance with the existentialist concern with the situatedness of human experience, I make no claim to the universality of this typicality of the bodily comportment of women and the phenomenological description based on it. The account developed here claims only to describe the modalities of feminine bodily existence for women situated in contemporary advanced industrial, urban, and commercial society. Elements of the account developed here may or may not apply to the situation of woman in other societies and other epochs, but it is not the concern of this essay to determine to which, if any, other social circumstances this account applies.

The scope of bodily existence and movement with which I am concerned here is also limited. I concentrate primarily on those sorts of bodily activities which relate to the comportment or orientation of the body as a whole, which entail gross movement, or which require the enlistment of strength and the confrontation of the body's capacities and possibilities with the resistance and malleability of things. Primarily the kind of movement I am concerned with is movement in which the body aims at the accomplishment of a definite purpose or task. There are thus many aspects of feminine bodily existence which I leave out of account here. Most notable of these is the body in its sexual being. Another aspect of bodily existence, among others, which I leave unconsidered is structured body movement which does not have a particular aim—for example, dancing. Besides reasons of space, this limitation of subject is based on the conviction, derived primarily from Merleau-Ponty, that it is the ordinary purposive orientation of the body as a whole toward things and its environment which initially defines the relation of a subject to its world. Thus focus upon ways in which the feminine body frequently or typically conducts itself in such comportment or movement may be particularly revelatory of the structures of feminine existence.[6]

Before entering the analysis, I should clarify what I mean here by "feminine" existence. In accordance with de Beauvoir's understanding, I take "femininity" to designate not a mysterious quality or essence which all women have by virtue of their being biologically female. It is, rather, a set of structures and conditions which delimit the typical *situation* of being a woman in a particular society, as well as the typical way in which this situation is lived by the women themselves. Defined as such, it is not necessary that *any* women be "feminine"—that is, it is not necessary that there be distinctive structures and behavior typical of the situation of women.[7] This understanding of "feminine" existence makes it possible to say that some women escape or transcend the typical situation and definition of women in various degrees and respects. I mention this primarily to indicate that the account offered here of the modalities of feminine bodily existence is not to be falsified by referring to some individual women to whom aspects of the account do not apply, or even to some individual men to whom they do.

The account developed here combines the insights of the theory of the lived body as expressed by Merleau-Ponty and the theory of the situation of women as developed by de Beauvoir. I assume that at the most basic descriptive level, Merleau-Ponty's account of the relation of the lived body to its world, as developed in the *Phenomenology of Perception*, applies to any human existence in a general way. At a more specific level, however, there is a particular style of bodily comportment which is typical of feminine existence, and this style consists of particular *modalities* of the structures and conditions of the body's existence in the world.[8]

As a framework for developing these modalities, I rely on de Beauvoir's account of woman's existence in patriarchal society as defined by a basic tension between immanence and transcendence.[9] The culture and society in which the female person dwells defines woman as Other, as the inessential correlate to man, as mere object and immanence. Woman is thereby both culturally and socially denied by the subjectivity, autonomy, and creativity which are definitive of being human and which in patriarchal society are accorded the man. At the same time, however, because she is a human existence, the female person necessarily is a subjectivity and transcendence and she knows herself to be. The female person who enacts the existence of women in patriarchal society must therefore live a contradiction: as human she is a free subject who participates in transcendence, but her situation as a woman denies her that subjectivity and transcendence. My suggestion is that the modalities of feminine bodily comportment, motility, and spatiality exhibit this same tension between transcendence and immanence, between subjectivity and being a mere object.

Section I offers some specific observations about bodily comportment, physical engagement with things, ways of using the body in performing tasks, and bodily self-image, which I find typical of feminine existence. Section II gives a general phenomenological account of the modalities of feminine bodily comportment and motility. Section III develops these modalities further in terms of the spatiality generated by them. Finally, in Section IV, I draw out some of the implications of this account for an understanding of the oppression of women, as well as raise some further questions about feminine Being-in-the-world which require further investigation.

I

The basic difference which Straus observes between the way boys and girls throw is that girls do not bring their whole bodies into the motion as much as the boys. They do not reach back, twist, move backward, step, and lean forward. Rather, the girls tend to remain relatively immobile except for their arms, and even the arm is not extended as far as it could be. Throwing is not the only movement in which there is a typical difference in the way men and women use their bodies. Reflection on feminine comportment and body movement in other physical activities reveals that these also are frequently characterized, much as in the throwing case, by a failure to make full use of the body's spatial and lateral potentialities.

Even in the most simple body orientations of men and women as they sit, stand, and walk, one can observe a typical difference in body style and extension. Women generally are not as open with their bodies as men in their gait and stride. Typically, the masculine stride is longer proportional to a man's body than is the feminine stride to a woman's. The man typically swings his arms in a more open and loose fashion than does a woman and typically has more up and down rhythm in his step. Though we now wear pants more than we used to, and consequently do not have to restrict our sitting postures because of dress, women still tend to sit with their legs relatively close together and their arms across their bodies. When simply standing or leaning, men tend to keep their feet further apart than do women, and we also tend more to keep our hands and arms touching or shielding our bodies. A final indicative difference is the way each carries books or parcels; girls and women most often carry books embraced to their chests, while boys and men swing them along their sides.

The approach persons of each sex take to the performance of physical tasks that require force, strength, and muscular coordination is frequently different. There are indeed real physical differences between men and women in the kind and limit of their physical strength. Many of the observed differences between men and women in the performance of tasks requiring coordinated strength, however, are due not so much to brute muscular strength, but to the way each sex *uses* the body in approaching tasks. Women often do not perceive themselves as capable of lifting and carrying heavy things, pushing and shoving with significant force, pulling, squeezing, grasping, or twisting with force. When we attempt such tasks, we frequently fail to summon the full possibilities of our muscular coordination, position, poise, and bearing. Women tend not to put their whole bodies into engagement in a physical task with the same ease and naturalness as men. For example, in attempting to lift something, women more often than men fail to plant themselves firmly and make their thighs bear the greatest proportion of the weight. Instead, we tend to concentrate our effort on those parts of the body most immediately connected to the task— the arms and shoulders—rarely bringing the power of the legs to the task at all. When turning or twisting something, to take another example, we frequently concentrate effort in the hand and wrist, not bringing to the task the power of the shoulder, which is necessary for its efficient performance.[10]

The previously cited throwing example can be extended to a great deal of athletic activity. Now most men are by no means superior athletes, and their sporting efforts more often display bravado than genuine skill and coordination. The relatively untrained man nevertheless engages in sport generally with more free motion and open reach than does his female counterpart. Not only is there a typical style of throwing like a girl, but there is a more or less typical style of running like a girl, climbing like a girl, swinging like a girl, hitting like a girl. They have in common, first, that the whole body is not put into fluid and directed motion, but rather, in swinging and hitting, for example, the motion is concentrated in one body part; and second, that the woman's motion tends not to reach, extend, lean, stretch, and follow through in the direction of her intention.

For many women as they move in sport, a space surrounds them in imagination which we are not free to move beyond; the space available to our movement is a constricted space. Thus, for example, in softball or volley ball women tend to remain in one place more often than men, neither jumping to reach nor running to approach the ball. Men more often move out toward a ball in flight and confront it with their own countermotion. Women tend to wait for and then *react* to its approach rather than going forth to meet it. We frequently respond to the motion of a ball coming toward us as though it were coming *at* us, and our immediate bodily impulse is to flee, duck, or otherwise protect ourselves from its flight. Less often than men, moreover, do women give self-conscious direction and placement to their motion in sport. Rather than aiming at a certain place where we wish to hit a ball, for example, we tend to hit it in a "general" direction.

Women often approach a physical engagement with things with timidity, uncertainty, and hesitancy. Typically, we lack an entire trust in our bodies to carry us to our aims. There is, I suggest, a double hesitation here. On the one hand, we often lack confidence that we have the capacity to do what must be done. Many times I have slowed a hiking party in which the men bounded across a harmless stream while I stood on the other side warily testing out my footing on various stones, holding on to overhanging branches. Though the others crossed with ease, I do not believe it is easy for *me*, even though once I take a committed step I am across in a flash. The other side of this tentativeness is, I suggest, a fear of getting hurt, which is greater in women than in men. Our attention is often divided between the aim to be realized in motion and the body that must accomplish it, while at the same time saving itself from harm. We often experience our bodies as a fragile encumberance, rather than the media for the enactment of our aims. We feel as though we must have our attention directed upon our body to make sure it is doing what we wish it to do, rather than paying attention to what we want to do *through* our bodies.

All the above factors operate to produce in many women a greater or lesser feeling of incapacity, frustration, and self-consciousness. We have more of a tendency than men to greatly underestimate our bodily capacity.[11] We decide beforehand—usually mistakenly—that the task is beyond us, and thus give it less than our full effort. At such a half-hearted level, of course, we cannot perform the tasks, become frustrated, and fulfill our own prophecy. In entering a task we frequently are self-conscious about appearing awkward, and at the same time do not wish to appear too strong. Both worries contribute to our awkwardness and frustration. If we should finally release ourselves from this spiral and really give a physical task our best effort, we are greatly surprised indeed at what our bodies can accomplish. It has been found that women more often than men underestimate the level of achievement they have reached.[12]

None of the observations which have been made thus far about the way women typically move and comport their bodies applies to all women all of the time. Nor do those women who manifest some aspect of this typicality do so in the same degee. There is no inherent, mysterious connection between these sorts of typical comportments and being a female person. Many of them result, as will be developed later, from lack of practice in using the body and performing tasks. Even given these qualifications, one can nevertheless sensibly speak of a general feminine style of body comportment and movement. The next section will develop a specific categorical description of the modalities of the comportment and movement.

II

The three modalities of feminine motility are that feminine movement exhibits an *ambiguous transcendence*, an *inhibited intentionality*, and a *discontinuous unity* with its surroundings. A source of these contradictory modalities is the bodily self-reference of feminine comportment, which derives from the woman's experience of her body as a *thing* at the same time that she experiences it as a capacity.

1. In his *Phenomenology of Perception*,[13] Merleau-Ponty takes as his task the articulation of the primordial structures of existence, which are prior to and the ground of all reflective relation to the world. In asking how there can be a world for a subject, Merleau-Ponty reorients the entire tradition of that questioning by locating subjectivity not in mind or consciousness, but in the *body*. Merleau-Ponty gives to the lived body the ontological status which Sartre, as well as "intellectualist" thinkers before him, attribute to consciousness alone: the status of transcendence as being-for-itself. It is the body in its orientation toward and action upon and within its surroundings which constitutes the initial meaning giving act (p. 121; pp. 146–147). The body is the first locus of intentionality, as pure presence to the world and openness upon its possibilities. The most primordial intentional act is the motion of the body orienting itself with respect to and moving within its surroundings. There is a world for a subject just insofar as the body has capacities by which it can approach, gasp, and appropriate its surroundings in the direction of its intentions.

While feminine bodily existence is a transcendence and openness to the world, it is an *ambiguous transcendence*, a transcendence which is at the same time laden with immanence. Now once we take the locus of subjectivity and transcendence to be the lived body rather than pure consciousness, all transcendence is ambiguous because the body as natural and material is immanence. But it is not the ever present possibility of any lived body to be passive, to be touched as well as touching, to be grasped as well as grasping, which I am referring to here as the ambiguity of the transcendence of the feminine lived body. The transcendence of the lived body which Merleau-Ponty describes is a transcendence which moves out from the body in its immanence in an open and unbroken directedness upon the world in action. The lived body as transcendence is pure fluid action, the continuous calling forth of capacities, which are applied to the world. Rather than simply beginning in immanence, feminine bodily existence remains in immanence, or better is *overlaid* with immanence, even as it moves out toward the world in motions of grasping, manipulating, and so on.

In the previous section, I observed that a woman typically refrains from throwing her whole body into a motion, and rather concentrates motion in one part of the body alone while the rest of the body remains relatively immobile. Only a part of the body, that is, moves out toward a task while the rest remains rooted in immanence. I also observed earlier that a woman frequently does not trust the capacity of her body to engage itself in physical relation to things. Consequently, she often lives her body as a burden, which must be dragged and prodded along, and at the same time protected.

2. Merleau-Ponty locates intentionality in motility (pp. 110–112); the possibilities which are opened up in the world depend on the mode and limits of the bodily "I can" (p. 137, p. 148). Feminine existence, however, often does not enter bodily relation to possibilities by its own comportment toward its surroundings in an unambiguous and confident "I can." For example, as noted earlier, women frequently tend to posit a task which would be accomplished relatively easily once attempted as beyond their capacities before they begin it. Typically, the feminine body underuses its real capacity, both as the potentiality of its physical size and strength and as the real skills and coordination which are available to it. Feminine bodily existence is an *inhibited intentionality*, which simultaneously reaches toward a projected end with an "I can" and withholds its full bodily commitment to that end in a self-imposed "I cannot."[14]

An uninhibited intentionality projects the aim to be accomplished and connects the body's motion toward that end in an unbroken directedness which organizes and unifies the body's activity. The body's capacity and motion structure its surroundings and project meaningful possibilities of movement and action, which in turn call the body's motion forth to enact them: "To understand is to experience the harmony between what we aim at and what is given, between the intention and the performance . . . "

(p. 144; see also pp. 101, 131, 132). Feminine motion often severs this mutually conditioning relation between aim and enactment. In those motions which when properly performed require the coordination and directedness of the whole body upon some definite end, women frequently move in a contradictory way. Their bodies project an aim to be enacted, but at the same time stiffen against the performance of the task. In performing a physical task the woman's body does carry her toward the intended aim, but often not easily and directly, but rather circuitously, with the wasted motion resulting from the effort of testing and reorientation, which is a frequent consequence of feminine hesitancy.

For any lived body, the world appears as the system of possibilities which are correlative to its intentions (p. 131). For any lived body, moreover, the world also appears as populated with opacities and resistances correlative to its own limits and frustrations. For any bodily existence, that is, an "I cannot" may appear to set limits to the "I can." To the extent that feminine bodily existence is an inhibited intentionality, however, the same set of possibilities which appears correlative to its intentions also appears as a system of frustrations correlative to its hesitancies. By repressing or withholding its own motile energy, feminine bodily existence frequently projects an "I can" and an "I cannot" with respect to the very same end. When the woman enters a task with inhibited intentionality, she projects the possibilities of that task—thus projects an "I *can*"—but projects them merely as the possibilities of "someone," and not truly *her* possibilities— and thus projects an "*I cannot*."

3. Merleau-Ponty gives to the body the unifying and synthesizing function which Kant locates in transcendental subjectivity. By projecting an aim toward which it moves, the body brings unity to and unites itself with its surroundings; through the vectors of its projected possibilities it sets things in relation to one another and to itself. The body's movement and orientation organizes the surrounding space as a continous extension of its own being (p. 143). Within the same act that the body synthesizes its surroundings, moreover, it synthesizes itself. The body synthesis is immediate and primordial. "I do not bring together one by one the parts of my body; this translation and this unification are performed once and for all within me: they are my body itself" (p. 150).

The third modality of feminine bodily existence is that it stands in *discontinuous unity* with both itself and its surroundings. I remarked earlier that in many motions which require the active engagement and coordination of the body as a whole to be performed properly, women tend to locate their motion in a part of the body only, leaving the rest of the body relatively immobile. Motion such as this is discontinuous with itself. That part of the body which is transcending toward an aim is in relative disunity from those which remain immobile. The undirectedness and wasted motion which is often an aspect of feminine engagement in a task also manifests this lack of body unity. The character of the inhibited intentionality whereby feminine motion severs the connection between aim and enactment, between possibility in the world and capacity in the body, itself produces this discontinuous unity.

According to Merleau-Ponty, for the body to exist as a transcendent presence to the world and the immediate enactment of intentions, it cannot exist as an *object* (p. 123). As subject, the body is referred not onto itself, but onto the world's possibilities. "In order that we may be able to move our body towards an object, the object must first exist for it, our body must not belong to the realm of the 'in-itself' " (p. 139). The three contradictory modalities of feminine bodily existence—ambiguous transcendence, inhibited intentionality, and discontinuous unity—have their root, however, in the fact that for feminine existence the body frequently is both subject and object for itself at the same time and in reference to the same act. Feminine bodily existence is frequently not a pure presence to the world because it is referred onto *itself* as well as onto possibilities in the world.[15]

Several of the observations of the previous section illustrate this self-reference. It was observed, for example, that women have a tendency to take up the motion of an object coming *toward* them as coming *at* them. I also observed that women tend to have a latent and sometimes conscious fear of getting hurt, which we bring to a motion. That is, feminine bodily existence is self-referred in that the woman takes herself as the *object* of the motion rather than its originator. Feminine bodily existence is also self-referred to the extent that a woman is uncertain of her body's capacities and does not feel that its motions are entirely under her control. She must divide her attention between the task to be performed and the body which must be coaxed and manipulated into performing it. Finally, feminine bodily existence is self-referred to the extent that the feminine subject posits her motion as the motion that is *looked at*. In Section IV, we will explore the implications of the basic fact of the woman's social existence as the object of the gaze of another, which is a major source of her bodily self-reference.

In summary, the modalities of feminine bodily existence have their root in the fact that feminine existence does not experience the body as a mere thing—a fragile thing, which must be picked up and coaxed into movement, a thing which exists as *looked at and acted upon*. To be sure, any lived body exists as a material thing as well as a transcending subject. For feminine bodily existence, however, the body is often lived as a thing which is other than it, a thing like other things in the world. To the extent that feminine existence lives her body as a thing, she remains rooted in immanence, is inhibited, and retains a distance from her body as transcending movement and from engagement in the world's possibilities.

III

For Merleau-Ponty there is a distinction between lived space, or phenomenal space, and objective space, the uniform space of geometry and science in which all positions are external to one another and interchangeable. Phenomenal space arises out of motility and lived relations of space are generated by the capacities of the body's motion and the intentional relations which that motion constitutes. "It is clearly in action that the spatiality of our body is brought into being and an analysis of one's own movement should enable us to arrive at a better understanding" (p. 102; cf. pp. 148, 149, p. 249). On this account, if there are particular modalities of feminine bodily comportment and motility, then it must follow that there are also particular modalities of feminine spatiality. Feminine existence lives space as *enclosed* or confining, as having a *dual* structure and the feminine existent experiences herself as *positioned* in space.

1. There is a famous study which Erik Erikson performed several years ago in which he asked several male and female pre-adolescents to construct a scene for an imagined movie out of some toys. He found that girls typically depicted indoor settings, with high walls and enclosures, while boys typically constructed outdoor scenes. He concluded that females tend to emphasize what he calls "inner space," or enclosed space, while males tend to emphasize what he calls "outer space," or a spatial orientation which is open and outwardly directed. Erikson's interpretation of these observations is psychoanalytical: girls depict "inner space" as the projection of the enclosed space of their wombs and vaginas; boys depict "outer space" as a projection of the phallus.[16] I find such an explanation wholly unconvincing. If girls do tend to project an enclosed space and boys to project an open and outwardly directed space, it is far more plausible to regard this as a reflection of the way each sex lives and moves their bodies in space.

In the first section, I observed that women tend not to open their bodies in their everyday movements, but tend to sit, stand, and walk with their limbs close to or enclosed around them. I also observed that women tend not to reach, stretch, bend, lean, or stride to the full limits of their physical capacities, even when doing so would better accomplish a task or motion. The space, that is, which is *physically* available to the feminine body is frequently of greater radius than the space which she uses and inhabits.

Feminine existence appears to posit an existential enclosure between herself and the space surrounding her, in such a way that the space which belongs to her and is available to her grasp and manipulation is constricted, and the space beyond is not available to her movement.[17] A further illustration of this confinement of feminine lived space is the observation already noted that in sport, for example, women tend not to move out and meet the motion of a ball, but rather tend to stay in one place and react to the ball's motion only when it has arrived within the space where she is. The timidity, immobility, and uncertainty which frequently characterize feminine movement project a limited space for the feminine, "I can."

2. On Merleau-Ponty's account, the body unity of transcending performance creates an immediate link between the body and the outlying space. "Each instant of the movement embraces its whole space, and particularly the first which, by being active and initiative, institutes the link between a here and a yonder . . . " (p. 140). In feminine existence, however, the projection of an enclosed space severs the continuity between a "here" and a "yonder." In feminine existence there is a *double spatiality* as the space of the "here" which is distinct from the space of the "yonder." A distinction between space which is "yonder" and not linked with my own body possibilities, and the enclosed space which is "here," which I inhabit with my bodily possibilities, is an expression of the discontinuity between aim and capacity to realize the aim which I have articulated as the meaning of the tentativeness and uncertainty which characterize the inhibited intentionality of feminine motility. The space of the "yonder" is a space in which feminine existence projects possibilities in the sense of understanding that "someone" could move within it, but not I. Thus the space of the "yonder" exists for feminine existence, but only as that which she is looking into, rather than moving in.

3. The third modality of feminine spatiality is that feminine existence experiences itself as *positioned in* space. For Merleau-Ponty, the body is the original subject which constitutes space; there would be no space without the body (pp. 102, 142). As the origin and subject of spatial relations, the body does not occupy a position coequal and interchangeable with the positions occupied by other things (p. 143, pp. 247–249). Because the body as lived is not an *object*, it cannot be said to exist *in* space as water is *in* the glass (pp. 139–140). "The word 'here' applied to my body does not refer to a determinate position in relation to other positions or to external coordinates, but the laying down of the first coordinates, the anchoring of the active body in an object, the situation of the body in the face of its tasks" (p. 100).

Feminine spatiality is contradictory insofar as feminine bodily existence is both spatially constituted and a constituting spatial subject. Insofar as feminine existence lives the body as transcendence and intentionality, the feminine body actively constitutes space and is the original coordinate which unifies the spatial field and projects spatial relations and positions in accord with its intentions. But to the extent that feminine motility is laden with immanence and inhibited, the body's space is lived as constituted. To the extent, that is, that feminine bodily existence is self-referred and thus lives itself as an *object*, the feminine body does exist *in* space. In Section I, I observed that women frequently react to motions, even our own motions, as though we are the object of the motion which issues from an alien intention, rather than taking ourselves as subject of motion. In its immanence and inhibition, feminine spatial existence is *positioned* by a system of coordinates which does not have its origin in her own intentional capacities. The tendency for the feminine body to remain partly immobile in the performance of a task which requires the movement of the whole body illustrates this characteristic of feminine bodily existence as rooted *in place*. Likewise does the tendency for women to wait for an object to come within their immediate bodily field rather than move out toward it.

Merleau-Ponty devotes a great deal of attention to arguing that the diverse senses and activities of the lived body are synthetically related in such a way that each stands in a mutually conditioning relation with all the others. In particular, visual perception and motility stand in a relation of reversability; an impairment in the functioning of one, for example, leads to an impairment in the functioning of the other (pp. 133–137). If we assume that reversability of visual perception and motility, the above account of the modalities of feminine motility and the spatiality which arises from them suggests that visual space will have its own modalities as well.

There have been numerous psychological studies which have reported differences between the sexes in the character of spatial perception. One of the most frequently discussed of these conclusions is that females are more often "field dependent." That is, it has been claimed that males have a greater capacity for lifting a figure out of its spatial surroundings and viewing relations in space as fluid and interchangeable, whereas females have a greater tendency to regard figures as embedded within and fixed by their surroundings.[18] The above account of feminine motility and spatiality gives some theoretical intelligibility to these findings. If feminine body spatiality is such that the woman experiences herself as rooted and enclosed, then on the reversability assumption it would follow that visual space for feminine existence also has its closures of immobility and fixity. The objects in visual space do not stand in a fluid system of potentially alterable and interchangeable relations correlative to the body's various intentions and projected capacities. Rather, they too have their own *places* and are anchored in their immanence.

IV

The modalities of feminine bodily comportment, motility, and spatiality which I have described here are, I claim, common to the existence of women in contemporary society to one degree or another. They have their source, however, in neither anatomy nor physiology, and certainly not in a mysterious feminine "essence." Rather, they have their source in the particular *situation* of women as conditioned by their sexist oppression in contemporary society.

Women in sexist society are physically handicapped. Insofar as we learn to live out our existence in accordance with the definition that patriarchal culture assigns to us, we are physically inhibited, confined, positioned, and objectified. As lived bodies we are not open and unambiguous transcendences which move out to master a world that belongs to us, a world constituted by our own intentions and projections. To be sure, there are actual women in contemporary society to whom all or part of the above description does not apply. Where these modalities are not manifest in or determinative of the existence of a particular woman, however, they are definitive in a negative mode—as that which she has escaped, through accident or good fortune, or more often, as that which she has had to overcome.

One of the sources of the modalities of feminine bodily existence is too obvious to dwell upon at length. For the most part, girls and women are not given the opportunity to use their full bodily capacities in free and open engagement with the world, nor are they encouraged as much as boys to develop specific bodily skills.[19] Girl play is often more sedentary and enclosing than the play of boys. In school and after school activities girls are not encouraged to engage in sport, in the controlled use of their bodies in achieving well-defined goals. Girls, moreover, get little practice at "tinkering" with things, and thus at developing spatial skill. Finally, girls are not asked often to perform tasks demanding physical effort and strength, while as the boys grow older they are asked to do so more and more.[20]

The modalities of feminine bodily existence are not merely privative, however, and thus their source is not merely in lack of practice, though this is certainly an important element. There is a specific positive style of feminine body comportment and movement, which is learned as the girl comes to understand that she is a girl. The young girl acquires many subtle habits of feminine body comportment—walking like a girl, tilting her head like a girl, standing and sitting like a girl, gesturing like a girl, and so on. The girl learns actively to hamper her movements. She is told that she must be careful not to get hurt, not to get dirty, not to tear her clothes, that the things she desires to do are dangerous for her. Thus she develops a bodily timidity which increases with age. In assuming herself as a girl, she takes herself up as fragile. Studies have found that young children of both sexes categorically assert that girls are more likely to get hurt than boys,[21] and that girls ought to remain close to home while boys can roam and explore.[22] The more a girl assumes her status as feminine, the more she takes herself to be fragile and immobile, and the more she actively enacts her own body inhibition. When I was about thirteen, I spent hours practicing a "feminine" walk which was stiff, closed, and rotated from side to side.

Studies which record observations of sex differences in spatial perception, spatial problem solving, and motor skills have also found that these differences tend to increase with age. While very young children show virtually no differences in motor skills, movement, spatial perception, etc., differences seem to appear in elementary school and increase with adolescence. If these findings are accurate, they would seem to support the conclusion that it is in the process of growing up as a girl that the modalities of feminine bodily comportment, motility, and spatiality make their appearance.[23]

There is, however, a further source of the modalities of feminine bodily existence which is perhaps even more profound than these. At the root of those modalities, I have stated in the previous section, is the fact that the woman lives her body as *object* as well as subject. The source of this is that patriarchal society defines woman as object, as a mere body, and that in sexist society women are in fact frequently regarded by others as objects and mere bodies. An essential part of the situation of being a woman is that of living the ever present possibility that one will be gazed upon as a mere body, as shape and flesh that presents itself as the potential object of another subject's intentions and manipulations, rather than as a living manifestation of action and intention.[24] The source of this objectified bodily existence is in the attitude of others regarding her, but the woman herself often actively takes up her body as a mere thing. She gazes at it in the mirror, worries about how it looks to others, prunes it, shapes it, molds and decorates it.

This objectified bodily existence accounts for the self-consciousness of the feminine relation to her body and resulting distance she takes from her body. As human, she is a transcendence and subjectivity, and cannot live herself as mere bodily object. Thus, to the degree that she does live herself as mere body, she cannot be in unity with herself, but must take a distance from and exist in discontinuity with her body. The objectifying regard which "keeps her in her place" can also account for the spatial modality of being positioned and for why women frequently tend not to move openly, keeping their limbs enclosed around themselves. To open her body in free active and open extension and bold outward directedness is for a woman to invite objectification.

The threat of being seen is, however, not the only threat of objectification which the woman lives. She also lives the threat of invasion of her body space. The most extreme form of such spatial and bodily invasion is the threat of rape. But we are daily subject to the possibility of bodily invasion in many far more subtle ways as well. It is acceptable, for example, for women to be touched in ways and under circumstances that it is not acceptable for men to be touched, and by persons—i.e., men—whom it is not acceptable for them to touch.[25] I would suggest that the enclosed space which has been described as a modality of feminine spatiality is in part a defense against such invasion. Women tend to project an existential barrier enclosed around them and discontinuous with the "over there" in order to keep the other at a distance. The woman lives her space as confined and enclosed around her at least in part as projecting some small area in which she can exist as a free subject.

This essay is a prolegomenon to the study of aspects of women's experience and situation which have not received the treatment they warrant. I would like to close with some questions which require further thought and research. This essay has concentrated its attention upon the sort of physical tasks and body orientation which involve the whole body in gross movement. Further investigation into woman's bodily existence would require looking at activities which do not involve the whole body and finer movement. If we are going to develop an account of the woman's body experience in situation, moreover, we must reflect on the modalities of a woman's experience of her body in its sexual being, as well as upon less task-oriented body activities, such as dancing. Another question which arises is whether the description given here would apply equally well to any sort of physical task. Might the kind of task, and specifically whether it is a task or movement which is sextyped, have some effect on the modalities of feminine bodily existence? A further question is to what degree we can develop a theoretical account of the connection between the modalities of the bodily existence of women and other aspects of our existence and experience. For example, I have an intuition that the general lack of confidence that we frequently have about our cognitive or leadership abilities is traceable in part to an original doubt in our body's capacity. None of these questions can be dealt with properly, however, without first per-

forming the kind of guided observation and data collection that my reading
has concluded, to a large degree, is yet to be performed.

NOTES

This essay was first presented at a meeting of the Mid-West Division of the Society
for Women in Philosophy (SWIP) in October 1977. Versions of the essay were
subsequently presented at a session sponsored by SWIP at the Western Division
meetings of the American Philosophical Association, April 1978; and at the Third
Annual Merleau-Ponty Circle meeting, Duquesne University, September 1978.
Many people in discussions at those meetings contributed gratifying and helpful
responses. I am particularly grateful to Professors Sandra Bartky, Claudia Card,
Margaret Simons, J. Davidson Alexander, and William McBride for their criticisms
and suggestions. Final revisions of the essay were completed while I was a fellow
in the National Endowment for the Humanities Fellowship in Residence for College
Teachers program at the University of Chicago.

1. Erwin W. Straus, "The Upright Posture," *Phenomenological Psychology* (New
York: Basic Books, 1966), 137–65. References to particular pages are indicated in
the text.

2. Studies continue to be performed which arrive at similar observations. See,
for example, Lolas E. Kalverson, Mary Ann Robertson, M. Joanne Safrit, and
Thomas W. Roberts, "Effect of Guided Practice on Overhand Throw Ball Velocities
of Kindergarten Children," *Research Quarterly* 48(May 1977):311–18. The study found
that boys had significantly greater velocities than girls.

See also F. J. J. Buytendijk's remarks in *Woman: A Contemporary View* (New York:
Newman Press, 1968), 144–45. In raising the example of throwing, Buytendijk is
concerned to stress, as am I in the essay, that the important thing to investigate is
not the strictly physical phenomena, but rather the manner in which each sex
projects her or his Being-in-the-world through movement.

3. Simone de Beauvoir, *The Second Sex* (New York: Vintage Books, 1974), xxxv.
See also Buytendijk, 275–76.

4. See de Beauvoir, *The Second Sex*, chap. 1, "The Data of Biology."

5. Firestone claims that de Beauvoir's account served as the basis of her own
thesis that the oppression of women is rooted in nature, and thus requires the
transcendence of nature itself to be overcome. See *The Dialectic of Sex* (New York:
Bantam Books, 1970). De Beauvoir would claim that Firestone is guilty of desituating
woman's situation by pinning a source on nature as such. That Firestone would
find inspiration for her thesis in de Beauvoir, however, indicates that perhaps de
Beauvoir has not steered away from causes in "nature" as much as is desirable.

6. In his discussion of the "dynamics of feminine existence," Buytendijk focuses
precisely on those sorts of motions which are aimless. He claims that it is through
these kinds of expressive movements—e.g., walking for the sake of walking—and
not through action aimed at the accomplishment of particular purposes, that the
pure image of masculine or feminine existence is manifest (*Woman: A Contemporary
View*, 278–79). Such an approach, however, contradicts the basic existentialist assumption that Being-in-the-world consists in projecting purposes and goals which
structure one's situatedness. While there is certainly something to be learned from
reflecting upon feminine movement in noninstrumental activity, given that accom-
plishing tasks is basic to the structure of human existence, it serves as a better
starting point for investigation of feminine motility. As I point out at the end of

this essay, a full phenomenology of feminine existence must take account of this noninstrumental movement.

7. It is not impossible, moreover, for men to be "feminine" in at least some respects, according to the above definition.

8. On this level of specificity there also exist particular modalities of masculine motility, inasmuch as there is a particular style of movement more or less typical of men. I will not, however, be concerned with those in this essay.

9. See de Beauvoir, *The Second Sex*, chap. 21, "Woman's Situation and Character."

10. It should be noted that this is probably typical only of women in advanced industrial societies, where the model of the Bourgeois woman has been extended to most women. It would not apply to those societies, for example, where most people, including women, do heavy physical work. Nor does this particular observation, of course, hold true of those women in our own society who do heavy physical work.

11. See A. M. Gross, "Estimated versus actual physical strength in three ethnic groups," *Child Development* 39(1968):283–90. In a test of children at several different ages, at all but the youngest age-level, girls rated themselves lower than boys rated themselves on self-estimates of strength, and as the girls grow older, their self-estimates of strength become even lower.

12. See Marguerite A. Cifton and Hope M. Smith, "Comparison of Expressed Self-Concept of Highly Skilled Males and Females Concerning Motor Performance," *Perceptual and Motor Skills* 16(1963): 199–201. Women consistently underestimated their level of achievement in skills like running and jumping far more often than men did.

13. Maurice Merleau-Ponty, *Phenomenology of Perception*, trans. Colin Smith (New York: Humanities Press, 1962). All references to this work are noted in parentheses within the text.

14. Much of the work of Seymour Fisher on various aspects of sex differences in body image correlates suggestively with the phenomenological description developed here. It is difficult to use his conclusions as confirmation of that description, however, because there is something of a "speculative" aspect to his reasoning. Nevertheless, I shall refer to some of these findings, with that qualification in mind.

One of Fisher's findings is that women have a greater anxiety about their legs than men, and he cites earlier studies which have come to the same results. Fisher interprets such leg-anxiety as anxiety about motility itself, because in body conception and body image it is the legs which are the body part most associated with motility. See Seymour Fisher, *Body Experience in Fantasy and Behavior* (New York: Appleton-Century-Crofts, 1970), 537. If his findings and his interpretation are accurate, this tends to correlate with the sort of inhibition and timidity about movement which I am claiming is an aspect of feminine body comportment.

15. Fisher finds the most striking difference between men and women in their general body image is that women have a significantly higher degree of what he calls "body prominence," awareness of and attention to the body. He cites a number of different studies which have come to the same results. The explanation Fisher gives for this finding is that women have a higher degree of body awareness because they are socialized to pay attention to their bodies, to prune and dress them, and to worry about how they look to others. Ibid., 524–25. See also Fisher, "Sex Differences in Body Perception," *Psychological Monographs* 78(1964), no. 14.

16. Erik H. Erikson, "Inner and Outer Space: Reflections on Womanhood," *Daedelus* 3(1964):582–606. Erikson's interpretation of his findings is also sexist. Having in his opinion discovered a particular significance that "inner space"—which he takes to be space *within* the body—holds for girls, he goes on to discuss the womanly "nature" as womb and potential mother which must be made compatible with anything else the woman does.

17. Another of Fisher's findings is that women experience themselves as having a more clearly articulated body *boundary* than men. More clearly than men they distinguish themselves from their spatial surroundings and take a distance from them. See Fisher, *Body Experience in Fantasy and Behavior*, 528.

18. The number of studies coming to these results is enormous. See Eleanor E. Maccoby and Carol N. Jacklin, *The Psychology of Sex Differences* (Palo Alto: Stanford University Press, 1974), 91–98. For a number of years psychologists used the results from tests of spatial ability to generalize about field independence in general, and from that to general "analytic" ability. Thus it was concluded that women have less analytical abiltiy than men. More recently, however, such generalizations have been seriously called into question. See, for example, Julia A. Sherman, "Problems of Sex Differences in Space Perception and Aspects of Intellectual Functioning," *Psychological Review* 74(1967):290–99. She notes that while women are consistently found to be more field dependent than men in spatial tasks, on nonspatial tests measuring field independence women generally perform as well as men.

19. Nor are girls provided with examples of girls and women being physically active. See Mary E. Duquin, "Differential Sex Role Socialization Toward Amplitude Appropriation," *Research Quarterly* (American Alliance for Health, Physical Education, and Recreation) 48(1977):288–92. Survey of textbooks for young children revealed that children are thirteen times more likely to see a vigorously active man than a vigorously active woman, and three times more likely to see a relatively active man than a relatively active woman.

20. Sherman, (see note 18) argues that it is the differential socialization of boys and girls in being encouraged to "tinker," explore, etc., that accounts for the difference between the two in spatial ability.

21. See L. Kolberg, "A Cognitive-Developmental Analysis of Children's Sex-Role Concepts and Attitudes," in E. E. Maccoby, ed., *The Development of Sex Differences* (Palo Alto: Stanford University Press, 1966), 101.

22. Lenore J. Weitzman, "Sex Role Socialization," in Jo Freeman, ed., *Woman: A Feminist Perspective* (Palo Alto: Mayfield Publishing Co., 1975), 111–12.

23. Maccoby and Jacklin, *The Psychology of Sex Differences*, 93–94.

24. The manner in which women are objectified by the gaze of the Other is not the same phenomenon as the objectification by the Other which is a condition of self-consciousness in Sartre's account. See *Being and Nothingness*, trans. Hazel E. Barnes (New York: Philosophical Library, 1956), Part Three. While the basic ontological category of being-for-others is an objectified for-itself, the objectification which women are subject to is that of being regarded as a mere in-itself. On the particular dynamic of sexual objectification, see Sandra Bartky, "Psychological Oppression," in Sharon Bishop and Margorie Weinzweig, ed., *Philosophy and Women* (Belmont, Calif: Wadswoth Publishing Co., 1979), 33–41.

25. See Nancy Henley and Jo Freeman, "The Sexual Politics of Interpersonal Behavior," in Freeman, ed., *Woman: A Feminist Perspective*, 391–401.

AN INTRODUCTION TO
PATRIARCHAL EXISTENTIALISM
A PROPOSAL FOR A WAY OUT
OF EXISTENTIAL PATRIARCHY

Jeffner Allen

The excitement of existentialism, for a feminist philosopher such as myself, is its unwavering affirmation of change. Existential emphasis on the primacy of existence over essence shows that I have no "nature": I am not destined to enact the dictates of biology, social custom, or political institutions. I am what I become through my choices to resist fixity and to create a new freedom. The death of God, boldly proclaimed by Nietzsche, makes possible a decision to assume the responsibility, dread, and joy for shaping my life in a historical context that is the outcome of individual and collective undertakings.[1] Simone de Beauvoir's *The Second Sex*, Jean-Paul Sartre's *Anti-Semite and Jew*, and Claude Lanzmann's recent cinematic production, *Shoah*, are major existential works which share the belief that change is effected through an intense focus on the possibilities which lie, albeit ambiguously, in my worlds of experience.

The transformation of philosophical perspective that existentialism portends may, nevertheless, be difficult or impossible to realize in the context within which existentialism has established itself. Simone de Beauvoir's remark, "man represents both the positive and the neutral, as is indicated by the common use of *man* to designate human beings in general," is incisive in this regard.[2] Existentialism, by its own admission, sets out to understand *human* being-in-the-world. A salient accomplishment of existentialism is its contribution to present-day humanism and its critique of methodologies which generate reductive accounts of human experience. Beauvoir's comment, and its far-reaching implications, undermine the existential-humanist alliance and point to a fundamental failure of the existential project. To the extent that existential description and the concepts which animate that description equate the masculine with the human, existentialism renders a reductive and misleading account of experience, specifically, of women's experience.

A disquieting dilemma emerges: existentialism, which seems to present unique possibilities for feminist philosophizing, may, as a consequence of its humanism, have little or nothing to offer women. The existential criteria of relevance, that one cannot jump over one's shadow, that is, that no ideas are entirely free of contextual relativism, may be applied to existentialism itself.[3] I will take up this dilemma by asking: by whom and for whom is existentialism written? Or, what is the scope and validity of existential thought?

An Introduction to Patriarchal Existentialism

At first it might seem that this question may readily be answered. Surely existentialism applies to all twentieth-century Western culture. Nietzsche's aphorism, "The Madman,"[4] tells us that with the death of God we find ourselves in an empty space of infinite nothingness. Hence the need to light our own lanterns in the morning and the freedom to invent new games and festivals of celebration. "God" is an ideal truth, or lie, which we once created and which we now destroy. Zarathustra, the godless, speaks to all of us.

If, however, I proceed from this general statement to the particular, that is, myself, I may persist in asking: does existentialism speak to me, a woman? Does existentialism address women?

The existential life cycle, which lies at the heart of existential theory, is central to discussion of this question. For existentialists, the cyclic enactment of change is a primary disposition of human beings. Since nothing is fixed, this cycle is the arena for all constitution of meaning. It enables creation of a life that stretches out from birth to death, and of the social world in which that life is lived. In this cycle there is constituted a historical past, future, and present. Without the existential life cycle, existence would fall into essence; human beings would be reduced to mere objects. If the existential life cycle were to represent the human as that which applies solely to the lives of men, it would exclude women from the existential project.

The existential life cycle is vividly depicted by the work of Albert Camus, whose literary philosophical style combines descriptions of daily life with theoretical concepts. Camus presents three moments of an existential cycle in which one endeavors to "live without appeal."[5] A solitary "I" emerges in the experience of the absurd, when an individual's demand for meaning in the face of nihilism is met by the world's silence. Through revolt against the absurd a solidary "we" stands forth. Revolt makes possible a "we" in which there are neither victims nor executioners, a situation in which freedom and lucidity are born. In artistic creation, the solitary "I" and solidary "we" are interwoven in a culminating, though fleeting, moment of creation which Camus designates as itself the evidence of man's dignity.

Yet I am absent from all the above mentioned moments. Analysis of the female characters in Camus's work shows that there are no women who partake in any aspect of the existential life cycle. Given the way that Camus describes women, women cannot participate in the existentialist endeavor.

In Camus's early writings, *The Stranger* and *The Myth of Sisyphus*, there are only dead women, a robot-woman, a battered woman, and an absent woman. Dead are Meursault's mother and Salamano's wife. Robotized is the "odd-looking little woman," the "little robot" who dines at Celeste's.[6] Battered is a Moorish woman. Wanting to teach her some "home truths," Raymond remarks that, "He'd beaten her til the blood came. Before that he'd never beaten her, 'Well, not hard, anyhow; only affectionately like. . . . Only to my mind I ain't punished her enough.' "[7] Absent is Marie. Her "presence" is really an absence, for her single, repeated question has no meaning for Meursault, who states, "She asked me if I loved her. I said that sort of question had no meaning, really; but I supposed I didn't."[8] Marie is likewise absent from *The Stranger*'s moment of existential crisis, for she is inside, washing dishes, when Meursault kills the Arab man on the beach.[9] Thus Camus's statement that, "Sisyphus teaches the higher fidelity that negates the gods and raises rocks," must be juxtaposed with his affirmation that, "His rock is his thing."[10] Sisyphus's "rock" is the sole evidence of man's "dignity," but it has nothing to do with the dignity of the women whom men have embalmed, robotized, battered, and rendered absent.

The Plague and *The Rebel*, central texts from Camus's middle writings, present a world from which women have been shut out. At the beginning of the plague, Rieux sends a telegram to his wife, "telling her that the town was closed . . . and that she was in his thoughts."[11] Rambert has "left his wife in Paris."[12] Only Rieux's mother stays in Oran, and at the end of a nearly three-hundred-page book, we know only of her highly regarded capacity for "self-effacement."[13] *The Plague* describes the "we," the public world in which three symbolic figures, Rieux, a rebel, Tarrou, a revolutionary, and Panelou, a priest, join in a male camaraderie that is to persist after the plague has been controlled, after each survivor has returned to his own private life.[14] These works of protest and rebellion never suggest that "invisible" women, the women who have been shut out, can "raise rocks" or "move mountains."

Camus's later work, *Exile and the Kingdom*, portrays male characters who are able to engage in existential creation only because female characters do not. In "The Artist at Work," it is Louise, the wife of Jonas, who by her "treasures of self-sacrifice"[15] enables her artist husband to remain in sublime isolation on a loft erected above the hubble-bubble of daily familial life, never to come down again, and hence, to be free to create. Even in "The Adulterous Woman," Camus's only writing which focuses on a female character, the main figure, Janine, has nothing to do with an existential life cycle. While traveling with her husband on his business trip, Janine walks out under the evening sky, has an orgasmic communion with the world, and returns, weeping, to her husband, who looks at her "without understanding."[16] Janine does not enter into the existential experience of the absurd. Although surrounded by solitude and silence, she does not ask the world for meaning. Camus does not portray Janine as acting to change her situation. She never rebels and, accordingly, cannot engage in artistic creation.

The male characters in Camus's writings indicate, moreover, that were women present at crucial moments of the existential experience, men would be "hindered" from developing an existential perspective. In *The Fall*, Clamence mentions that at times women are of interest to him. He is "stirred" by the nape of the neck of a woman who leaps suicidally from a bridge.[17] When he feels forsaken by the world, he desires "to be loved" by women and "to receive" what in his opinion is "due" him.[18] Yet the unavoidable conclusion to be drawn from Clamence's statement, "It hurts to confess it, but I'd have given ten conversations with Einstein for an initial rendezvous with a pretty chorus girl. It's true that at the tenth rendezvous I was looking for Einstein or a serious book,"[19] is that only when Clamence is without women is he able to *exsistere*, to stand out in the world, that is, the world of men.

Examination of the principal female characters in Camus's major works shows how existentialism views women as essentially non-existential beings and as impediments to men's existential progress. Since existentialism uses, profits from, but does not speak to, its female characters, is it possible to claim that existentialism addresses me, a woman?

One positive response might suggest that existentialism simply needs to be reformed. Perhaps fully developed female characters need only be invented and placed in an existential framework. The remarks of Kierkegaard's aesthete might be disregarded: "Woman's most profound destiny is to be a companion to man. If I were to imagine my ideal girl, she would always be alone in the world, and thereby be self-centered, and especially she would not have girl friends."[20] The comments of Kierkegaard's ethicist might be set aside, though not without difficulty: "She [woman] is man's deepest life, but a life which should always be concealed and hidden as the root of life always is. For this reason I hate all talk about the emancipation of woman. God forbid that ever it may come to pass. I cannot tell you . . . what hate I feel toward everyone who gives vent to such talk."[21] A deaf ear would necessarily be turned to Nietzsche's aphorism on women: "She [woman] is beginning to enlighten men about 'woman as such': *this* is one of the worst developments of the general *uglification* of Europe . . . so far all this was at bottom best repressed and kept under control by *fear* of man. . . . whatever women write about 'woman,' we may in the end reserve a healthy suspicion."[22] But, all to no avail. Just as the presence of a new figure makes a significant change in any context, an attempt to write women into the existentialist script necessarily ends by rewriting that script altogether.

In principle, existentialism cannot be reformed, for its first principle, a tacit but ever present foundation of its entire structure, is that man must make himself god. The existential man-become-god waylays the death of the God. The existential hero intercepts the decline of the rule of essence. Counter to the initial pronouncement of Nietzsche's "Madman," existentialism sustains the shadow of God. In this existential drama, women are eclipsed.

There are at least four senses in which God is not dead for the existentialists, and in which existentialism cannot address women:

1. *The rule of essence.* The initial promise of existentialism is evoked by Sartre when he writes that there is no human nature, or essence, because there is no God to have a conception of it.[23] Margery Collins and Christine Pierce, authors of "Holes and Slime: Sexism in Sartre's Psychoanalysis," point out the apparent implications of Sartre's existential perspective: "One would not expect to find sexism in Sartrian psychology because Sartre denies the concept of human nature and therefore its legitimacy as a source of human values. Such a view disallows the argument that roles are natural as a basis for assigning particular roles to women."[24] Yet, as Collins and Pierce note, Sartre's portrayal of women is "gravely disappointing."

The slip between the existential promise and its fulfillment lies in the existential reversal, by which man appropriates for himself the rule of essence. Just as the God of tradition functions as an ideal spectator who creates the essence of man, the existential man-become-god is an ideal spectator and legislator of essence for women. The existential hero imposes on women a womanly nature and womanly values.

Søren Kierkegaard writes that the existential artist creates the ideal image of women and judges its realization.[25] In the eyes of Kierkegaard's existential artist, a woman's rejection of the image in which she is created, even by cutting her long hair, turns her into a "crazy woman, like a criminal, a horror to men."[26] If the "contagion" of women's emancipation were to spread to his wife, Kierkegaard's ethicist declares, he would "sit down in the marketplace and weep, weep like that artist whose work has been destroyed and who did not even remember what he himself had painted."[27] Upon discovering that Regina, whom he considers "his" work of art, always will be lacking precisely because she "is" a woman, Kierkegaard's aesthete desires to act as a divinity and place her among those beings he perceives as leading active, interesting lives: "I have loved her, but from now on she can no longer engross my soul. If I were a god, I would do for her what Neptune did for a nymph: I would change her into a man."[28]

Existentialism attempts to displace the God of tradition, but not the desire which created that God. Such desire constitutes the man-god, who takes in his own hands the rule of essence. The desire to be God, characterized by Sartre as man's nostalgic search for unity, as man's search for the absolute, is unchallenged. The desire to be God is renamed: the desire for transcendence.[29]

2. *Transcendence*. With the death of God, Nietzsche urges a faithfulness to the earth.[30] Zarathustra, Nietzsche's central existential figure, passes his life in quest of earthly fidelity and friendship. Yet, paradoxically, a strong connection with the earth is interdicted by the priority that existentialists, including Nietzsche, give to transcendence.

Transcendence outstrips the earth, which existentialism posits as the site of immanence. Sartre's being-for-itself, the movement of desire or consciousness, "annihilates" being-in-itself, the plenitude of that which "is." The existentialist voices the belief that birthing is "sick" and "unclean,"[31] and comes himself miraculously into existence, seemingly without nurturance of any kind. Just as God created the world *ex nihilo*, the existentialist attempts to create himself out of nothing. By separating himself from "the given," the existential hero is omnipotently what he makes himself.

The earth as the site of daily life is transcended by the existential fascination with non-being. The profoundly necrophilic tendency of this fascination is expressed by the "wisdom of Silenus": "What is best of all is utterly beyond your reach: not to be born, not to *be*, to be *nothing*. But the second best is for you to die soon."[32] Here the Christ and the existential Antichrist both are rooted in the transcendent God of tradition. The Christian saint leaves earthly life by a death in which he becomes God-like. The existential antihero, condemned to carry the weight of the world on his shoulders,[33] evades the complexities of that world by immersion in melancholy, despair, and dread.

Existential preoccupation with non-being leaps over the concerns that I, a woman, have for my life. Rather than prepare myself for an encounter with dread, is it not the case that I, a woman, face a possible nothingness brought about by concrete acts of power over me: physical and mental harassment, incest, rape? If I am anxious, it is because a definite action threatens my life. Violence by men against women makes me fear for myself and other women. As Adrienne Rich writes, that nothingness over which existentialists despair has never been mine.[34]

3. *Identity.* Existentialism seeks to affirm the unique experiences and choices of each individual. The existential insistence that each individual choose and take responsibility for that individual's actions endeavors to undermine, ontologically and politically, the forfeiture of responsibility in the anonymous "they," the unreflective social and political climate of the times. The existential conception of self-identity does not achieve its aim, however, for its adherence to phallocentric assumptions leads it to dismiss the individual and collective identities of women.

The existential subordination of women's sexuality to men's self-identity is a salient instance of this dismissal. Existential drama, short stories, and novels extend the unquestioning faith that once upheld the identity of the God of tradition to the romantic love that the existential man-become-god expects of women. From Kierkegaard's Regina to Sartre's Lizzie the "respectful prostitute," women are represented as passive, reactive characters whose lives are intended to serve and support the desires of men.

Just as the God of tradition is alone in his omniscience and yet everywhere present, the existentialist enjoys a solitude accompanied by the presence of himself to himself wherever he turns. The existential life cycle affirms man's identity with himself, "he is himself the heart and center of his transcendence," and man's bond with other men, as in Zarathustra's celebratory "Last Supper," at which men, and only men, are present.[35] Such male-identification institutes a false universality in which the masculine is equated with all forms of "human" identity. Throughout his metaphysical rebellion against God, his historical rebellion against the state, and his artist's rebellion against the sheer contingency of existence, the existential hero preserves and perpetuates the identity of men's heritage. Existentialists may commemorate dwelling but not housework, psychological rebirth but not physical pregnancy, the lives of male painters, writers, and barrel makers, but not the accomplishments of women. Women's history as friends, sisters, midwives, laborers, and teachers is not discussed.

4.*The eclipse of women's lives.* So integral to existentialism are the rule of essence, transcendence, and identity, that without them the existential life cycle cannot be conceived. Were existentialism to dispense with these three characteristics, the death of God might be achieved, though at the risk of the end of the existential hero and the existential project.

The limits of existentialism are defined, however, not only by what it sets out to accomplish, but by what it fails to undertake: the presentation of a philosophical analysis from the perspective of women's lives. Existentialism's limits are evidenced precisely by what it renders absent: reflection, both conceptual and descriptive, which situates itself within the cycles of life which are lived by women.

Existentialism is, in principle, patriarchal existentialism. By perpetuating fundamental characteristics of the God of tradition, existentialists continue the humanist fallacy: the equation of men with human beings in general. Existentialism thereby establishes itself as a patriarchal endeavor that ignores women's existence, that dismisses the past, future, and present of women's culture.

Removal of existentialism's first principle, that man must make himself god, constitutes the deconstruction of its foundation. No longer is it necessary to engage in methodolatry of any sort. With the theoretical (although at this time in history not yet entirely actual) destruction of existential patriarchy, women need no longer see ourselves as the existential hero sees us.

A Proposal for a Way Out of Existential Patriarchy

Women's lives, out of reach for existential patriarchy, remain no longer in a hiddenness that presages survival, but open in their diversity to other worlds of philosophical inquiry. The foundational aspects of existentialism and their implications for women, delineated above, need not lead to a dead end. Such a critique dislodges new methods and concepts for reflection on women's experience.

I suggest a paradigm of women's lives that emerges in the turning of women to one another. Such a paradigm is apart from that of the existentialists: it seeks neither to be "equal" to the existential position nor to be a feminine inversion of existentialism, affirming the merits of what existentialism denies or neglects. I hold in common with existentialism, nevertheless, the paramount importance of change and the claim that philosophy is a sustained reflection on lived experience.

The work of Simone de Beauvoir is instrumental for the development of such a paradigm. Beauvoir, who stands both outside and within existen-

tialism, brings patriarchal existentialism to—though not through and beyond—the moment of its dissolution.

A distinctive trait of Beauvoir's writing is its grounding of existentialism
and feminist theory in women's experience. Beauvoir affirms women's
recovery of lived experience in passages such as this, in which she writes
of Violette Leduc, "She turned her life into the raw material of her works,
and that gave her life meaning."[36] An overriding concern of Beauvoir in
The Second Sex, as well as in her autobiographies and in several of her novels,
is to discover the connectedness of women's experiences or, as she states,
"to describe the common basis that underlies every individual feminine
existence."[37] The world of women's lives that is unearthed by Beauvoir's
studies is so unlike that represented by men that she boldly asserts, in
agreement with the seventeenth century feminist Poulain de la Barre,
"Everything written about women by men ought to be suspect, for these
men are at the same time the judge and the litigant."[38]

The astute analysis Beauvoir offers of the existential concepts "essence"
and "existence" gives rise to her most radical thesis: One is not born a
woman, rather, one becomes, and is forced to become, a woman.[39] One
is a woman not by essential necessity, but as a consequence of a cycle of
experiences that are lived and interpreted in a male-dominated political,
educational, and economic situation.

Ironically, Beauvoir challenges the equation of the masculine with the
human, but falls into patriarchal existentialism when her analysis of wom-
en's experiences commits a similar humanist fallacy. Key to this failure is
her identification of transcendence with men, and her valuation of transcendence over its twin concept, immanence, which she attributes to
women. Beauvoir writes that throughout history men have been the subject, the absolute, and women have been the other; men have acted and
transcended their situations, and women have passively repeated life.[40]
Yet the dualistic conceptual framework of transcendence/immanence does
violence to the complexity of women's experience. Beauvoir's exhortation
to women to affirm a brotherhood with men and become "full scale human
beings"[41] is precariously close to viewing women as liberated only when
women have taken on the characteristics attributed by existentialism to
men.

The Turning

The course of women's lives frequently is represented not as extending
from birth to death, but from birth to men and male institutions. Even
today, women's lives often end by absorption through marriage, or by

death in childbirth (the only social activity "short of war" that presents such a great danger of death).[42]

Women's actions that prioritize women's needs and concerns customarily appear as brief, unrelated spurts of energy subsumed in the omnipresent lives of men. At the crucial and all too dangerous angles of this broken zigzag, we turn, and are forced to turn, out of our lives and into men functioning as father, husband, teacher, or employer.

As pervasive patriarchal patterns assume the guise of the "natural," women come to be judged in relation to men, the absolute. From such a point of observation women often are characterized as inadequate, a failure. How many times is a woman asked, "What's wrong with you anyway?" Taught by patriarchy that women's lives have no meaning in and of themselves, we may come to perceive ourselves as "essentially incomplete being."[43] Even women's so-called "positive characteristics"—resilience, the ability to bounce back in the face of untoward conditions; perseverance, the tenacious and caring endurance of difficult situations—tend to be posited as compensatory actions that offset the excesses of women's deficient, and hence, undesirable, being-in-the-world. Yet just as all paths do not lead to Rome, the course of women's lives need not point to patriarchy.

In Hélène de Beauvoir's paintings there is a turning that brings to light a feminist politics of experience for which recovery of one's life and shared history constitutes a significant form of survival and resistance. The paintings depict, "Women who had formerly been bound, wrapped like mummies, or buried . . . freeing each other from their bandaged burial vestments."[44] The communal unwrapping effects a shift to a female subjectivity which acts with the power of knowledge that has arisen from personal experience. A correlate to this politics of experience is "consciousness raising" in the contemporary women's movements. The precondition of consciousness raising, according to one of its initiators, Kathie Sarachild, is "the decision to emphasize our own feelings and experiences as women and to test all generalizations and reading . . . by our own experience . . . to put all theories to the test of living practice and action."[45]

The turning of women to women portrayed in Hélène de Beauvoir's work shows how each action brings with it a unique world of connections. The women who will no longer be bound act not according to the expectations of a patriarchal order, but with an experience of past, future, and present that is constitutive of other lifeworlds. The resilience and perseverance designated by patriarchy as compensatory modes of being are freed to assume new connotations. "Gynecomyopia," which has been termed by Mary Carruthers as the failure to see women as "full, strong, mortal beings," is overturned by the powerful perception of women's lives as "a multidimensional shape rightfully culminating in old age and death."[46]

If the turning is represented as the isolated actions of women who live on the fundamentally alien ground of patriarchy, its transformative power is missed. The belief that women connect with women by weaving cleverly in and out of patriarchal society does not recognize sufficiently the displacement of patriarchal presence that such actions bring about. Patriarchy profits from this belief by expecting women to fulfill roles which revolve around male presence in ways that are scheming, devious, witch-like, and crafty: the female receptionist, secretary, homemaker, who must make skillful detours to keep all lines of communication open; the female nurse, waitress, wife, who must follow a circuitous route to keep everything running smoothly in the most complex of situations; the female textile worker, librarian, maker of printed circuits, who is supposedly "endowed" with extraordinary finger dexterity and ability for intricate maneuvers.

The turning of women to women is not a development within the patriarchal world, but a constitution of other worlds. The existential being-in-the-world is, in fact, being in a specific world which may or may not be that of patriarchal culture. Here it is by way of insinuation, by a positive sinister wisdom, that women break free of patriarchal interpretation and experience the tangible overlapping of women's lives.

Sinuosity

A paradigm for the turning of women to women may be articulated by a reflective description of one mode of female existence: sinuosity. *Sinuosity is a pattern of connectedness that constitutes women's experiences of being in a world. Sinuosity is a dynamic structure that enables the emergence of a positive women-identified sensibility and feminist experience.*

Sinuosity can be approached from the perspective of experiential description. It is not a formal category and attempts to avoid the rule of essence, identity, and transcendence typical of formal categories. The French deconstructive critique of terms such as "connection" and "wholeness," on the grounds that these terms lead to closed, self-referential systems which reduce diversity to an ideal identity, applies convincingly when these terms are employed as formal categories of experience. Western metaphysics is aptly portrayed by deconstruction as using "connection" and "wholeness" with the at least tacit assumption that all parts of an entity can be held in one's grasp and represented in their totality like the parts of an architect's drawing.[47] Yet deconstruction dismisses too quickly lived experience of connection and wholeness, claiming that appeal to such experience replicates the same closed system.

Some recent French writers, notably Cixous, Irigaray, Wittig, and Barthes, have argued that certain experiences of bodily connection overcome problematic issues that characteristically confront Western metaphysics. From a post-existential stance, the sinuous connectedness of women's lives also crosses the bounds of Western metaphysics.

There is no pre-established ideal for sinuosity, for the turning of women to women is constantly in transition. Precisely because such a turning is free, and thus, unpredictable, it cannot be identified by an index of behaviors or analyzed by prescriptive definition.

Nor is there an absolute, objective guarantee for when sinuosity is present. That "there is" sinuosity is experienced only when "guarantee" (from Old High German "guarantor," *werēnto*) is *felt* in its root meaning: to trust and to care (*wāra*). The sinuous "is" in the connectedness of the trusting, caring lives of women friends (Old High German, *frēond*) who love (*frēon*), caress (*fría*), and free (*frēo*) one another.[48]

Sinuosity is constituted not from the outside, as an attempt to impress a fixed mold on life events, but by a gathering of memories and projects. There emerges in this gathering the curving, winding, folding of women's lives. The sinuous, in its folding (*sinus*) reconnects with a once lost etymological sense: the fold of a garment, the folds of a breast, the fold—gulf or great bay—of the sea.[49] The sinuous undulates, ripples, in the breeze. It slithers silvery on moonlit nights. The sinuous billows in the waving fields of corn, the flowing of a mane, the rolling in laughter of joyous celebration.

At the same time, the sinuous names the sinew, the tendon, tough and strong. Here anger and revolt are embedded in women's muscles, giving us the endurance to shape a world of our priorities and delights. The determinations of resistance and survival which women make daily craft the sinuous by a bold taking of risks.

The linguistic field of the sinuous retrieves connection with etymological groundings and challenges the monopoly on meaning by which Western metaphysics has maintained its power. Language for naming the sinuous is felt by an experience of wholeness (Old English, *hal*): those connections which are sound and unbroken; connections which are being healed; connections which now are free of injury. Whole is that aspect of the sinuous which spreads healing and strength. A whole (Old Norse, feminine, *heil*) is good luck and happiness.[50]

Yet sinuosity is never a paradigm for a metaphysical paradise, promising perfection or an ideal existence. The sinuous is tortuous—because it is tortured by the judgmental actions of patriarchy, and because it is difficult, necessitating the constant decision to emphasize one's own feelings and experiences. Having unchained the earth from its sun, the man-become-god, women are free, even, from any necessity to experience our lives as sinuous.

To see existentialism as patriarchal and to suggest a way out of existential patriarchy raises in an unaccustomed light the question: What is philosophy? The powerful connections of women's lives have been repressed in the development of Western philosophy, with its monotheistic trend toward the rule of essence. Philosophical wisdom that has arisen in the midst of such connections has survived, for the most part, only secretly, and on heretical, revolutionary bypaths.[51]

Thinking in existential patriarchy brings forth, at least in part, a ground of philosophy in which women live, act, and speak with one another. Perhaps most urgent at present is a new acoustics in which, as women, we listen to and respond to each other. The feelingful, thoughtful voices which speak from out of this ground have a love of Sophia, free of all godly shadows.

NOTES

1. Friedrich Nietzsche, *The Gay Science*, trans. Walter Kaufmann (New York: Random House, 1974), 181, 182.

2. Simone de Beauvoir, *The Second Sex*, trans. H. M. Parshley (New York: Random House, 1953), xviii.

3. Friedrich Neitzsche, *Thus Spake Zarathustra*, trans. Walter Kaufmann (New York: Random House, 1954), 272–75.

4. Nietzsche, *The Gay Science*, 181, 182.

5. Albert Camus, *The Myth of Sisyphus*, trans. Justin O'Brien (New York: Random House, 1955), 39.

6. Albert Camus, *The Stranger*, trans. Stuart Gilbert (New York: Random House, 1946), 55, 56.

7. Ibid., 38.

8. Ibid., 44, 52.

9. Ibid., 66.

10. Camus, *The Myth of Sisyphus*, 91.

11. Albert Camus, *The Plague*, trans. Stuart Gilbert (New York: Random House, 1948), 76.

12. Ibid., 77.

13. Ibid., 248.

14. Ibid., 265, 396.

15. Albert Camus, *Exile and the Kingdom*, trans. Justin O'Brien (New York: Random House, 1957), 116.

16. Ibid., 150, 33.

17. Albert Camus, *The Fall*, trans. Justin O'Brien (New York: Random House, 1956), 70.

18. Ibid., 67.

19. Ibid., 59, 60.

20. Søren Kierkegaard, *Either/Or*, vol. 1, trans. David F. Swenson and Lillian Marvin Swenson (New Jersey: Princeton University Press, 1944), 335.

21. Kierkegaard, *Either/Or*, vol. 2, trans. Walter Lowrie (New Jersey: Princeton University Press, 1944), 316.

22. Friedrich Nietzsche, *Beyond Good and Evil*, trans. Walter Kaufmann (New York: Random House, 1966), 162, 163.

23. Jean-Paul Sartre, "Existentialism is a Humanism," trans. Hazel E. Barnes, in *Existentialism from Dostoevsky to Sartre*, 2nd. ed., Walter Kaufmann, ed. (New York: American Library, 1975), 349.

24. Margery Collins and Christine Pierce, "Holes and Slime: Sexism in Sartre's Psychoanalysis," in *Woman and Philosophy: Toward a Theory of Liberation*, Carol C. Gould and Max W. Wartofsky, eds. (New York: Putnam's Sons, 1976), 113, 125.

25. Kierkegaard, *Either/Or*, vol. 1, 384.

26. Ibid., vol. 2, 318.

27. Ibid., vol. 2, 317.

28. Ibid., vol. 1, 440.

29. Jean-Paul Sartre, *Being and Nothingness*, trans. Hazel E. Barnes (New York: Citadel Press, 1956), 535, 544.

30. Nietzsche, *Thus Spake Zarathustra*, 13.

31. Ibid., 291.

32. Friedrich Nietzsche, *The Birth of Tragedy*, trans. Walter Kaufmann (New York: Random House, 1967), 42.

33. Sartre, *Being and Nothingness*, 677.

34. Adrienne Rich, "Power and Danger: The Work of a Common Woman by Judy Grahn," in Judy Grahn, *The Work of a Common Woman* (California: Diana Press, 1978), 20.

35. Sartre, "Existentialism is a Humanism," in *Existentialism from Dostoevsky to Sartre*, 368. Nietzsche, *Thus Spake Zarathustra*, 284–86.

36. Beauvoir, *The Second Sex*, xxxv, 694.

37. Simone de Beauvoir, *All Said and Done*, trans. Patrick O'Brian (New York : Putnam's Sons, 1974), 52.

38. Beauvoir, *The Second Sex*, xxv.

39. Ibid., xxxv, 694; Beauvoir, *All Said and Done*, 448. See also Monique Wittig, "One is Not Born a Woman," *Feminist Studies* 1:2 (Winter 1981):47–54. *Conference* (New York), 71.

40. Beauvoir, *The Second Sex*, xix, 72.

41. Ibid., 810; Beauvoir, *All Said and Done*, 458, 459.

42. Jeffner Allen, "Motherhood: The Annihilation of Women," in *Mothering: Essays in Feminist Theory*, ed. Joyce Trebilcot, (New Jersey: Roman and Allanheld, 1984), 315–30.

43. Mary Carruthers, "Imagining Woman: Notes Towards a Feminist Poetic," *Massachusetts Review* (Summer 1979), 284, 290.

44. Gloria Orenstein, "Exorcism/Protest/Rebirth," *Womanart* (Winter 1977–78):10.

45. Kathie Sarachild, "Consciousness-Raising: A Radical Weapon," in *Feminist Revolution*, Redstockings, inc. (New York: Random House, 1978), 145.

46. Carruthers, "Imagining Women," 289.

47. Martin Heidegger, *Being and Time*, trans. John MacQuarrie and Edward Robinson (New York: Harper & Row, 1962), 226, 277, 280.

48. From a cluster of derivative etymologies: love [old English *frēon*], caress [old Norse *friá*], and free [old English *frēo*]. See *Oxford English Dictionary* and *Websters International Dictionary*.

49. Ibid.

50. Ibid.

51. This theme is developed by Eric Neumann, *The Great Mother: An Analysis of the Archetype*, trans. Ralph Manheim (New Jersey: Princeton University Press, 1963), 331.

SEXUAL IDEOLOGY AND PHENOMENOLOGICAL DESCRIPTION

A FEMINIST CRITIQUE OF MERLEAU-PONTY'S *PHENOMENOLOGY OF PERCEPTION*

Judith Butler

Theories of sexuality which tend to impute natural ends to sexual desire are very often part of a more general discourse on the legitimate locations of gender and desire within a given social context.* The appeal to a natural desire and, as a corollary, a natural form of human sexual relationships is thus invariably normative, for those forms of desire and sexuality which fall outside the parameters of the natural model are understood as unnatural and, hence, without the legitimation that a natural and normative model confers. Although Merleau-Ponty does not write his theory of sexuality within an explicitly political framework, he nevertheless offers certain significant arguments against naturalistic accounts of sexuality that are useful to any explicit political effort to refute restrictively normative views of sexuality. In arguing that sexuality is coextensive with existence, that it is a mode of dramatizing and investigating a concrete historical situation, Merleau-Ponty appears to offer feminist theory a view of sexuality freed of naturalistic ideology, one which restores both the historical and volitional components of sexual experience and, consequently, opens the way for a fuller description of sexuality and sexual diversity.

In the section of Merleau-Ponty's *Phenomenology of Perception* entitled "The Body in its Sexual Being," the body is termed a "historical idea" rather than "a natural species."[1] Significantly, Simone de Beauvoir takes

---

*This essay was originally written in 1981.

up this claim in *The Second Sex*,[2] quoting Merleau-Ponty to the effect that woman, like man, is a historical construction bearing no natural telos, a field of possibilities that are taken up and actualized in various distinctive ways. To understand the construction of gender, it is not necessary to discover a normative model against which individual instances can be gauged, but, rather, to delimit the field of historical possibilities which constitute this gender, and to examine in detail the *acts* by which these possibilities are appropriated, dramatized, and ritualized. For Merleau-Ponty, the body is a "place of appropriation" and a mechanism of "transformation" and "conversion," an essentially dramatic structure which can be 'read' in terms of the more general life that it embodies. As a result, the body cannot be conceived of as a static or univocal fact of existence, but, rather, as a modality of existence, the 'place' in which possibilities are realized and dramatized, the individualized appropriation of a more general historical experience.

And yet, the potential openness of Merleau-Ponty's theory of sexuality is deceptive. Despite his efforts to the contrary, Merleau-Ponty offers descriptions of sexuality which turn out to contain tacit normative assumptions about the heterosexual character of sexuality. Not only does he assume that sexual relations are heterosexual, but that the masculine sexuality is characterized by a disembodied gaze that subsequently defines its object as mere body. Indeed, as we shall see, Merleau-Ponty conceptualizes the sexual relation between men and women on the model of master and slave. And although he generally tends to discount natural structures of sexuality, he manages to reify cultural relations between the sexes on a different basis by calling them 'essential' or 'metaphysical'. Hence, Merleau-Ponty's theory of sexuality and sexual relations at once liberates and forecloses the cultural possibility of benign sexual variation. Insofar as feminist theory seeks to dislodge sexuality from those reifying ideologies which freeze sexual relations into 'natural' forms of domination, it has both something to gain and something to fear from Merleau-Ponty's theory of sexuality.

Merleau-Ponty's Criticisms of Reductive Psychology

In arguing that "sexuality is coextensive with existence," Merleau-Ponty refutes those theoretical efforts to isolate sexuality as a "drive" or a biological given of existence. Sexuality cannot be reduced to a specific set of drives or activities, but must be understood as subtending all our modes of engagement in the world. As an inexorable "aura" and "odour," sexuality is an essentially malleable quality, a mode of embodying a certain existential relation to the world, and the specific modality of dramatizing that relation in corporeal terms. According to Merleau-Ponty, there are two prominent theoretical attitudes toward sexuality which are fundamentally mistaken. The one regards sexuality as a composite set of drives which occupy some interior biological space and which, consequent to the emergence of these drives into conscious experience, become attached to representations. This contingent relation between drive and representation results in the figuration of drives as 'blind' or motored by an internal teleology or naturalistic mechanism. The objects to which they become attached are only arbitrary foci for these drives, occasions or conditions for their release and gratification, and the entire life of the drive takes place within a solipsistic framework. The other theory posits sexuality as an ideational layer which is projected onto the world, a representation which is associated with certain stimuli and which, through habit, we come to affirm as the proper domain of sexuality. In the first instance, the reality of sexuality resides in a set of drives which pre-exist their representation, and in the second case, the reality of sexuality is a production of representation, a habit of association, a mental construction. In both cases, we can see that there is no intentional relation between what is called a 'drive' and its 'representation'. As intentional, the drive would be referential from the outset; it could only be understood in the context of its concrete actualization in the world, as a mode of expressing, dramatizing, and embodying an existential relation to the world. In the above two cases, however, sexuality is solipsistic rather than referential, a self-enclosed phenomenon which signals a rupture between sexuality and existence. As a drive, sexuality is "about" its own biological necessity, and as a representation, it is a mere construct which has no necessary relation to the world upon which it is imposed. For Merleau-Ponty, sexuality must be intentional in the sense that it modalizes a relationship between an embodied subject and a concrete situation: "bodily existence continually sets the prospect of living before me . . . my body is what opens me out upon the world and places me in a situation there."[3]

Written in 1945, *The Phenomenology of Perception* offered an appraisal of psychoanalytic theory both appreciative and critical. On the one hand, Freud's contention that sexuality pervades mundane existence and structures human life from its inception is accepted and reformulated by Merleau-Ponty in the latter's claim that sexuality is coextensive with existence. And yet, in Merleau-Ponty's description of psychoanalysis, we can discern the terms of his own phenomenological revision of that method. Note in the following how Freud's theory of sexuality comes to serve the phenomenological and existential program:

> For Freud himself the sexual is not the genital, sexual life is not a mere effect
> of the processes having their seat in the genital organs, the libido is not an

> instinct, that is, an activity naturally directed towards definite ends, it is the general power, which the psychosomatic subject enjoys, of taking root in different settings, of establishing himself through different experiences . . . It is what causes a man (sic) to have a history. In so far as a man's (sic) sexual history provides a key to his life, it is because in his sexuality is projected his manner of being towards the world, that is, towards time and other men (sic).[4]

Merleau-Ponty's presumption that the Freudian libido is "not an instinct" does not take into account Freud's longstanding ambivalence toward a theory of instinctual sexuality, evident in the 1915 essay, "Instincts and Their Vicissitudes," in *Beyond the Pleasure Principle* (1920), and in his later speculative writings.[5] Unclear, for instance, is how strictly Freud maintained the distinction between drive (*Trieb*) and instinct (*Instinkt*), and the extent to which drives are viewed as a necessary mythology or part of the framework of a naturalistic ideology. Freud's theory of psychosexual development very often relies on a naturalistic theory of drives whereby the normal development of a sexual drive culminates in the restriction of erotogenic zones to the genital and the normative valorization of heterosexual coitus. Although complicated and varied in its methodological style, Freud's book *Three Essays on the Theory of Sexuality* nevertheless tends to subject the analysis of the body in situation to a description of the internal teleology of instincts which has both a natural and normal life of its own.[6] Indeed, as a drive which develops along natural and normal lines, sexuality is figured as precisely the kind of naturalistic construction that Merleau-Ponty views as contrary to his intentional view. And as a "psychical representative of an endosomatic, continuously flowing source of stimulation,"[7] the sexual drive is precisely the kind of arbitrary construct that Merleau-Ponty also wants to repudiate.

But even more curious is Merleau-Ponty's attribution to Freud of a unified agent whose reflexive acts are manifest in his/her sexual life. In arguing that "the psychosomatic subject" takes root and establishes him/herself in different settings and situations, Merleau-Ponty glosses over the psychoanalytic critique of the conscious subject as a product of unconscious desires and the mechanism of repression. In effect, Merleau-Ponty assimilates the psychoanalytic subject to a reflexive Cartesian ego, a position that psychoanalytic theory sought to criticize as much more limited in its autonomy than rationalist philosophy had presumed.

In light of Merleau-Ponty's curious appropriation of psychoanalysis, it seems clear that he rejects any account of sexuality which relies upon causal factors understood to precede the concrete situation of the individual, whether those factors are natural or unconscious. Moreover, he refuses to accept any normative conception of sexuality such that particular social organizations of sexuality appear either more normal or more natural than others. We will later see, however, that while he does not assert such a telos, he nevertheless assumes one at various crucial points in the theory. Despite the alleged openness and malleability of sexuality in Merleau-Ponty's view, certain structures emerge as existential and metaphysical necessities which ultimately cast doubt upon Merleau-Ponty's nonnormative pretensions. Indeed, despite his trenchant critique of naturalistic accounts of sexuality, it becomes unclear whether Merleau-Ponty is himself wholly freed of naturalistic ideology.

The Constitution of Sexuality: Nature, History, and Existence

For Merleau-Ponty, the various expressions of human sexuality constitute possibilities arising from bodily existence in general; none can claim ontological priority over any other. Sexuality is discussed in general terms as a mode of situating oneself in terms of one's intersubjectivity. Little more is said, not because Merleau-Ponty thinks sexuality is abstract, but because the multifarious expressions of sexuality have only these expressive and intersubjective qualities in common. In its fundamental structure, sexuality is both reflexive and corporeal and signifies a relation between the embodied subject and others. The individual who is clinically considered asexual is misunderstood by the vocabulary that names him or her; 'asexuality' reveals a definite sexual orientation, what Merleau-Ponty describes as "a way of life—an attitude of escapism and need of solitude— . . . a generalized expression of a certain state of sexuality . . . the fact remains that this existence is the act of taking up and making explicit a sexual situation."[8] On the other hand, sexuality is never experienced in a pure form such that a purely sexual state can be achieved: "Even if I become absorbed in the experience of my own body and in the solitude of sensations, I do not succeed in abolishing all reference of my life to a world. At every moment some intention springs afresh from me."[9]

As "a current of existence," sexuality has no necessary forms, but presents itself as having-to-be-formed. Sexuality is not a choice inasmuch as it is a necessary expression of bodily existence and the necessary medium of 'choice'. In opposition to Sartre's claim in *Being and Nothingness* that the body represents a factic limitation to choice, the constraining material perspective, Merleau-Ponty argues that the body is itself a modality of reflexivity, a specifically corporeal agency. In this sense, then, sexuality cannot be said to 'represent' existential choices which are themselves pre- or nonsexual, for sexuality is an irreducible modality of choice. And yet, Merleau-Ponty acknowledges that sexuality cannot be restricted to the various reflexive acts that it modalizes; sexuality is always there, as the medium for existential projects, as the ceaseless 'current' of existence. Indeed, in the following, Merleau-Ponty appears to invest sexuality with powers that exceed those of the individual existence which gives it form:

> Why is our body for us the mirror of our being, unless it is a natural self, a current of given existence, with the result that we never know whether the forces that bear on us are its or ours—or with the result rather that they are never entirely either its or ours. There is no outstripping of sexuality any more than there is any sexuality enclosed within itself.[10]

This 'natural' current is thus taken up through the concrete acts and gestures of embodied subjects and given concrete form, and this form thus becomes its specific historical expression. Thus, sexuality only becomes historical through individual acts of appropriation, "the permanent act[s] by which man [sic] takes up, for his own purposes, and makes his own a certain de facto situation."[11]

Here it is clear that while each individual confronts a natural sexuality and a concrete existential situation, that situation does not include the history of sexuality, the legacy of its conventions and taboos. It seems we must ask whether individuals do not confront a *sedimented* sexuality, and if so, are not the individual acts of appropriation less transformations of a natural sexuality into a historically specific sexuality than the transformation of past culture into present culture? It is unclear that we could ever confront a 'natural' sexuality which was not already mediated by language and acculturation and, hence, it makes sense to ask whether the sexuality we do confront is always already partially formed. Merleau-Ponty is doubtless right in claiming that there is no outstripping sexuality, that it is there, always to be reckoned with in one way or another, but there seems no *prima facie* reason to assume that its inexorability is at once its naturalness. Perhaps it is simply the case that a specific formation of culturally constructed sexuality has come to *appear* as natural.

According to his own arguments, it would seem that Merleau-Ponty would discount the possibility of a subject in confrontation with a natural sexuality. In his words, "there is history only for a subject who lives through it, and a subject only insofar as he is historically situated."[12] Yet, to say that the subject is historically situated in a loose sense is to say only that the decisions a subject makes are delimited—not exclusively constituted—by a given set of historical possibilities. A stronger version of historical situatedness would locate history as the very condition for the constitution of the subject, not only as a set of external possibilities for choice. If this stronger version were accepted, Merleau-Ponty's above claim with regard to a natural sexuality would be reversed: individual existence does not bring natural sexuality into the historical world, but history provides the conditions for the conceptualization of the individual as such. Moreover, sexuality is itself formed through the sedimentation of the history of sexuality, and the embodied subject, rather than an existential constant, is itself partially constituted by the legacy of sexual relations which constitute its situation.

Merleau-Ponty's anthropological naiveté emerges in his view of how cultural conventions determine how the lived body is culturally reproduced. He distinguishes, mistakenly I believe, between biological subsistence and the domain of historical and cultural signification: " 'living' (*leben*) is a primary process from which, as a starting point, it becomes possible to 'live' (*erleben*) this or that world, and we must eat and breathe before perceiving and awakening to relational living, belonging to colours and lights through sight, to sounds through hearing, to the body of another through sexuality, before arriving at the life of human relations."[13] When we consider, however, the life of the infant as immediately bound up in a set of relationships whereby it receives food, shelter, and warmth, it becomes impossible to separate the fact of biological subsistence from the various ways in which that subsistence is administered and assured. Indeed, the very birth of the child is already a human relation, one of radical dependence, which takes place within a set of institutional regulations and norms. In effect, it is unclear that there can be a state of sheer subsistence divorced from a particular organization of human relationships. Economic anthropologists have made the point various times that subsistence is not prior to culture, that eating and sleeping and sexuality are inconceivable apart from the various social forms through which these activities are ritualized and regulated.

In accounting for the genesis of sexual desire, Merleau-Ponty once again reverts to a naturalistic account which seems to contradict his own phenomenological procedure. In the following, he attributes the emergence of sexuality to the purely organic function of the body: "there must be, immanent in sexual life, some function which insures its emergence, and the normal extension of sexuality must rest on internal powers of the organic subject. There must be an Eros or Libido which breathes life into an original world."[14] Once again, it appears that sexuality emerges prior to the influence of historical and cultural factors. And yet theorists such as Michel Foucault have argued that cultural conventions dictate not only when sexuality becomes explicit, but also in what form. What leads Merleau-Ponty, then, to safeguard this aspect of sexuality as prior to culture and history? What dimensions of 'natural' sexuality does Merleau-Ponty wish to preserve such that he is willing to contradict his own methodology in the ways that he has? Although Merleau-Ponty is clearly concerned with sexuality as the dramatic embodiment of existential themes, he distinguishes between those existential themes that are purely individual, and those that are shared and intersubjective. Indeed, it appears, for him, that sexuality dramatizes certain existential themes that are universal in character, and which, we will see, dictate certain forms of domination between the sexes as 'natural' expressions of sexuality.

Misogyny as an Intrinsic Structure of Perception

Not only does Merleau-Ponty fail to acknowledge the extent to which sexuality is culturally constructed, but his descriptions of the universal features of sexuality reproduce certain cultural constructions of sexual normalcy. The case of the sexually disinterested Schneider is a rich example. In introducing the reader to Schneider, Merleau-Ponty refers to his "sexual incapacity," and throughout the discussion it is assumed that Schneider's state is abnormal. The evidence that Merleau-Ponty provides in support of this contention is considered to be obvious: "Obscene pictures, conversations on sexual topics, the sight of a body do not arouse desire in him."[15] One wonders what kind of cultural presumptions would make arousal in such contexts seem utterly normal. Certainly, these pictures, conversations, and perceptions already designate a concrete cultural situation, one in which the masculine subject is figured as viewer, and the yet unnamed feminine subject is the body to be seen.

In Merleau-Ponty's view, evidence of Schneider's "sexual inertia" is to be found in a general lack of sexual tenacity and willfulness. Deemed abnormal because he "no longer seeks sexual intercourse of his own accord," Schneider is subject to the clinical expectation that sexual intercourse is intrinsically desirable regardless of the concrete situation, the other person involved, the desires and actions of that other person. Assuming that certain acts necessitate a sexual response, Merleau-Ponty notes that Schneider "hardly ever kisses, and the kiss for him has no value as sexual stimulation." "If orgasm occurs first in the partner and she moves away, the half-fulfilled desire vanishes"; this gesture of deference signifies masculine "incapacity," as if the normal male would seek satisfaction regardless of the desires of his female partner.[16]

Central to Merleau-Ponty's assessment of Schneider's sexuality as abnormal is the presumption that the decontextualized female body, the body alluded to in conversation, the anonymous body which passes by on the street, exudes a natural attraction. This is a body rendered irreal, the focus of solipsistic fantasy and projection; indeed, this is a body that does not *live*, but a frozen image which does not resist or interrupt the course of masculine desire through an unexpected assertion of life. How does this eroticization of the decontextualized body become reconciled with Merleau-Ponty's insistence that "what we try to possess is not just a body, but a body brought to life by consciousness?"[17]

Viewed as an expression of sexual ideology, *The Phenomenology of Perception* reveals the cultural construction of the masculine subject as a strangely disembodied voyeur whose sexuality is strangely non-corporeal. Significant, I think, is the prevalence of visual metaphors in Merleau-Ponty's descriptions of normal sexuality. Erotic experience is almost never described as tactile or physical or even passionate.[18] Although Merleau-Ponty explains that 'perception' for him signifies affective life in general, it appears that the meaning of perception occasionally reverts to its original denotation of sight. Indeed, it sometimes appears as if sexuality itself were reduced to the erotics of the gaze. Consider the following: "In the case of the normal subject, a body is not perceived merely as an object; this objective perception has within it a more intimate perception: the visible body is subtended by a sexual schema which is strictly individual, emphasizing the erogenous areas, outlining a sexual physiognomy, and eliciting the gestures of the masculine body which is itself integrated into this emotional totality."[19]

As Merleau-Ponty notes, the schema subtending the body emphasizes the erogenous zones, but it remains unclear whether the "erogenous areas" are erogenous to the perceiving subject or to the subject perceived. Perhaps it is significant that Merleau-Ponty fails to make the distinction, for as long as the erotic experience belongs exclusively to the perceiving subject, it is of no consequence whether the experience is shared by the subject perceived. The paragraph begins with the clear distinction between a perception which objectifies and decontextualizes the body and a perception which is 'more intimate', which makes of the body more than 'an object'. The schema constitutes the intimate perception, and yet, as the schema unfolds, we realize that as a focusing on erogenous parts it consists in a further decontextualization and fragmentation of the perceived body. Indeed, the 'intimate' perception further denies a world or context for this body, but reduces the body to its erogenous (to whom?) parts. Hence, the body is objectified more drastically by the sexual schema than by the objective perception.

Only at the close of the paragraph do we discover that the "normal subject" is male, and "the body" he perceives is female. Moreover, the sexual physiognomy of the female body "elicit[s] the gestures of the masculine body," as if the very existence of these attributes 'provoked' or even necessitated certain kinds of sexual gestures on the part of the male. Here it seems that the masculine subject has not only projected his own desire onto the female body, but then has accepted that projection as the very structure of the body that he perceives. Here the solipsistic circle of the masculine voyeur seems complete. That the masculine body is regarded as "integrated into this emotional totality" appears as a bizarre conclusion considering that his sole function has been to fulfill a spectatorial role.

In contrast to this normal male subject is Schneider, for whom it is said "a woman's body has no particular essence." Nothing about the purely physical construction of the female body arouses Schneider: "It is, he says, predominately character which makes a woman attractive, for physically they are all the same."[20] For Merleau-Ponty, the female body has an "essence" to be found in the "schema" that invariably elicits the gestures of masculine desire, and although he does not claim that this perception is conditioned by a natural or mechanistic causality, it appears to have the same necessity that such explanations usually afford. Indeed, it is difficult to understand how Merleau-Ponty, on other occasions in the text, makes general claims about bodies which starkly contradict his specific claims about women's bodies, unless by 'the body' he means the male body, just as earlier the 'normal subject' turned out to be male. At various points, he remarks that "bodily existence . . . is only the barest raw material of a genuine presence in the world,"[21] a 'presence' which one might assume to be the origin of attractiveness, rather than the sexual schema taken alone. And rather than posit the body as containing an 'essence', he remarks that "the body expresses existence."[22] To maintain, then, that the female body has an essence qua female and that this essence is to be found in the body contradicts his more general claim that "the body expresses total existence, not because it is an external accompaniment to that existence, but because existence comes to its own in the body."[23] And yet, female bodies appear to have an essence which is itself physical, and this essence designates the female body as an object rather than a subject of perception. Indeed, the female body is seemingly never a subject, but always denotes an always already fixed essence rather than an open existence. She is, in effect, already formed, while the male subject is in exclusive control of the constituting gaze. She is never seeing, always seen. If the female body denotes an essence, while bodies in general denote existence, then it appears that bodies in general must be male—and existence does not belong to women.

That Schneider finds only women with character arousing is taken as proof that he suffers from a sublimation of his true desires, that he has rationalized the object of his desire as a bearer of virtue. That Schneider conflates a moral and a sexual discourse is, for Merleau-Ponty, evidence of repression, and yet it may be that after all Schneider is more true to Merleau-Ponty's phenomenological account of bodily existence than Merleau-Ponty himself. By refusing to endow a woman with an essence, Schneider reaffirms the woman's body as an expression of existence, a 'presence' in the world. Her body is not taken as a physical and interchangeable fact, but expressive of the life of consciousness. Hence, it appears that Schneider is a feminist of sorts, while Merleau-Ponty represents the cultural equation of normalcy with an objectifying masculine gaze and the corollary devaluation of moral concerns as evidence of pathology.

The Sexual Ideology of Master and Slave

The ideological character of *The Phenomenology of Perception* is produced by the impossible project of maintaining an abstract subject even while describing concrete, lived experience. The subject appears immune from the historical experience that Merleau-Ponty describes, but then reveals itself in the course of the description as a concrete cultural subject, a masculine subject. Although Merleau-Ponty intends to describe the universal structures of bodily existence, the concrete examples he provides reveal the impossibility of that project. Moreover, the specific cultural organization of sexuality becomes reified through a description that claims universality. On the one hand, Merleau-Ponty wants sexuality to be intentional, in-the-world, referential, expressive of a concrete, existential situation, and yet he offers a description of bodily experience clearly abstracted from the concrete diversity that exists. The effect of this abstraction is to codify and sanction one particular cultural organization of sexuality as legitimate. Hence, the promise of his phenomenological method to provide a nonnormative framework for the understanding of sexuality proves illusory.

Central to his argument is that sexuality instates us in a common world. The problem arises, however, when the common world he describes is a reification of a relation of domination between the sexes. Although he argues that sexuality makes us a part of a universal community, it becomes clear that this 'universality' characterizes a relationship of voyeurism and objectification, a nonreciprocal dialectic between men and women. In claiming that this universal dialectic is to be found in lived experience, Merleau-Ponty prefigures the analysis of lived experience, investing the body with an ahistorical structure which is in actuality profoundly historical in origin. Merleau-Ponty begins his explanation of this structure in the following way: "The intensity of sexual pleasure would not be sufficient to explain the place occupied by sexuality in human life or, for example, the phenomenon of eroticism, if sexual experience were not, as it were, an opportunity vouchsafed to all and always available, of acquainting oneself with the human lot in its most general aspects of autonomy and dependence."[24]

The dynamics of autonomy and dependence characterize human life universally and "arise from the metaphysical structure of my body." Moreover, this dynamic is part of "a dialectic of the self and other which is that of master and slave: insofar as I have a body, I may be reduced to the status of an object beneath the gaze of another person, and no longer count as a person for him, or else I may become his master and, in my turn, look at *him*."[25]

Master-slave is thus a metaphysical dynamic insofar as a body is always an object for others inasmuch as it is perceived. Perception designates an affective relation and, in the context of sexuality, signifies desire. Hence, a body is an object to the extent that it is desired, and is, in turn, a subject, inasmuch as it desires. Hence, being desired is equivalent to enslavement, and desiring is equivalent to mastering. Taken yet further, this dialectic suggests that the master, as the one who desires, is essentially without a body; indeed, it is a body which he desires to have. In other words, active desire is a way of dispensing with the existential problematic of being a body-object. In phenomenological terms, active desire is a flight from embodiment. The slave is thus designated as the body that the master lacks. And because the slave is a body-object, the slave is a body without desire. Hence, in this relationship, neither master nor slave constitute a *desiring body*; the master is desire without a body, and the slave is a body without desire.

We can speculate yet further upon this 'metaphysical' structure of bodily existence. The desire of the master must always be the desire to possess what he lacks, the body which he has denied and which the slave has come to *em*body. The slave, on the other hand, is not a person—a body expressive of consciousness—much less a person who desires. Whether or not the slave desires is irrelevant to the master, for his desire is self-sufficient; it posits the object of its desire and sustains it; his concern is not to *be* a body, but to have or possess the body as an object. But what does it mean to say that the master does not have a body? If the body is a "situation," the condition of perspective and the necessary mediation of a social existence, then the master has denied himself the condition for a genuine presence in the world and has become worldless. His desire is thus both an alienation of bodily existence and an effort to recapture the body from this self-imposed exile, not to be this body, but this time to possess and control it in order to nurse an illusion of transcendence. Desire thus signifies an effort at objectification and possession, the master's bizarre struggle with his own vulnerability and existence that requires the slave to be the body the master no longer wants to be. The slave must be the Other, the exact opposite of the Subject, but nevertheless remain his possession.

If the slave is a body without desire, the very identity of the slave forbids desire. Not only is the desire of the slave irrelevant to the master, but the emergence of the slave's desire would constitute a fatal contradiction in the slave's identity. Hence, the liberation of the slave would consist in the moment of desire, for desire would signal the advent of a subject, a body expressive of consciousness.

Although Merleau-Ponty does not equate the master with the male body or the slave with the female body, he does tend, as we have seen, to identify the female body with a sexual schema of a decontextualized and fragmented body. Read in light of Simone de Beauvoir's later claim in *The Second Sex*, that women are culturally constructed as the Other, reduced to their bodies and, further, to their sex, Merleau-Ponty's description of the 'metaphysical' structure of bodily existence appears to encode and reify that specific cultural dynamic of heterosexual relations. Strangely enough, Merleau-Ponty's effort to describe lived experience appeals to an abstract metaphysical structure devoid of explicit cultural reference, and yet once this metaphysical structure is properly contextualized as the cultural construction of heterosexuality, we do, in fact, seem to be in the presence of a widely experienced phenomenon. In effect, *The Phenomenology of Perception* makes gestures toward the description of an experience which it ultimately refuses to name. We are left with a metaphysical obfuscation of sexual experience, while the relations of domination and submission that we do live remain unacknowledged.

Toward a Phenomenological Feminism

In his incomplete and posthumously published *The Visible and the Invisible*, Merleau-Ponty criticizes Sartre for maintaining the subject-object distinction in his description of sexuality and bodily existence. In the place of a social ontology of the look, Merleau-Ponty suggests an ontology of the tactile, a description of sensual life which would emphasize the interworld, that shared domain of the flesh which resists categorization in terms of subjects and objects. It may well be that by the time Merleau-Ponty undertook that study at the end of his life, he had achieved philosophical distance from the sexual Cartesianism of his phenomenological colleagues, and that the reification of voyeurism and objectification that we have witnessed would no longer conform to that later theory. At the time of *The Phenomenology of Perception*, however, Merleau-Ponty accepts the distinction in a limited but consequential way. As a result, he accepts the dialectic of master and slave as an invariant dynamic of sexual life. Both 'subject' and 'object' are less givens of lived experience than metaphysical constructs that inform and obfuscate the theoretical 'look' that constitutes sexuality as a theoretical object. Indeed, the greatest obfuscation consists in the claim that this constructed theoretical vocabulary renders lived experience transparent.

Merleau-Ponty's conception of the 'subject' is additionally problematic in virtue of its abstract and anonymous status, as if the subject described were a universal subject or structured existing subjects universally. Devoid of a gender, this subject is presumed to characterize all genders. On the one hand, this presumption devalues gender as a relevant category in the description of lived bodily experience. On the other hand, inasmuch as the subject described resembles a culturally constructed male subject, it consecrates masculine identity as the model for the human subject, thereby devaluing, not gender, but women.

Merleau-Ponty's explicit avoidance of gender as a relevant concern in the description of lived experience, and his implicit universalization of the male subject, are aided by a methodology that fails to acknowledge the historicity of sexuality and of bodies. For a concrete description of lived experience, it seems crucial to ask *whose* sexuality and *whose* bodies are being described, for 'sexuality' and 'bodies' remain abstractions without first being situated in concrete social and cultural contexts. Moreover, Merleau-Ponty's willingness to describe a 'natural sexuality' as a lived experience suggests a lamentable naiveté concerning the anthropological diversity of sexual expressions and the linguistic and psychosomatic origins of human sexuality. In the end, his version of 'lived experience' commits the fallacy of misplaced concreteness, giving life to abstractions, and draining life from existing individuals in concrete contexts. What is the historical genesis of the 'subject' that Merleau-Ponty accepts as an a priori feature of any description of sexuality? Does this 'subject' not denote a given history of sexual relations which have produced this disembodied voyeur and his machinations of enslavement? What social context and specific history have given birth to this idea and its embodiment?

Merleau-Ponty's original intention to describe the body as an expressive and dramatic medium, the specifically corporeal locus of existential themes, becomes beleaguered by a conception of 'existence' which prioritizes hypothetical natural and metaphysical structures over concrete historical and cultural realities. A feminist critique of Merleau-Ponty necessarily involves a deconstruction of these obfuscating and reifying structures to their concrete cultural origins, and an analysis of the ways in which Merleau-Ponty's text legitimates and universalizes structures of sexual oppression. On the other hand, a feminist appropriation of Merleau-Ponty is doubtless in order. If the body expresses and dramatizes existential themes, and these themes are gender-specific and fully historicized, then sexuality becomes a scene of cultural struggle, improvisation, and innovation, a domain in which the intimate and the political converge, and a dramatic opportunity for expression, analysis, and change. The terms of this inquiry, however, will not be found in the texts of Merleau-Ponty, but in the works of philosophical feminism to come.

NOTES

1. Maurice Merleau-Ponty, *Phenomenology of Perception*, trans. Colin Smith (New York: Routledge & Kegan Paul, 1962), 170.

2. Simone de Beauvoir, *The Second Sex*, trans. H. M. Parshley (New York: Vintage, 1952), 38.

3. Merleau-Ponty, *Phenomenology of Perception*, 165.

4. Ibid., 158.

5. Sigmund Freud, "Instincts and their Vicissitude," *General Psychological Theory*, Philip Rieff, ed. (New York: Macmillan, 1976), 84–90; *Beyond the Pleasure Principle*, trans. James Stracheby (London: William Brown, 1950), 43, 44, 55–57; *Civilization and its Discontents*, Philip Rieff, ed. (New York: Macmillan, 1961).

6. Sigmund Freud, *Three Essays on the Theory of Sexuality*, trans. James Strachey (New York: Basic Books, 1962). See pages 13–14, "we have been in the habit of regarding the connection between the sexual instinct and the sexual object as more intimate than it in fact is. Experience of the cases that are considered abnormal has shown us that in them the sexual instinct and the sexual object are soldered together—a fact which we have been in danger of overlooking in consequence of the uniformity of the normal picture, where the object appears to be part and parcel of the instinct." Not only is the instinct ontologically independent of the object, but it follows a development toward a reproductive telos whereby "the sexual object recedes into the background" (p. 15). The normal development of this 'instinct' dictates active sexual behavior for the male, and passive sexual behavior for the female (p. 26) with the consequence that the reversal of roles signifies an abnormal sexuality, i.e., one which has not developed according to the proper internal teleology. Sexuality which is not restricted to the erotogenic zones characterizes "obsessional neurosis" (p. 35). The perversions thus characterize underdeveloped stages of instinctual development, and are in that sense 'normal' inasmuch as these stages must be lived through. For Freud, however, they come to represent abnormalities when they are not relinquished in favor of heterosexual coitus. This link between normal sexuality and reproduction is recast in his theory of Eros in *Civilization and its Discontents*.

7. Freud, *Three Essays on the Theory of Sexuality*, 34.

8. Merleau-Ponty, *Phenomenology of Perception*, 169.

9. Ibid., 165.

10. Ibid., 171.

11. Ibid., 172.

12. Ibid., 173.

13. Ibid., 160.

14. Ibid., 156.

15. Ibid., 155.

16. Ibid.

17. Ibid., 167.

18. In *The Visible and the Invisible*, Merleau-Ponty's posthumously published work,

his discussion of sexuality focuses on tactile experience and marks a significant departure from the visual economy of the *Phenomenology of Perception*.

19. Merleau-Ponty, *Phenomenology of Perception*, 156.
20. Ibid.
21. Ibid., 165.
22. Ibid., 166.
23. Ibid.
24. Ibid., 167.
25. Ibid.

THE LOOK IN SARTRE AND RICH

Julien S. Murphy

Crucial to feminist theory is an understanding of the oppression we experience as women in patriarchal society. The category "woman," which dooms us to sexist oppression, is a category which none of us can entirely escape. "Woman" is also a category that none of us can deny if we are to understand our lives in patriarchy. We make even the most liberating of choices in the midst of sexist constraint. No matter how we shape ourselves, we live in a society in which we are seen by others as women.

The oppression we experience is so ever present that any feminist theory needs clear and concrete insights into its structure. As feminist philosophers, moreover, we are immersed in oppression even as we theorize about it. A phenomenological approach to the nature of sexist oppression can reveal the lived situation by which the oppression of women is maintained through daily acts that manifest an oppressive kind of seeing. Enlightening views on the experience of oppression can be found in the phenomenological work, *Being and Nothingness* by Jean-Paul Sartre, especially Sartre's theory of "the look." Although Sartre does not address sexist oppression and has only the barest sketch of a theory of liberation, his theory of "the look" is integral to a feminist phenomenological analysis of oppression and liberation. Without intending to, Sartre has provided us with a particularly useful description of women's experience of devaluation in a world where men are dominant. I will show the relevance of Sartre's theory of "the look" for feminist philosophy by juxtaposing his analysis with images of women's oppression in the early work of a feminist poet—Adrienne Rich—tracking the development of women's consciousness through a phenomenological style. By moving through the Sartrian look and beyond to images of liberating vision among women in Rich's recent works, *The Dream of a Common Language, A Wild Patience Has Taken Me This Far*, and *Your Native Land, Your Life*, we can develop an incisive analysis of the movement out of oppression: *that movement in which we are not born women, must recognize ourselves as women, and need be women no longer.*[1]

The movement beyond oppression requires new eyes for the oppressor and the oppressed. Sartre writes of the oppressor: "In order for the oppressor to get a clear view of an unjustifiable situation, it is not enough to look at it honestly, he must also change the structure of his eyes."[2] Sartre's claim implies that one must choose those actions which radically disrupt the present system of judging and call into question how one is to be in the future. Rich writes of women's project as oppressed: "The act of looking-back, of seeing with fresh eyes, of entering another text from a new critical direction—is for women—an act of survival."[3] The act of examining our lives anew is presented by Rich as central to the realization of our freedom. Yet, precisely because new ways of seeing are needed by both oppressor and oppressed, we find ourselves in a problematic situation: How can we "look back" with "fresh eyes" when even our backward glance is shaped by the look of the oppressor? Feminism and feminist philosophy exist not outside, but in the midst of, patriarchy, giving rise to the perplexing dilemma: If we are seen as belonging to that group of individuals having "women's eyes," through looks that blind our vision in advance and against our will, how can we claim to see with "fresh eyes?" What fresh views of ourselves can we develop—without illusion—while existing within societies which assert emphatically that we are less than men?

Distance, Desire, and Destruction in "The Look"

Analysis of our oppression in patriarchy begins with an examination of how we are seen as "women." Our awareness of falling under the construct "woman" often occurs in individual encounters in daily social life. The work of Sartre and Rich is instrumental in demonstrating the lived situation of the look, and the ways in which this oppressive kind of seeing effect a fundamental difference in our existence. The movement of oppression begins with the look of the oppressor, a look whose *distance, desire,* and *destruction* frame the context for our lives.

The look of the oppressor is, as Marilyn Frye points out, centered around arrogance.[4] Indeed, from a Sartrian perspective, the look of the other can rob us of our possibilities, alienate us from ourselves and our options for choice, and make us feel in the service of the other. The impact of the look can be so devastating that it reduces us, at a glance, to powerlessness, to the status of a thing. The recognition that we are always under the gaze of the other evidences that our freedom is held in constant check. We live, to varying degrees, as objects in the world of others.

The power of the look to rob us of our possibilities is in the looker who negates the freedom of the individual looked at. The look, be it one of vehement degradation, or mild interest, presents a moment of conscious life in which we are aware of existing for others as merely concrete bodies. For Sartre, any individual, irrespective of gender, experiences the anguish of being objectified in the experience of being seen. Insofar as each person is capable of receiving and returning the gaze, each person can function as oppressor and oppressed. Sartre writes that "being-seen-by-the-Other" is the truth of "seeing-the-Other."[5] The mutual oppression of the looker and the looked-at is not unlike the power play common to male forms of competition, as illustrated by Sartre's all male examples of spy and warfare scenes: a man peeping through a keyhole feels the look when he hears footsteps suddenly approaching, a man hiding in a dark corner experiences the look when another circles the area with a bright light; men crawling through the brush in the midst of an attack encounter the look of others when they come upon an ominous farmhouse. In the look, individuals engage in a social war of mutual objectification.[6]

Rich's instances of the look directed at women show that the objectification can strike at the very core of one's being and can be more devastating than Sartre described in his warfare examples. For Rich, the look of the other can so interrupt our lives that we may not be able to stare back. So foreboding is our experience of the "eye of the glass" that we may hide behind our eyeball like "a woman waiting behind grimed blinds slatted across a courtyard / she never looks into."[7] The force of the stare marks, as an incision, our power to see: "Walking, I felt my eyes like wounds / raw in my head, / so postal-clerks, I thought, must stare."[8] The eye as a wound, does not yet see, but rather experiences only the pain of being looked at.

Within oppressive vision, distance is established by the looker in order to be saved from objectification. The looker creates distance by entering into a vacuous isolation. Sartre notes the remoteness of the looker in the look: "The Other's look is the disappearance of the Other's eyes . . . one hides his eyes; he seems to go in front of them." Rich illustrates the experience of being seen by one who is hidden in his gaze: "your eyes are stars of a different magnitude / they reflect lights that spell out: EXIT."[9]

Desire is the most familiar element of the look directed toward women. Rich writes of the conjunction of distance and desire, "How many men have touched me with their eyes / more hotly than they later touched me with their lips."[10] Distance and desire can work together to reduce women in the eyes of men to objects for violation. In a discussion of desire, Sartre writes of desire for women much in the way that one would desire an inanimate object. He can "desire a woman in the world, standing near a table, lying naked on a bed, or seated at my side."[11] Even the most casual instance of desire assumes the violation of women in Sartre's work. He writes of an "absent-minded desire," enacted when one "undresses a woman with his look."[12] Such a metaphor suggests action at a distance—undressing a woman with one's eyes—reflects the presumed all-encompassing power of the oppressor's gaze.

The alienation that the looked at experiences through the desire of the looker is found in the poetry of Rich: "I am trying to imagine how it feels to you / to want a woman / trying to hallucinate desire centered in a cock / focused like a burning glass, desire without discrimination: to want a woman like a fix."[13]

The destructive nature of the look lies in its capacity to annihilate the freedom of the individual who is looked at. The desire of the look is inevitably linked to an act of destruction. Sartre claims that the desiring look always seeks the destruction of its object.[14] In the suddenness of the look, "I experience a subtle alienation of all of my possibilities."[15] Rich states, "You look at me like an emergency."[16] To be seen as an "emergency," is to experience oneself in the look of another as a thing to be controlled, stopped, extinguished. The destructive aspect of oppressive seeing constitutes a view of women that presupposes our extinction as autonomous beings and disconnects us from an array of possibilities we fashion for ourselves. The look directed toward women within patriarchy distances women from positions of power, focuses on women as objects of male sexual desire, and seeks the destruction of women as free subjects.

The Eyes of the Group

When the look is analyzed in terms of groups of individuals of *unequal* power the complexity of the movement out of oppression becomes evident. Collective awareness of a shared social situation brings with it a shift in perception such that the group looked at need no longer view itself under the guise of limiting social constructs. Our recognition of the look of oppressive seeing is accompanied by the possibility that we need not be women, that our eyes need not be shaped by the oppressor.

The look between political and economic groups of unequal social standing is aptly described by Sartre in terms of the look of "the Third" and the "Us-object."[17] The Third, be it God, capitalism, the white race, or patriarchy constitutes a series of individuals as a totality by impressing on those individuals a social construct comprised of an arbitrary collection of traits. The Third maintains its position of power in society by restricting the possibilities of the Us-object to the range of characteristics attributed to it. Frye's notion of coercion, as a "manipulation of the circumstances and manipulation of the options" is central to the power of the Third.[18] If the Third is understood as patriarchy, the Third would be said to maintain itself by a grand scheme involving manipulation of circumstances and choices which require females to do what is deemed fitting and proper for "women."

The Us-object comes into existence through the look of the Third. The oppression of an individual as "woman" is no longer seen as a random act of misplaced aggression, but is recognized as pertaining to a shared situation of collective oppression. The entire series of individuals seen as "women" becomes an Us-object in which each member of the Us-object shares in common the awareness of being looked at by the Third. Yet, no member of the Us-object can actually *be* that object, for the collection of traits that form the Us-object depends entirely on the judgment of the Third. We can never *be* women, for "woman" is a form of existence that is forced upon us from the outside by the Third with the demand that we see ourselves through the eyes of the Us-object and do not claim a vision of our own.

The emergence of the Us-object from the look of the Third entails a change in perception in which the Us acts, in light of its awareness of the gaze of the Third, to bring forth its own, new eyes. In Rich's "The Phenomenology of Anger," female consciousness emerges into self-consciousness through recognition of its anger at the look of the Third: "I hate you. / I hate the mask you wear, your eyes / assuming a depth / they do not possess, drawing me / into the grotto of your skull."[19] In Rich's "Burning Oneself Out," the eye of female consciousness, "the eye sunk inward / the eye bleeding with speech,"[20] struggles to speak the language which it sees for itself: "a pair of eyes imprisoned for years inside my skull / is burning its way outward, the headaches are terrible."[21]

Action taken by the Us, when it perceives the look of the Third, runs a perilous course between falling back into and thereby perpetuating the constructs created by the Third, and transcending those constructs altogether. For Sartre, we cannot actually be the constructs created by the Third, and hence he calls such constructs "unrealizables."[22] We can only attempt to claim those constructs in our daily lives. Such attempts are always projects of "bad faith." They assume we could actually exist in terms of their demands. It would mean, as Frye writes, that "she has assumed *his* interest. She now sees with *his* eye, his arrogant eye."[23] In bad faith we slip into seeing ourselves primarily through the eyes of the others. In bad faith, we may attempt to ignore the historical and political context of the constructs created by the Third. We may even deny the restriction of choice that such constructs impose on our lives. Or we can reject the constructs entirely and avoid bad faith by authentically claiming responsibility for our situation.

To avoid bad faith, we must recognize that we are the object of the gaze of the Third. The first step in freeing ourselves is to claim our oppressive situation. Sartre writes, a Jew must demand "full rights as a Jew," a worker must "demand to be liberated as a worker."[24] It is only through a political identification with the oppressive construct, that the oppressed can begin to render that construct meaningless. Any attempt to disassociate ourselves from our historical situation is but an inauthentic attempt at assimilation. We must claim we are "women," not because any one of us really *is* a "woman," but rather because we all are immersed within a historical situation of *being seen as* "women." It is only from acting within our historical situation, that true liberation can be brought about. However, although authenticity entails claiming our oppression, it does not require that we negate any possible moments of freedom within our situation. Authenticity demands an acute awareness that we must be free in *this* world, that we must choose ourselves by taking into account *these* circumstances. As long as there are choices within our situation, we have some freedom, and since situations always afford some range of choices, Sartre claims we are "wholly and forever free."[25] We must use our freedom to not only claim our rights but we must act "to go beyond that situation to one that is fully human."[26]

An authentic appraisal of our situation as women, requires a commitment to taking up our lives in the midst of the patriarchal gaze. How we are seen as "women" in patriarchy is part of our reality. As Rich writes in "Twenty-One Love Poems": "Wherever in this city, screens flicker / with pornography, with science-fiction vampires, / victimized hirelings bending to the lash, / we also have to walk." Our lives occur, unmistakably, within our historical situation. Our freedom is inseparable from the oppressive context that sees us as "women."[27]

We take up our freedom when we look closely at ourselves in a situation which is, in part, forced upon us. In "The Images" Rich asks, "But when did we ever choose to see our bodies strung / in bondage and crucifixion across exhausted air / when did we choose / to be lynched on the queasy electric signs."[28] We have not chosen the crude depictions of ourselves or to live in a world that oppresses us. Yet, we do choose how we see ourselves. Rich writes, "I recollect myself in that presence."[29]

That our eyes need not be shaped by the oppressor becomes increasingly evident as we claim our freedom in the midst of our historical situation. In the refusal to exist for others and in the development of our consciousness as oppressed beings there emerges a new mode of seeing by which we move out of oppression.

Feminist Vision

Feminist vision claims that women must be free and proposes, as central to that goal, a revisioning of how we see ourselves and each other under the patriarchal gaze. The "look" of feminist vision in Rich's later poetry is grounded in the development of women's consciousness through a solidarity among women that is at once both sexual and political. Rich envisions a gynocentric movement in her lesbian feminism. She describes the discovery of women seeing each other as lovers: "that two women / . . . should think it possible / now for the first time / perhaps, to love each other / neither as fellow-victims / nor as a temporary shadow of something better."[30]

Feminist vision enables us to take a fresh look at ourselves, at each other, and at our situation. In the "look" of feminist vision we discover that our eyes need be neither those of the victim nor those of the oppressor. *Feminist seeing, through its boldness and freedom, confronts and moves beyond the distance, destruction, and desire that permeate the look of oppression.*

Rich uses *hereness as a confrontation with distance.* She writes of the choice to act "here," that is, in our own bodies and from our own situations. We take up our vision and our lives, as she entitles one poem, "Not Somewhere Else but Here."[31] The choice to be "here," to be for ourselves, is depicted by Rich in "Phantasia for Elvira Shatayev," a celebration of the women's climbing team that perished on Lenin's Peak. Rich reflects, in the person of Elvira, "for months for years each one of us / had felt her own *yes* growing in her . . . that *yes* gathered its forces." Yet, the climbers' consciousness expands only to encounter limits, "to meet a *No* of no degrees / the black hole sucking the world in."[32] The women's collective vision, woven together with the mountain and the blue sky, is described by Rich, "our frozen eyes unribboned through the storm / we could have stitched that blueness together like a quilt." The real danger is not mountain climbing, but the isolation of women from each other: "We know now we have always been in danger / down in our separateness / and now up here together but till now / we had not touched our strength."

The choice to confront the distance of patriarchal oppression with acting *here*, within our situation, does not alleviate our oppression. Hereness can manifest, however, a movement toward wholeness. In "Origins and History of Consciousness," Rich writes of women's consciousness, of the "drive to connect," the urge to assemble the pieces of ourselves into a meaningful web of experience.[33] The look of the oppressor is broken when the oppressed connect with each other for understanding and transforming our lives. Rich presents a wholistic and tactile image of feminist vision:

"the water / is mild, I sink and float / like a warm amphibious animal / that has broken the net." We take up our lives "here" within our situations when we break through the netting and no longer transcribe the differences between women as barriers to a common womanly vision.

In *A Wild Patience Has Taken Me This Far* Rich acknowledges the differences that exist between women and that may impede solidarity, specifically, racism, family roles, physical limitations, politics, and failings in friendships. All the while Rich stretches language across these barriers trying to understand how we are divided from each other. In her poem on racism, "Frame," Rich describes the experience of a white woman seeing a white policeman assault a black woman, writing, *"I don't know her. I am / standing though somewhere just outside the frame / of all this, trying to see."* The family differences between women emerge in the distance between a daughter-in-law and her mother-in-law in "Mother-in-Law," with the mother-in-law asking *"tell me something true,"* and the daughter-in-law responding, "Ask me something." The difference of physical limitations are described in "Transit" when the impaired skier, knowing the other woman will soon pass her by, looks for something common between them: "And when we pass each other I look into her face / wondering what we have in common / where our minds converge, . . . as I halt beside the fence tangled in snow, / she passes me as I shall never pass her / in this life." In "For Ethel Rosenberg" Rich confronts political differences between women asking, "Ethel Greenglass Rosenberg would you / have marched to take back the night / collected signatures / for battered women who kill / . . . would you have burst the net." The pain of failures in friendships is found in "For Julia in Nebraska," when Rich speaks of "when our maps diverge, when we miss signals, fail" and in "Rift" a break between friends, "I have in my head some images of you: / your face turned awkwardly from the kiss of greeting" and mentions the pain of missed signals, divergence, "when we fail each other / there is no exorcism. The hurt continues." Yet, despite the differences in women's situations, Rich seeks common ground through the barriers that have separated us.[34]

The "look" of the oppressor denies women's freedom by positing us as objects in the patriarchal world. In the "looks" of feminist consciousness we discover new forms of subjectivity and power through *action that refuses destruction.* By choosing to act, we align ourselves with moments of freedom at the core of our subjectivity. Although we are seen as powerless, we claim power within ourselves by refusing, whenever possible, to allow patriarchy to limit our possibilities. Our freedom to act in small or great ways constitutes our rebellion. To take up our lives against patriarchy moves us to new ground. As Rich writes, "No one who survives to speak / new language, has avoided this: / the cutting-away of an old force that held her / rooted to an old ground."[35]

Feminist vision sees the source of our power to act within patriarchy as lying with ourselves. Through feminist vision, each of us sees in new ways the daily actions required to retain our freedom amidst oppressive constraints. In "A Vision" Rich thinks of the gaze of Simone Weil, "You. There, with your gazing eyes / Your blazing eyes / . . . You with your cornea and iris and their power / you with your stubborn lids that have stayed open / at the moment of pouring liquid steel."[36] Feminist vision brings us to see ever more forcefully, ever more deeply. The look can reshape the world such that we, along with Rich, may dare to wonder what it would be like "to take and use our love, / to hose it on a city, on a world."[37] With every act that springs from consciousness of our situation as women, we make a reality for ourselves.

Feminist vision recasts desire to encompass a passion for our freedom. The desire between women need not be bounded by patriarchy. Rich writes of the look between women, "Two women, eye to eye, measuring each other's spirit, each other's limitless desire / . . . Vision begins to happen in such a life."[38] Vision enables us to see our possibilities.

With integrity we create ourselves in the midst of patriarchal desire. Integrity is not loyalty to an absolute principle, but commitment to our freedom that expresses steadfastness to the project of moving out of oppression. In Rich's poem "Integrity," anger and tenderness are summoned so that we can pursue our projects from our own ground.[39] Integrity presents a way of looking at ourselves and each other that places as central the projects we choose within our situations. As we cast aside external standards for evaluating ourselves, each of us discovers unique patterns for assuming our situational freedom. The steadfastness of integrity enables us to steer a course through and out of oppression.

Vision's Voice

Feminist vision acquires voice in Rich's most recent poetry, *Your Native Land, Your Life,* bringing full circle the hints of a feminist theory of oppression and liberation. Although there is still look imagery in *Your Native Land,* "And if my look becomes the bomb that rips / the family home apart," it is *voice* that emerges as a central metaphor allowing the "eyes bleeding with speech" to break open. Rich speaks from the center, defying her marginal woman's situation: "from the center of my body / a voice bursts," speaking through and beyond women's situation, "speaking from, and of, and to, my country." The emergence of voice is marked in "North American Time" which begins by breaking through the net of politically correct poetry, "When my dreams showed signs / of becoming / politically correct / no unruly images / escaping beyond borders / when walking in the street I found my / themes cut out for me / . . . then I began to wonder," towards the affirmation of feminist voice bold enough to address any injustice, "out of the Bronx, the Harlem River / the drowned towns of the Quabbin / the pilfered burial mounds / the toxic swamps, the testing-grounds / and I start to speak again."[40]

Rich gives voice to her feminist vision and offers glimpses of liberation by thinking through connections common to diverse forms of oppressions, interweaving sexism, racism, heterosexism, anti-semitism into experience. For instance, in "Yom Kippur 1984" women and men are fellow-sufferers as Jews, Blacks, and homosexuals: "What is a Jew in solitude? / . . . What is a woman in solitude: a queer woman or man? . . . faggot kicked into the icy / river, woman dragged from her stalled car / . . . young scholar shot at the university . . . nothing availing his Blackness." The poem goes on to connect two forms of oppression in a single experience: "Jew who has turned her back / . . . hiking alone / found with a swastika carved in her back at the foot of the cliffs / (did she die as queer or as Jew?)."[41]

The voice of feminist vision chooses to confront the world's suffering, the world's injustice, to move outward from a feminist politic to embrace the "edges that blur," "to connect . . . the pain of anyone's body with the pain of the body's world / for it is the body's world / they are trying to destroy forever / the best world is the body's world / filled with creatures filled with dread."[42] To confront the world's body does not mean "withdrawing from difference with whose pain we can choose not to engage,"[43] but rather knowing the world through our women's situation, our "womanly lens." "When / I speak of an end to suffering . . . I mean knowing the world, and my place in it, . . . as a powerful and womanly series of choices: and here I write these words, in their fullness: powerful, womanly."[44] For Rich, we are at the same time, womanly, powerful, responsible and accountable to a vision that cannot ignore injustices that may escape feminist analysis. "Try telling yourself" she writes in another poem, "you are not accountable / to the lie of your tribe / the breadth of your planet."[45] Feminist vision needs to speak from the center of our lives, and we, as feminists, need to see our lives as centered in, and central to the world in which we live.

Rich sees ways out of oppression and towards liberation as both recognizing our womanly situation as a lens through which we see the world, and as defying our womanly situation by referring to "the breaker of rules . . . the one / who is neither a man nor a woman," and later "when we who refuse to be women and men as women and men are / chartered, tell our stories of solitude spent in multitude / . . . what will solitude mean?"[46]

The movement out of oppression involves constant reexamination of the category "woman" as integrally linked to all other oppressive constructs, such that we see that at one moment, *we are not born women*, but become women when under the patriarchal gaze. At another moment, *we must recognize ourselves as women*. We must confront "woman" as the construct under which we are seen, and which attempts to shape our reality. And, as yet another moment, *we need to be women no longer*. The hereness, power, and integrity of feminist vision respond to the distance, desire, and destruction of oppression by demonstrating that our vision need not be that of the oppressor.

Vision's voice presents new ways of speaking about ourselves and refuses to be silent to the limits patriarchy has placed on our situation. The voice of fresh eyes is possible when we lay aside "woman," while not forgetting that we take up our lives in the center of a world that continues to see us under that construct. With fresh eyes, we appraise our possibilities for freedom within and on the ground where we find ourselves. Within our situation, we speak as subjects, for ourselves, and others in the midst of our movement out of oppression.

NOTES

1. Simone de Beauvoir, *The Second Sex*, trans. H. M. Parshley (New York: Bantam, 1953), 249; Monique Wittig, "One is Not Born a Woman," *Feminist Issues*, 1(2):47–54.

2. Jean-Paul Sartre, *The Writings of Jean-Paul Sartre*, trans. Richard C. McLeary, ed. Michel Conat and Michel Rybalka (Evanston, Illinois: Northwestern University Press, 1974), 229 (hereafter cited as *Writings*).

3. Adrienne Rich, *On Lies, Secrets and Silence* (New York: Norton, 1979), 35.

4. Marilyn Frye, "In and Out of Harm's Way: Arrogance and Love," in *The Politics of Reality: Essays in Feminist Theory* (Trumansburg, New York: The Crossing Press, 1983), 66–72 (hereafter cited as *Politics*).

5. Jean-Paul Sartre, *Being and Nothingness*, trans. Hazel E. Barnes (New York: Washington Square Press, 1953), 345 (hereafter cited as *Being*).

6. Ibid., 350, 257, 353.

7. Adrienne Rich, *Poems: Selected and New, 1950–1974* (New York: Norton, 1975), 177 (hereafter cited as *Poems*).

8. Ibid., 62.

9. Sartre, *Being*, 258.

10. Rich, *Poems*, 185.

11. Ibid., 124.

12. Sartre, *Being*, 258.

13. Rich, *Poems*, 227.

14. Sartre, *Being*, 756, 757.

15. Ibid., 258.

16. Rich, *Poems*, 186.

17. Sartre, *Being*, 543.

18. Frye, *Politics*, 56.

19. Rich, *Poems*, 201.

20. Ibid., 170.

21. Ibid., 125.

22. Sartre, *Being*, 675.

23. Frye, *Politics*, 74.

24. Sartre, *Writings*, 145.

25. Sartre, *Being*, 629.

26. Sartre, *Writings*, 145.

27. Adrienne Rich, *The Dream of a Common Language* (New York: Norton, 1978), 25 (hereafter cited as *Dream*).

28. Adrienne Rich, *A Wild Patience has Taken Me This Far, 1978–1981* (New York: Norton, 1981), 3 (hereafter cited as *Patience*).

29. Ibid., 5.

30. Rich, *Poems*, 133, 134.

31. Rich, *Dream*, 39.

32. Ibid., 6.

33. Ibid., 8.

34. Rich, *Patience*, 46, 31, 19, 29, 18, 49.

35. Rich, *Dream*, 75.

36. Rich, *Patience*, 50.

37. Rich, *Dream*, 13.

38. Ibid., 76.

39. Rich, *Patience*, 9.

40. Adrienne Rich, *Your Native Land, Your Life* (New York: Norton, 1986), 16, 94, jacket flap, 33–36 (hereafter cited as *Native*).

41. Ibid., 75–78.

42. Ibid., 100.

43. Adrienne Rich, "Notes for a Magazine: What does Separatism Mean?," *Sinister Wisdom*, 18: 90.

44. Rich, *Native*, 8, 27.

45. Ibid., 34.

46. Ibid., 57, 78.

IN-DIFFERENT CRITICISM
THE DECONSTRUCTIVE "PAROLE"

Linda Kintz

> How does one formulate an understanding
> of a structure that insists on our absence
> even in the face of our presence?
>
> —Ruby Rich

Deconstruction as a strategy to destabilize the hierarchical oppositions that structure Western metaphysics has helped critics sift out the logical presuppositions which construct a text's boundaries. But deconstruction has its own economy, its own boundaries, and its own limitations. Its logical presuppositions may constitute serious difficulties for feminist theory, difficulties which center on the problem of gender differentiation.

Derrida has warned feminists to avoid putting their energies into describing a specifically female subject, differentiating the experience of female readers and writers from that of men. Such advice is based on the assumption that an attempt to conceptualize the female subject is a remnant of the metaphysical opposition of male to female which has supported idealism in philosophy; the One, which is male, has been made possible by the negation of the Other, which is female. For Derrida, the attempt to describe the construction of the female subject as specifically different from the male subject continues that idealist, logocentric tradition.

But we might wonder whether Derrida's advice is not posed from the very terrain of the binary oppositions he warns us against and whether a reading which does not take into account the gender differentiation of writer and critic, at least for a while as we make our way toward indifferentiation, or "choreographic texts with polysexual signatures,"[1] leaves Derrida and us unwittingly on the ground that supported idealism all along: the familiar generic "he" that claims to speak for us all. The problem is a vexing one and structures much feminist debate, both here and in France. I hope to use the metaphor of theater as a heuristic device to investigate a few of the presuppositions that lend coherence to the Derridean argument and to see whether or not those presuppositions are familiar ones.

Theater has been an important concept in Derrida's writing, particularly as it is compared to metaphor, which claims to imitate and re-present a hidden truth that occurs offstage. In some ways, both theater and metaphor work like Hegel's *Aufhebung*, the idealizing concept par excellence of Continental philosophy. Metaphor, like theater, can claim to contain within itself the interiorized memory of what has gone before; it tries, like the signifier, to remember the signified in its purity. Thus theater can claim to perform meaning, to enact the connection between what is represented and itself as representation. But at the same time, it raises the representation to an abstraction, which, in the hierarchy established in this system of the *logos*, can claim to exist at a higher level than the matter that has been interiorized. Unmediated matter, in this idealist schema, is redeemed by being abstracted.

Derrida's project investigates the way in which the theatrical representation, like metaphor, the signifier, or the Idea, also plays a duplicitous role as a substitute, a stand-in for the truth which tries to enforce its uniqueness. The representation always constitutes both truth's possibility and the risk that truth, or meaning, will not return to its original site but will be spirited away by the substitute. The theatrical representation or the metaphor might, by chance, run away from the Father's guidance, stealing from his truth its self-identity and wreaking havoc on his truth's system of logic, while simultaneously disrupting that system of logic's truth.

Derridean deconstruction reveals the desire for presence, or wholeness and singularity, in all such theatrical concepts: mimesis, theory, dialectics, metaphor. The desire for presence is a desire for a proximity to meaning that allows the thinker to overlook, or misrecognize, her own role, as well as the role of language, in the truth discovered. The thinker can claim a connection to truth, all the while missing the fact that Writing has always made the connection to absolute truth impossible, because the thinker has been constructed as a subject through the structure of language. The form and historical contents of language partially predetermine the relative truth she can find or miss.

Writing in its large sense refers to the way all meaning is a result of systems of differences. Like the sound of a long *e* which can only be identified by differentiating it from short *e*'s and from other sounds which are not long *e*'s, meaning can only be arrived at by comparing one idea to another. To know what cold is, to identify it, I must compare it to hot.

Hot, therefore, is a part of the meaning of cold since cold cannot make itself known without it.

The thought, the inner voice, and the referent are always shattered by the differential nature of Writing, though, paradoxically, that shattering makes the concepts of thought, the inner voice, and the referent possible. The fact that cold and hot cannot be separated so that I can finally, in reality, reach the meaning of cold completely separated from hot is, ultimately, the only way I can understand cold at all. The "shattering" of the uniqueness of cold, the fact that it can never be found alone, is the only way it can be available to my understanding. Thus the content of thought is always marked by having come into existence within Writing, fissured by what can never be captured: death, the unconscious, heterogeneity.

Historically, deconstruction grew out of the resistance to a European intellectual climate overdetermined by positivism and, later, by a rather mechanical structuralism. Because of that historical background, it focused on a critique of reference and of system. As a result, we are now acutely aware of the dangers of a presumed immediacy of match between a word or concept and a thing or body, an immediacy that could take into account neither the linguistic and historical tradition nor the differential nature of signification. Such a critique of immediacy can be extended to the self, as Derrida has shown; we have no direct, unambiguous line to what we call our subjectivity. That, too, emerges into and because of Writing and the symbolic meanings carried by language. Certain forms of subjectivity and not others are made possible because of the symbolic system there waiting for us and into which we are born.

But in Derrida's reading of subjectivity and reference, there is a tendency to overlook the fact that, as Paul de Man reminded us, just as we can never prove reference, neither can we ever completely *disprove* it. Undercutting reference has led to a new intellectual position which is unquestioningly and dizzily accepted, leading to a forgetfulness of the importance of context. At this point in history, given the different critical context that now faces us, it might be radical to redefine referentiality in its cultural context, focusing on the gender of the subject doing the reading and writing through an analysis of the different *symbolic capacities* which characterize the male and female subject's relation to language.

Derrida's brilliant readings have been centered on a Subject who is male, white, European; then that critique of subjectivity has been generalized, like a metaphor that substitutes the genus for the species. The Subject, the general term, covers the more limited one, the male of the dominant class, but it claims universality, a pattern or experience characteristic of all human beings. The deconstruction of the Subject has thus been generalized to cover all subjects, even those who were never included in that core group of Subjects. We have gone from Subject to subject, with no pause for gender differentiation, or for race and class distinctions.

There has been a conflation enacted here, one based on the bothersome generic "he" and its repression of differentiated subjectivity, its erasure of thé female as a locus of experience or subjectivity.[2] We have received, rather than a deconstruction of subjectivity, a deconstruction of male, white, bourgeois subjectivity, the "I" generalized to the universality of the "we," with the concomitant extension of the applicability of deconstruction to all, indifferently, undifferentiatedly. This carries with it a suspicion of all investigations of female subjectivity and a denigration of research concerning spaces in history for women as agents.

But can we talk about subjectivity and its crises as if we all experienced them in the same way? Are we ready at this point in history for the question Derrida asks: "What if we were to approach here [in deconstruction] (for one does not arrive at this as one would at a determined location) the area of a relationship to the other where the code of sexual marks would no longer be discriminating?"[3] The teleology is tempting, a world where neither male nor female identity were limiting, but could be freely chosen and passed into and out of, a utopia of gender freedom, a polysexual chorus. But can we start from where we would like to end up without losing sight of some very important historical differences? To what extent do cultural determinations make these tempting in-different positions impossible even as reading strategies, in spite of what would appear to be their theoretical necessity to keep us out of the clutches of idealism? Are we leaping over that missing first chapter, the disappearance of women as active subjects yet again, only more subtly this time?

A certain historical perspective might help us work our way into an analysis of these very difficult concepts. Pierre Bourdieu describes one particular example of a historical situation in which an undecidable, reciprocal, permanently moving alternation between male and female positions was possible and allowed the female an active space, an in-different possibility of movement. That alternation was one of the various consequences of marriage, property, and fertility strategies among the residents of Bearn, in the Pyrenees: "The question of political authority within the family became the most acute . . . when an eldest son married an eldest daughter, especially if the heiress was the wealthier of the spouses . . . this type of marriage tended to create a permanent back-and-forth between the two homes or even led the spouses to maintain their separate residences."[4]

In this example, the give-and-take between sites, the movement back and forth between the male and female "home," as a metaphor for the proper space of each, the disruption of Oedipal hierarchy within that particular family was possible. But it is obvious that that internal ambiguity and indeterminacy is dependent on an external situation; there is a larger stage that contains it. The ambiguity of positions is clearly framed and kept decidable at another level. One step backward allows us to see the stage this drama of supposed power-sharing is played upon: the father's lineage and property, heterosexuality, sexuality as reproduction. The internal ambiguity, ambivalence, alternation of power, depends on external reassurance, as does a similar kind of equality described by Julia Kristeva. According to her, the tracing of genealogy through both husband and wife at the upper levels of society in India can only occur because of the rigid enforcement of caste divisions and separations in the rest of society, separations that provide security against whatever societal disruption might occur because of the risk allowed at the top.[5]

The question we want to pursue in terms of Derrida's advice about in-different criticism is this: Is the indeterminacy he advises, the "indiscriminate" concept of gender, possible within his system precisely because heterosexuality and the power of the male as speaker is guaranteed on a larger stage? Has the risk been guaranteed in such a way as to make this indeterminate subjectivity safe for the speaker which the culture identifies as masculine?

For the moment, we will leave these marriage strategies, which may set the stage for Derrida's argument before they recede, or efface themselves. We will return to them later on.

Derrida as Playwright

> Ce qu'exprime la représentation théâtrale, son message propre, ce n'est pas tant le discours des personnages que les conditions d'exercice de ce discours.
>
> —Anne Ubersfeld

> What the theatrical representation expresses, its proper message, is not so much the discourse of the characters as the operative conditions of that discourse.

Derrida's essay on metaphor, "White Mythology," can furnish us with a brief script for a dramatic scenario of deconstruction, whose staging, or conditions of enunciation, contain a good deal of information about its message, or utterance. What we will look for will be "the imprint of the process of enunciation in the utterance,"[6] that is, what the situation in which a word is spoken has to do with its message. The stage and the concept of marriage strategies will rejoin as we proceed.

The etymology of the word "script" places us in the deconstructive framework, as that etymology traces the socially constructed nature of meanings and serves as a history of the definitions judged worthy at various times of being preserved. An etymology is always a social product, just as its preservation in a twentieth-century dictionary is part of the history of institutions, reflecting, among other things, who occupies the positions of writer, publisher, scholar, or judge of preservation.

A script is a text given by a director to actors in traditional theater to be followed, played, enacted. It is both *descriptive* and, because of its location on a particular stage as an institution, it has a meaning in relation to that institutional space. As such, it is *prescriptive*, in that it speaks not just its own words but the words of the institution of theater. It is not given to us by just any writer from just any place in society; there are forces at work in the positioning of the script itself. And we know from reading Derrida that the word "script," from the Latin *scribere*, "to write," also has connections to nature as handwriting, to technology as a type of print which is the name of the printing material as well as its product, to money as script, to God through the Scriptures, and to metaphysics. A script always has a long and wide history.

Derrida's minute analyses have allowed him to link the broad structural level of etymology to individual texts, to show how words exhibit their history of hierarchy. But what we have to deal with is a kind of paralysis that that broadness can lead to. Because Derrida has undertaken such a broad and radical critique of reference as the support of metaphysics, he has left us in some ways immobilized within his system as we try to connect linguistic force to its physical manifestations in history, even if we have learned from him that we can no longer be confident we know exactly what history is. Much of Derrida's work has been an attempt to extricate himself in careful, subtle ways from Hegel's grasp; however, we find that his own system may have produced another, different kind of grasp upon us as we are contained within it, constrained by it, and unable to show how language applies differently to particular subjects in different contexts.

Perhaps, though, if we look at how the script is presented and by whom, and if we look at what texts are considered, we can reactivate what is missing by arguing strictly on Derrida's terms. There are several important questions that must be asked: Are there significations produced by the difference between what is said and who says it, that is, how it is said? Does one alter the other? What is the nature of the gap between the act of enunciation and the message of the utterance? What of the perlocutionary status of his writing—its *effects*? And what of its addressee? What kind of reading subject is assumed by his deconstructive text? We cannot return to a discredited immediacy of context, or of self-identical referents or points in time, but neither can we do without any analysis of context at all. Specifically, we cannot afford to overlook the fact that within this drama, every word is an act that has an effect.

"White Mythology"[7] is a long and complex discussion of texts by Aristotle, Fontanier, Anatole France, and Bachelard which deal with attempts to articulate the philosophy of metaphor, which is, Derrida says, the metaphor of philosophy. What we discover is the duplicitous nature of metaphor, which undoes every system because metaphors constitute the very possibility, or the ground, of the logic that tries to explain them. They reveal themselves to be a fold inherent in language, a fold that shows that the explanation is always contaminated by being a part of what it tries to explain or master.

The male writer of this argument focuses on texts by masters of the tradition he is out to decenter. "Woman" appears here only as a marginal, ghostly, reported echo, reminding us of Luce Irigaray's reference to Woman as the guarantor of exchange, an "echonomie." Women readers, writers, and critics are not a category that has anything to do, according to Derrida, with the category "Woman."[8] So we will initially notice the separation of "Woman" from "women."

But "Woman" appears in Derrida's text where the risks of metaphor are discussed, where there is a need for something to represent a gap, to unsettle the main text and by representing the unsettling, to settle it down a bit. Derrida quotes a passage from Diderot concerning Mademoiselle de l'Espinasse, followed by an excerpt from Nietzsche on the uselessness of believing in the masculinity or feminity of the sun. He then quotes a long passage from Freud's *Interpretation of Dreams*, in which Freud describes the dream of one of his female patients:

> Thus the flower symbolism in this dream included virginal feminity, masculinity and an allusion to defloration by violence. . . . She laid all the more emphasis on the preciousness of the 'centre' . . . on another occasion she used the words, "a centre-piece of flowers—that is to say, on her virginity. . . . Later on the dreamer produced an addendum to the dream . . . 'there is a gap, a little space in the flowers.'[9]

This shadowy means of evidence for the fold within metaphor, the gap, the fascinating risk that always unsettles metaphor's claim of fullness, is located on the text's borders as epigraphs to Derrida's "real" text, like ghostly echoes. The marginal space of the text's edges allows us to trace a dizzying set of displacements. To begin with, the female reader has always been displaced to a greater extent than the male reader because only a long tradition of texts by males is referred to by the male writer; female readers are somewhat like the female analysts in Freud's audience. They are spoken about but not directly addressed.[10] Second, however, the text is ostensibly addressed to all readers indifferently, so that readers are never expected to read as women or as men but from a generic space, that of "the reader." Third, women having disappeared, "Woman" as image becomes a textual necessity to represent what is absent, but as Derrida has said, this image has no connection to real women. The enigma of Woman is suggested without any marker to represent the absent "women." And finally, in that displaced, marginal text of the epigraph, it is men who speak Woman: she is filtered through their words, or rather she becomes the support and reason for those words. Thus in the main text, both Woman and women are absent. In the marginal epigraphs, the borderline texts, Woman is spoken about and spoken for, so it is women who are absent.

These marginal epigraphs are thus carefully controlled interruptions that propel Derrida's argument forward, like the eternal feminine in the text of history, the muse in literature, Woman in the Oedipal narrative. They are representations through which Derrida's narrative must pass in order to assure its coherence; they are the means, or the matter, of his argument. Woman in this essay is "spoken" just after a long treatment of Aristotle's discussion of ellipsis, the missing term that enlivens and makes pleasurable the activity of knowing, the elliptical enigma that interferes between the match of thought and speech, signifier and signified. The ellipsis sends the metaphoric equation off into dangerous implicit sentences; it is, as Derrida says, an "enigmatic division, that is, the interval which makes scenes and tells tales."[11] The pleasure of interpretation comes from bringing the ellipsis back into a circle, from correcting it, according to Aristotle; the Greek root of ellipsis means "defect," "something left out."

Pleasure increases because of the risk involved; the more unexpected the missing term of an ellipsis, according to Aristotle, the greater the profit on the speculation. This skill at ellipsis also proves genius; the philosopher who is the most natural of men when nature is defined as what is closest to *logos* will be the most adept at ellipsis because he best understands the truths of nature. He will, not surprisingly, have proved the necessity of his own position as interpreter of nature, as Derrida points out. Thus his speculation is specular; it mirrors back to him what he put into it plus an increase in his investment through the risky pleasures of knowledge.

The increase in pleasure brought about by Derrida's texts is its metonymic linkage of woman to this textual enigma. She is not located in the main text as a metaphor. Rather she is found beside the text, contiguous to it. Associated in this sideways manner with ellipsis, she is given added valorization as being somehow associated with what is absolutely heterogeneous, with alterity. Thus Woman is valorized obliquely by being linked to the indecidability of textuality while women are relegated to passivity and silence by male speech.

This suggests a change from an older tradition of the idealization of Woman, but the change is perhaps not very radical. In the tradition of courtly love, Woman as *metaphor* was idealized while the situation of women historically grew worse.[12] In Derrida's text, the sideways relation to Woman as *metonymy* updates the medieval pattern; Woman as textual enigma covers over the continuing absence of women as speakers and writers. What might at first appear to be an improvement begins to look very familiar.

But Derrida reminds us that we cannot make a connection between these terms and real women or men. The terms in his usage apply to neither men nor women but to both in varying and continually shifting degrees. And in "White Mythology," his primary metaphor is "dehiscence," from the infinitive "to dehisce," a botanical word whose definition would seem to make it the perfect choice for an active/passive indecidability, an asymmetrical alternation between male and female. It means "to burst or split open along a line or slit," as do the ripe capsules or pods of some plants; and it comes from roots meaning both "to propel or prick," and "to yawn or gape."[13] It provides us with a space in which positions can be filled indifferently by subjects whose very identification as male or female have been proved to be theoretically impossible.

As Derrida says, in an interview with Christie V. McDonald concerning the connection between metaphors having to do with Woman and real women:

> "Hymen" and "invagination," at least in the context into which these words have been swept no longer simply designate figures for the feminine body. They no longer do so, that is, assuming that one knows for certain what a feminine or masculine body is, and assuming that anatomy is in this instance the final recourse. . . . One could say quite accurately that the hymen does not exist. Anything constituting the value of existence is foreign to the "hymen." And if there were hymen—I am not saying if the hymen existed— property value would be no more appropriate to it for reasons that I have stressed. . . . How can one then attribute the existence of the hymen properly to woman?[14]

This indecidability of dehiscence and of terminology having to do with female body parts should perhaps be reassuring, as should Lacan's demonstration that there is no correspondence between the Phallus and the penis. But it is timely to remind ourselves of another of Derrida's statements: "one can never decide properly whether [a] particular term implies complicity with or a break from existent ideology."[15] Perhaps it is only the context, with all its difficulties, that can help us come to some sort of decision and help us out of this paralyzing indecidability. Context has something to do with another philosopher, who also puzzled over the logical difficulties and duplicities of language. We might compare what Derrida says about the indecidability of gender to my free paraphrase of what Zeno had to say about movement, logic, and language: Motion, said Zeno while out for a walk, is impossible.

Generic Erasure: A School for Wives

> Le dialogue de théâtre se fait sur la base d'un presupposé qui la gouverne: que l'un des interlocuteurs, par exemple, a qualité pour imposer la loi du dialogue.
>
> —Anne Ubersfeld

> The dialogue of theater is constituted on the basis of a presupposition that governs it: that, for example, one of the interlocutors has the capacity to impose the law of dialogue.

It is important to establish whether or not the deconstructive advice does what it says, to the extent we can make such a determination. But the first thing we notice is the ease with which one can move from the position of the in-difference of the subject to one which openly recognizes deconstruction's valorization of the male critic's position. Richard Klein, in a passage from an article on Julia Kristeva's work on the *semiotique* (her attempt to theorize a socially determined pre-symbolic level of signification that differs from Lacan's Imaginary and conceptualizes a feminine disruption of the Symbolic), is critical of Kristeva because she cannot give up a reliance on a certain "grounding" of her theory in the residual effects of a relationship to the maternal body. For Klein, this reliance limits Kristeva's theory as her earlier reliance on deconstruction did not. Through the methodology of deconstruction, Klein is able to locate the power in powerlessness:

> Suppose it were the case that what gives to women the power to understand better than men the nature of male oppression gives to men, better than to women, what Melanie Klein calls "an intuitive understanding of the feminine soul." Suppose it were only men who could finally understand the overweaning power of feminine weakness.[16]

Derrida's advice to women to be "self-less," in-different, not to seek to conceptualize an active female subjectivity, would thus accompany, in the ready use a male interpreter makes of his theory, a valorization of the male interpretation of the "powerful" space of their powerlessness; like Aristotle, the thinker has coincidentally proved the necessity of his position. A recognition, on Klein's part, of the difference between a male and female critic has quickly found its way back into the argument, which in Derrida's hands, denies the isolatable difference between readings. The space of the male critic, which then forgetfully poses as in-difference, proves to be the best vantage point for deconstructing a metaphysics which has left women no voice; the male speaks his knowledge of the power of weakness. Klein's deconstruction, like metaphysics and Derrida's script, would leave women speechless. And on a more immediate level, it is also difficult to imagine how Klein's characterization of the "power of feminine weakness" would go over with women trying to support themselves and their families in an economic and political system that disadvantages them.

It is perhaps not fair to blame Derrida for the claims of others about deconstruction. Nevertheless, the fact that such uses are so easily made of his theory might make us want to see if that use tells us something about a hidden presupposition of the theory. Perhaps the "he" that re-emerges in Klein's argument has been lying in wait all along in Derrida's advice that the critic not remind us that s/he comes in two genders. The neuter, "masterful" subject that Derrida wants to avoid may well have found its way back into the argument as we seem to have circled back around to something like a "generic" subject.

The definition of the word "generic" can help us here because it leads us back to the trail of history's force in the institution of the dictionary. "Generic" means two things: (1) it is an adjective relating to or descriptive of an entire class or group, in this case, perhaps, all writers or readers, all human beings; and (2) it also describes something commonly available; not protected by trademark; nonproprietary. The irony of the generic becomes clearer with a closer look at these two definitions and their relationship.

There is an insurance policy, a guarantee, underwriting the definition as a whole, and it can be found in the first definition. Certain persons can from the beginning locate themselves in the slot first described. If we place the adjective "male," or "masculine," and its noun "man" in that slot, we find both the Subject and the deconstructor of that Subject. A male writer could proceed to work toward the second part of the definition, toward non-identity, selflessness, the nonproprietary, as a radical project, a change in the *status quo*.

But he would have his first step, the first chapter of his argument, his own position legally, politically, symbolically grounded, even if he could not reach any absolute "truth" about that ground. He could take on the fight against this very grounding and work toward selflessness and powerlessness, but his risks would be covered by the fact that he already "belonged" in the general group and its identifications, however much he may have proved theoretically that that belonging is fictional. His allegory of non-identity would be concerned with the mismatch between the cultural representations of himself as powerful and meaningful, and his awareness of the impossibility of proving that meaning.

For women, the process has been quite different. Legally, they began from and belonged to the second definition as the *status quo*. Marked by men's names, in certain historical periods women have had no individual legal status separated from a man, whether father, husband, or brother. In many cases, they were and are common property, with little power. They have, at various times and places, been the property of men, available for trademark by male naming. Those who occupy the nonproprietary space, in varying degrees according to race and class, are frequently "commonly available," to violence, as well as to circulation in prostitution and in marriage. This is, too, the structure of pornography, which "denies the woman as a locus of experience."[17] Women's allegory of non-identity, unlike men's, is concerned with the fact that they may look into the symbolic mirror or the male text and see nothing of themselves as women.[18] They may see only male fantasies of themselves, spoken by males: Woman.

The *teleology* for men, as deconstructors, the direction of their action toward self-lessness, is thus already the *condition* of women; each gender begins from a different direction. Our argument has circled around to Emile Benveniste's tracing of the etymology of the verb "to marry" in Indo-European languages as an active verb for men, while "matrimony" refers to a condition to be accepted by women. The generic begins to reveal itself as the best description of the critical position Derrida recommends, and it is not neuter or indecidable. It is male.

Benveniste, in his study of the derivation of "to marry" and the condition of marriage, or "matrimony," found that the two have no etymological connection. The verb refers to men, the noun to women: "[F]or the man the terms are *verbal*, and for the woman *nominal*."[19] "To marry," for the man, is an act; for the woman, "matrimony" is a condition, or function to which she accedes—that of receptivity to the act of the male, to the process of reproduction from which the association between masculinity and activity seems to be derived.

Benveniste goes on to say: "If we now search for terms employed to designate the "marriage" from the woman's point of view, we find that there exists no verb denoting in her case the fact of marrying which is the counterpart of the expressions mentioned [to take, to lead, to give as actions of the male when he marries]. The only verb which can be cited is the Latin *nubere*. But apart from being confined to Latin, *nubere* properly applies only to the taking of the veil."[20]

For the woman, then, there is no active verb having to do with her entry into this marriage situation. Hers is what Benveniste calls a "negative lexical situation." She is legally led into wifehood, "the condition to which the young woman accedes," a condition named *matrimonium* that signifies the "legal status of the mater" and gets its full sense from "the point of view of the father, from the husband's point of view, and lastly from the woman's point of view." Her only *act*, in this etymology is, paradoxically, a passive one: she may "take the veil," not appropriate or grasp it, but accede to it because she herself has already been "taken." Ironically, she is given a *choice* that proves to be similar to what Freud will eventually describe as a characteristic of women, masochism. She can choose to accept what has been done to her.

Though Derrida has deconstructed arguments that claim to rest on biology, his own logic's boundaries uneasily situate themselves near the boundaries of biological reproduction, the marriage boundaries Benveniste describes. Excluded from taking an active part in marrying and in matrimony, the female subject is similarly excluded from taking a specifically female, active part in deconstruction. Reproduction, in mediated form, seems to establish in a roundabout way the ground of Derrida's advice against the construction of a female subject, advice which, in its misrecognition of what indifferentiated or "generic" subjectivity means, results in the symbolic reproduction of the male as critic and subject. In his study of "to marry" and "matrimony," Benveniste showed that "the situation of the man and the woman have nothing in common."[21] Perhaps that is also true of literary criticism. The stage upon which we write and speak makes sure of that—at least for now.

Staging the Enunciation

> Un dialogue de théâtre a donc une double couche de contenu, il delivre deux espèces de messages; le même systeme de signes (linguistiques) porte un double contenu: (*a*) le contenu même des énoncés du discours; (*b*) les informations concernant les conditions de production de ces énoncés.

Oublier cette seconde couche
d'information, parce qu'elle est moins
évidente, revient a mutiler le sens des
énoncés euxmêmes . . .

—Anne Ubersfeld

A theatrical dialogue has a double layer of
content; it delivers two types of messages.
The same system of linguistic signs carries
a double content: (*a*) the content itself of
the statements, (*b*) information concerning
the conditions of production of those
statements.
    To forget this second layer of
information because it is less evident
amounts to distorting the meaning of the
statements themselves.

The theatrical scene we began with can give us further help in evaluating
the Derridean admonition against a critical position linked to gender differentiation. It can also help us work toward a theoretical approach that
does not leave women silenced in the position of Other, passively acceding
to the veil. What is required is a step to the side for a better view.[22] As
Anne Ubersfeld writes in *Lire le theatre*, "theater speaks less a word than
how one can or cannot speak it. It is the conditions of the enunciation of
discourse that constitute the message."[23] Though referring specifically to
theater, Ubersfeld's description of the theatrical "parole" can be extended
to the "parole" of Derrida in a wider sense by requiring that we ask certain
questions about that word. Who speaks to whom? Under what conditions
can one speak or not speak? The conditions of enunciation, as Foucault
has shown, may carry as much information as the "contents" of the message; the two are inseparable but irreducible.

The stage of Derrida's "parole" is an institutional space which is charged
with its own reproduction, even as its occupants dissect claims of mastery.
All discourses are not the same, and a part of the message that rides along
within and makes possible deconstruction is the university as a paternal
institution within a highly centralized European capitalist state and concerning a highly selected *corpus* of texts. The "contexts" of deconstruction
aims at dismantling this very centralization; its enactment, however, locates
it within a position of pedagogic authority that continues to reproduce its
own conditions, with this scene of symbolic reproduction as its core. In
other words, the foremost deconstructor, its Father, occupies a pedagogic
position that "diverts an advantage of the office onto the office holder,"
and the female deconstructor then silently moves into the position of student to be trained to perform that type of criticism, to be "disciplined."

And, as Pierre Bourdieu says, "If the student fails to be what he ought to be, which is none other than his 'being-for-the-teacher,' then all the faults— whether of error or ill-will—are on his [the student's] side."[24] (The use of the pronoun "he" is especially appropriate here.)

The pedagogic message operates upon what Bourdieu calls "the prestigious fiction of an exchange,"[25] the assumption or pretense that in an academic situation, words go reciprocally both ways, hiding the fact that "no one acquires a language without thereby acquiring a relation to language. In cultural matters, the manner of acquiring perpetuates itself in what is acquired."

Bourdieu connects the institution to what he characterizes as the symbolic level of culture. The symbolic level, as I relate it to the engenderment of subjects as male or female, refers to the symbolic representations in which the dynamics of a society establish their meaning. A subject is born into and lives her or his body according to certain ways of representing male and female difference, and these representations are related to a broad variety of institutions. This description of the engenderment of subjects is not based on unmediated anatomical differences purely and simply, though these can never be wholly discounted in a complete erasure of the body. However, biological differences cannot be known in any way that is separated from the linguistic and representational means at our disposal to conceptualize them. And, as Bourdieu points out, "linguistic exchanges are also relations of symbolic power in which relations of force between interlocutors or their respective groups actualize themselves."[26] Because it is in language that engenderment takes place, i.e., subjects are "identified" as male or female, in our own historical situation males and females have different *symbolic capacities*, different relationships to language. And because the symbolic system we call language is a historical production, it is changeable.

Bourdieu is particularly interested in the determining and reproductive effect of culture that poses as universal though it is, in fact, the values of the dominant class, as Marx saw in *The German Ideology*. Bourdieu's investigations focus on lower-class and rural students who must learn to perform well in the urban academic institution, and his investigations, for my purposes, are somewhat limited by a certain mechanical application and an undeveloped awareness of gender as one of the most fundamental divisions in society. Nevertheless, his is an important theoretical approach to analyzing the nature of symbolic force. I will extend his category of working class students to include women as a specific category or caste which overlaps class. Obviously women from minority racial groups and from the working class are even further disadvantaged in very specific ways.

The institution demands a certain level of performance from its students, a performance which, in highly misrecognized ways, can only be given to those who already know how to perform, those who have formed their identities, however deconstructed those may be by now, within the space of the privileged subject. That space is occupied by the middle and upper classes for Bourdieu, and extended in my gloss, to the generic groups of our definition, the white males of those classes:

> It can be seen, first, that in not explicitly giving what it demands, the system demands uniformly what it does not give, i.e., the relation to language and culture exclusively produced by a particular mode of inculcation.
> Secondly, it . . . gives training and information which can be fully received only by those who have *had* the training it does not give.[27]

In other words, by demanding an in-different response on the part of students, in this case students of deconstruction, the institution presumes that they have entered the field in-differently. In fact, it requires that of them. And its training and information can be most adequately assimilated by those students who already have, because of their historical position, what the field of study demands but does not *provide*, an in-different position. Those who already occupy the privileged field of the male subject can hear the message best and use it best, as perhaps Klein's example illustrates. Those who hear and speak best hear and speak best in the tautological reasoning of the Oedipal space, which Aristotle's conceptualization of the *polis* has taught us.

Bourdieu connects the level of pedagogic authority to symbolic violence and makes a practical move in showing the levels of misrecognition that go into masking the force that is presumed but not articulated in the definition of the symbolic power of language.[28] The question of the social and institutional conditions capable of imposing misrecognition of this de facto power is central to his investigation of symbolic violence:

> [T]his general theory of actions of symbolic violence (whether exerted by the healer, the sorcerer, the priest, the prophet, the propagandist, the teacher, the psychiatrist, or the psychoanalyst) belongs to a general theory of violence and legitimate violence, and is directly attested by this interchangeability of the different forms of social violence and indirectly by the homology between the school system's monopoly of legitimate symbolic violence and the state's monopoly of the legitimate use of physical violence . . .[29]

We might add to this list the informal legitimate violence of men over women, both within the family and, as Elizabeth Fox-Genovese says, in history, "the informally licensed violence against women who trespassed upon the public space."[30]

Derrida is obviously not a violent man and neither is his ostensible message; in fact, it is quite the reverse. But it may still rest on unrecognized symbolic violence; as Gayatri Spivak says, we come to an "awareness that even the strongest personal goodwill on Derrida's part cannot turn him quite free of the massive enclosure of the male appropriation of [women's] voice."[31] The space of the enunciation surpasses its individual occupant, and it is the space of the Father, the theological space of knowledge *of* women, the space of the Father whose discursive authority is very much alive, even if the individual occupant of that space can always be proved to be a fraud.

Derrida's speech act takes place and has its effects in the paradoxical space of the inseparable but double subject of the message and the enunciation. The message is *what* is said; the enunciation refers to the conditions of its saying. The familiar example, "I am lying," shows us those two subjects: one, the subject of the message, lies. The other, the subject of the *act* of saying "I am lying," does not lie because it is true that she presents us with a lie.

The male deconstructor, the speech actor, must say he does not know, must claim that his meaning cannot be proven, and because of that, he can claim that he can always be shown to be lying in his position as subject when he advises women against that very position. But as he claims not to know the truth, he nevertheless *knows*. One subject, the subject of the utterance, does not know; the other subject, the subject of the enunciation, knows. As Michael Ryan has written of Nietzsche, and as I generalize to Derrida: "To act, for Nietzsche, to act out fate and to act with words, to teach others to do the same, to become actors, is also to act—to dramatize as well as to pose. And when one poses, even when one poses not to know, he knows in posing."[32]

Male/female undecidability, in-differentiation, might ideally result from a continuing, asymmetrical lying/not lying opposition as in our example, or in a meaning/meaninglessness alternation. But if the *space* of the enunciation adds its own weight, if the conditions of enunciation consistently outweigh the denial of knowledge, one of the two subjects will always have the loudest voice. The danger of deconstruction's faulty memory about its conditions of possibility is that it does not check to see *why* one of the subjects always speaks louder than the other. It does not ask itself the most important question, which Julia Kristeva formulates: "What is the meaning, interest, and benefit of the interpretive position itself, a position from which I wish to give meaning to an enigma?"[33]

What's the Difference?

> What does the we-bird see with who has
> lost its I's?
>
> —Audre Lorde

The success of deconstruction in undoing our reliance on interpretive authority has left us unwilling to acknowledge Derrida's authority. In my awareness of deconstruction's usefulness for feminist theory, I can hope, however, to go beyond a strict reliance on its techniques while at the same time recognizing a debt to Derrida for a methodology that emphasizes careful textual work and evaluation of the structure of logic. There is a great deal to be learned from the study of deconstruction.

But we are brought back to the question with which we started. If we do not try to work out a theoretical position from which we can analyze how men and women read and write differently, not because of any essence that either gender somehow possesses which would make their readings "truer" but because they enter with a different historical relation to language, in what way can women claim the right to speak at all as women in a system like deconstruction? The danger of not claiming that gender differentiation is important in strategies of reading and writing in that females who are, in fact, present and active on the critical scene, are forced into the rather mystical and mythical stance of writing as Other, as if they were not present, are forced to *react* in terms of some kind of ambiguous textuality, to write from Woman's place, to keep endlessly analyzing the absence of women writers and subjects from men's texts.

One obvious alternative to this, which Derrida seems to presume is the only way one can describe an active female subject, is the position of Phallic mother, of female critics who write "like men" and who, in his opinion, merely perpetuate the problem by leaving the ground of phallogocentrism untouched. But the fear that a feminist reading which tries to conceptualize the specificity of a female reader or writer automatically reproduces the idealist dialectic rests, ironically, on that very dialectic. The feared "Same" proves to be located in the conceptual space of that familiar generic subject, "he." Only if the deconstruction of the dialectic of idealism presumes a neuter or masculine speaker can a reproduction of that dialect be presumed and feared. But what does that mean?

If the feminist who tries to construct an active, specific female place in the conceptual scheme were able to write as a male subject, she would get into the same trouble Derrida fears; she would write like a man and make his same mistakes. But there are only a certain number of ways a woman could write like a man: (1) if she *were* a man, (2) if she were neuter or ambiguously gendered, since historically, neuter or androgynous or polymorphously perverse turned out to be masculine, or (3) if the symbolic level of Western culture were not structured on the opposition male/female and supported by the valorization of the visible. Western culture engenders its subjects so that appearance becomes visualized power, separating white from black, male from female, the penis from the envy.

Derrida's in-different point of view requires from female students of deconstruction precisely what they enter the classroom without: an in-different relation to power. Because women do enter the pedagogic scene engendered as not-male in this culture, their words are already marked by their bodies, whose lack, perceived from the direction of the male eye, supports the privilege of the male body and masculine speech. The female body signifies both the negative of masculinity and the abject, the border which enforces the division between positive and negative.

Her words, even if she speaks "like a man," are obviously mimicry. Their similarity to the words of men mark them as *not* the words of men; they are inappropriate. For a woman to speak from a Phallic position or for her to speak like a man, it must first be clear that she is *not* a man, just as in nineteenth-century India, to be Anglicized required that one *not* be English.[34] Hidden in the claim that she can, in fact, speak "like a man," that an Indian can be Anglicized, is the proof that they cannot, the proof that their difference from authentic subjects is already apparent. They are proved to be inappropriate by their very attempt to mimic, to be appropriate.

But this mimicry, far from reproducing the "Same," may be quite subversive. It may turn from *"mimicry*—a difference that is almost nothing but not quite—to *menace*—a difference that is almost total but not quite."[35] The reproduction of the symbolic by those it has disavowed and abjected— men of color and all women—contaminates and displaces the words reserved for the appropriate speaking subject. The reproduction of that symbolic may begin to founder when inappropriate subjects learn its language because they can only repeat it partially. As incomplete mirrors, as the waste of the system that produced the identity of the white male, they can only reflect back to the male subject a partial representation of himself, a reflection that is askew, flawed, not specular. The more the inappropriate subjects learn his language, the less dependable is his mirror. Rather than reacting, they may re-*act* to change both the language and the world.

Derrida's fears that women speaking like men will continue the Same dialectic thus rests on this oversight: he does not factor in gender or color as disruptive and inappropriate threats to the specular dialectic. His concern with the Same *presumes* the Same. By implicitly presuming, while denying, in-different or neuter readers and writers, he presumes a dialectic whose structure is an ahistorical constant, anchoring his theory to a dialectic that appears to be unsusceptible to transformation, rather than taking seriously the two subjects of enunciation we followed earlier, subjects whose relationship is historically changeable.

By insisting on in-difference, Derrida denies the differences that gender always introduces into the situation of the reader and writer; men and women enter that scene and act within it differently, with different symbolic capacities. But the fact that his words occur in the institutional academic setting of Western culture means that he simultaneously insists on differences. Women may participate in the "selfless" rhetoric of deconstructive democracy, but they are not the ones who write the texts he reads. Denying the importance of gender differentiation on the one hand, he includes it on the other.

This oversight is debilitating to women in another of its effects; like all cultivated discourse, this one "succeeds in obtaining from the dominated classes a recognition of legitimate knowledge and know-how, entailing the devaluation of the knowledge and know-how they [the dominated] effectively command."[36] At the same time it "confers on the privileged the supreme privilege of not seeing themselves as privileged and manages the more easily to convince the disinherited that they owe their scholastic and social destiny to their lack of gifts or merits."[37] The "ideology of the gift," as Bourdieu calls it, the ideology of superior intellectual ability, talent, genius, masks the way language and knowledge are acquired; it is "a negation of the social conditions of cultivated discourse."[38]

The discourse of the Subject should lead us to a reevaluation of the social conditions of cultivated discourse about subjectivity, in which our own class and race privileges are also factors. We must take seriously, even as we work to undermine them, the effects of gender differentiation, which is "translated by and translates a difference in the relation to power, language, and meaning."[39] We need time to conceptualize the activity of women, to pry apart the persistent "natural" association, even in the most perceptive criticisms of phallogocentrism, between passivity, being penetrated, and femininity, and between activity, the ability to penetrate, and masculinity, a "natural" association worthy of Aristotle. In such a conceptual system, we can assume, with Luce Irigaray, that "any theory of the subject has always been appropriated by the 'masculine.' "[40] But what we are beginning to notice is that there are (at least) two dramas of subjectivity,[41] and if we keep at it, if we keep refining our terms, we may find a way to talk about activity that is not simply an analogy for masculinity. Because we are past the time when women need to be shown our absence

from history and language, we might carry on a project that is a dialogue—
a continuing dream of utopian indifferentiation, of "incalculable choreographies," while we also take the time to find ways to theorize our activity
as culturally constructed, gendered subjects, speaking bodies, real fictions.
Such a dialogue may help us theorize what metaphysics has always missed:
"le moi corporeal."[42]

NOTES

1. Jacques Derrida and Christie B. McDonald, "Choreographies: Interview,"
Diacritics (Summer 1982):76.

2. The intersection, as Alice Jardine calls it, between French and American feminist criticism is nowhere more apparent and problematic than in the treatment of
"experience." It may help to historicize the concept of experience by considering
it as a semiotic concept. It can describe the particular historical context within which
an individual is "subjected," in which a particular form of subjectivity is made
possible. Though experience is unique to that individual, its form and interpretation
are nevertheless only possible because subjectivity occurs within a particular social
and linguistic context.

3. Derrida and McDonald, "Choreographies: Interview," 76.

4. Pierre Bourdieu, "Marriage Strategies as Strategies of Social Reproduction,"
Family and Society: Selections from the Annales, trans. Elborg Forster and Patricia M.
Ranum (Baltimore: Johns Hopkins University Press, 1976), 135.

5. Julia Kristeva, *Pouvoirs de L'horreur: essai sur l'abjection* (Paris: Éditions du seuil,
1980).

6. Oswald Ducrot and Tzvetan Todorov, *Dictionary of the Sciences of Language*,
trans. Catherine Porter (Baltimore: Johns Hopkins University Press, 1979), 324.

7. Jacques Derrida, "White Mythology," *Margins of Philosophy*, trans. Alan Bass
(Chicago: University of Chicago Press, 1982).

8. For a valuable account of the French use of woman as metaphor, see Alice
Jardine, "Theories of the Feminine: Kristeva," *Enclitic*, vol. 4 (Fall 1980) and *Gynesis:
Configurations of Woman and Modernity* (Ithaca: Cornell University Press, 1985).

9. Sigmund Freud, quoted in Derrida, "White Mythology," 246.

10. In a lecture on Nietzsche and the institution, Derrida scrupulously acknowledges the past of the discourse he repeats:

> . . . what indeed would we recognize but all of *us*, ourselves, a century later?
> I would say in French *'nous tous'*, not *'nous toutes'*—all of us men, not all of
> us women. For such is the profound complicity linking the protagonists in
> this situation or scene; such is the contract that masterminds all, even their
> conflicts: woman, if I have read correctly, never appears. Neither to engage
> in study nor to teach. . . . The great 'cripple,' perhaps. No women . . . .

Jacques Derrida, "All Ears: Nietzsche's Otobiography," *The Pedagogical Imperative:
Teaching As a Literary Genre*, ed. Barbara Johnson (New Haven: Yale University Press,
1983), 250.

11. Derrida, "White Mythology," 239.

12. A historian's investigation of this development can be found in Georges Duby,
The Knight, the Lady, and the Priest: The Making of Modern Marriage in Medieval France,
trans. Barbara Bray (New York: Random House, 1983).

13. Derrida, "Choreographies," 75.

14. Ibid., 75.

15. Ibid., 74.

16. Richard Klein, "In the Body of the Mother," *Enclitic*, 7(Spring 1983):74.

17. Timothy Beneke, *Men on Rape* (New York: St. Martin's Press, 1982), 23.

18. Hunter College Women's Studies Collective "The Family Circle," *Women's Realities, Women's Choices* (New York: Oxford University Press, 1983), 228.

19. Emile Benveniste, "The Indo-European Expression for 'Marriage,' " *Indo-European Language and Society* (New York: Faber and Faber, 1973), 193.

20. Ibid.

21. Ibid.

22. The use of visual metaphors connects us always to the necessity of psychoanalysis in the investigation of the juncture of the personal and the symbolic level of culture. It also always has to do with the angle of vision.

23. Anne Ubersfeld, *Lire le Théâtre* (Paris: Éditions sociales, 1978), 265.

24. Pierre Bourdieu, "Cultural Capital and Pedagogic Communication," *Reproduction in Education, Society, and Culture*, trans. Richard Nice (London: Sage Publication, 1977), see chap. 1.

25. Ibid., 119.

26. Ibid., 116.

27. Ibid., 128.

28. "These positions of male and female must be recognized for what they imply, namely that there are social conditions which concretely prevent any free or mutual access to 'other' positions, and these range from the outright cultural sanctions extended to masculine mobility in such matters, over and above the feminine counterpart, to the degrading civil fate of the trans-sexual." Andrew Ross, "The Eternal Varieties," *Diacritics*, (Winter 1983):11.

29. Bourdieu, "Cultural Capital and Pedagogic Communication," xi.

30. Elizabeth Fox-Genovese, "Placing Women in Women's History, *New Left Review*, 133 (May-June 1982):15.

31. Gayatri Chakravorty Spivak, "Displacement and the Discourse of Woman," *Displacement: Derrida and After*, ed. Mark Krupnick (Bloomington and London: Indiana University Press, 1983).

32. Michail Ryan, "The Act," *Glyph 2* (Baltimore: Johns Hopkins University Press, 1977):80.

33. Julia Kristeva, "Psychoanalysis and the Polis," *Critical Inquiry: The Politics of Interpretation*, 9(September 1982):78.

34. Homi Bhaba, "Of Mimicry and Man: The Ambivalence of Colonial Discourse," *October* 28(Spring 1984):129. Bhaba traces the repetition and displacement of the master's message by the colonized subject.

35. Bhaba, "Of Mimicry and Man," 132.

36. Bourdieu, "Culture Capital and Pedagogic Communication," 42.

37. Ibid., 210.

38. Ibid., 52.

39. Julia Kristeva, "Women's Time," *Signs*, 7(Autumn 1981):21.

40. Luce Irigaray, *Speculum of the Other Woman*, trans. Gillian C. Gill (Ithaca: Cornell University Press, 1985), 133.

41. There is little agreement over this point, with some feminists in both France and America opting for indifferentiation on the grounds that analyzing differences reinforces the cultural encoding of difference that marks women as inferior. A tolerant dialogue between various approaches can only enrich both. For a range of opinion which makes the term "feminism" very difficult to define, see Claire Duchen, *Feminism in France from May '68 to Mitterrand* (Boston: Routledge and Kegan

Paul) and Zillah R. Eisenstein, *Feminism and Sexual Equality: Crisis in Liberal America* (New York: Monthly Review Press, 1984).

42. Anne Ubersfeld uses this term in her materialist semiotics of theater, which is not a specifically feminist project. However, her work can be extended to a feminist semiotics of gender and the subject.

TRUE CONFESSIONS

CIXOUS AND FOUCAULT
ON SEXUALITY AND POWER

Linda Singer

Almost everything is yet to be written by
women about femininity: about their sexuality, that is, its infinite and mobile complexity, about their eroticization, sudden
turn-ons of a certain miniscule-immense
area of their bodies; not about destiny, but
about the adventure of such and such a
drive, about trips, crossings, trudges,
abrupt and gradual awakening, discoveries
of a zone, at once timorous and soon to be
forthright. A woman's body, with its thousand and one thresholds of ardor—once by
smashing yokes and censors, she lets it articulate the profusion of meanings that run
through in every direction—will make the
old single-grooved mother tongue reverberate with more than one language.

—Hélène Cixous[1]

It may well be that we talk about sex more
than anything else; we set our minds to
the task; we convince ourselves that we
have never said enough on the subject,
that, through inertia or submissiveness, we
conceal from ourselves the blinding evidence, and that what is essential always
eludes us—so that we must start out again
in search of it. It is possible that where sex
is concerned, the most long-winded, the
most impatient of societies is our own.

—Michel Foucault[2]

These excerpts from the work of Hélène Cixous and Michel Foucault mark a site of difference in contemporary sexual politics. The question is whether the discursive representation of woman's sexuality is, as Cixous asserts, still a vital liberatory practice or whether, as Foucault implies, such discourse is compatible with and contributory to the proliferation of operative hegemonies. One of the ironies of our age, according to Foucault, is our investment in the production of sexual discourse in the belief that "our 'liberation' is in the balance."[3] If liberation is not at stake in proliferating sexual discourse, what is?

These questions become all the more pressing in light of the contemporary AIDS epidemic which dramatically alters the stakes attached to sexual proliferation and circulation. When one of the possible consequences of sexuality is contracting a fatal, debilitating disease, we are all forced to question our investments in sexuality, to ask not only whether we can be liberated through and for sex, but also whether sex is worth dying for. Foucault notes, with an ironic and eerie prescience, that the dominant sexual politic of our age predisposes us to answer in the affirmative.

Foucault is not the only voice to raise questions about the state of contemporary sexual discourse. American feminists have raised questions about the ideological surplus produced by a representational apparatus which identifies women as the emblem of sex and uses that identification to market commodities and marginalize women. Debates continue in the public sphere around issues of access to sexual material including pornography, paraphernalia and information about contraception, abortion, and sexually transmitted diseases. The anxiety emerging from epidemic conditions, not only with respect to sexually transmitted diseases but also with respect to phenomena like the rising rate of teenage pregnancy and divorce, has also provided occasion for a revisionist critique of sexual discourse, and a revivification of a traditional rhetoric of repression.

Given Foucault's insight into the self-perpetuating character of sexual discourse, the question cannot be resolved within a logic of prohibition and permission. If Cixous is right about the absence of a sexual discourse adequate to women's libidinal economy, feminists and others critical of existing sexual arrangements will need to investigate the conditions responsible for producing this absence. As a culture we may be talking extensively about sex, but given the limits of our representational repertoire, we feminists may still need to find new ways to speak about sex. For as Cixous would argue, the contemporary state of affairs provides ample evidence that it is not yet being done right. Given Foucault's insights into the potentially fatal consequences of our contemporary sexual logic, the need to generate new sexual scripts and stories becomes all the more urgent.

Here I intend to read some of Foucault's and Cixous's texts as strategic responses to the problem of sexual discourse in the age of epidemic. In doing so, and this is my first confession, I subject them to my own purposes. Even though these texts do not address one another directly, both writers situate their work in what may fairly be described as a common turf. Both address the relationship between sex and power and the constitutive effects of discourse on these dynamics. Although neither can or should be read as pamphleteers or advocates in the conventional sense, both writers do engage in prescriptive rhetoric which attempts to address historical specificities from a position of resistance or opposition to the operative sexual hegemony. Both would agree on the need to reconstitute the terms and language of sexual interaction. Though their positions do not oppose one another, the differences point to the limits of their respective analyses. Foucault's reconsideration of the way sexual discourse functions to circulate and intensify the effects of sexual hegemony, raises questions with respect to Cixous's optimism about the transformative effects of women's writing of the body. But more significantly, from the standpoint of feminist concerns, Cixous's emphasis on the role of the asymmetrical configuration of sexual difference in maintaining male hegemony over the construction of sexuality and sexual desire, points to a blind spot in Foucault's analysis of how the sex-power system operates. Foucault's failure to consider male dominance as one of the effects produced by the circulation of sexual discourse results in a series of strategic recommendations that circumvent the issues of greatest concern to feminists. Feminists, therefore, ought to reconsider the merits of Foucault's prescriptions lest our efforts only end up contributing to the maintenance of a system that has historically circumscribed our powers and possibilities. While much of what Foucault writes is useful for developing liberatory strategies for addressing the political paradoxes that accompany the hegemony of sexual epidemic, we must also avoid identifying ourselves with what, in some sense, is yet another paternal discourse of instruction which claims preemptive entitlement to speak to and for women in their absence.

Sexual Discourse and Its Discontents

· Part of the difference in strategic emphasis can be attributed to the different ways in which Foucault and Cixous conceptualize the operations of the sex-power apparatus and its consequences. While both understand sexuality to be correlated with political formations, they differ in their assessments of how power has worked to produce sexuality and about the consequences of these historically specific constructions. As a result, their analyses operate with different strategic priorities that are worth considering for their differences.

Cixous's advocacy of women's writing proceeds from her analysis of the construction of sexuality in patriarchy as an asymmetrical opposition between "masculine" and "feminine" which functions as a mechanism for maintaining male privilege. Male dominance is maintained by a phallocentric organization, founded on a masculine economy which distributes pleasure and entitlement differentially according to gender in a way that disadvantages women, and which inscribes bodies of both genders with a logic of male dominance. This differential economy affects not only sexual practices but also sexual discourse which, Cixous argues, is organized by a structuring absence, an absence of a discourse of "feminine jouissance."[4] This absence serves and extends the logic of phallocentric sexuality. Women who do not know or are incapable of representing what they want are that much less likely to demand or pursue it. The absence of a female-identified discourse adequate to representing women's sexuality in its difference is both a symptom of and instrumental to the continued subjugation of women within the patriarchal order.

In patriarchy, male privilege is both marked and exercised, at least in part, by control over the production, circulation, and representation of pleasure. Such control is operative both at the level of the erotic choreography which structures heterosexual encounters, and at the level of cultural representations, which are designed to accommodate and normalize masculine preferences and patterns of gratification. Because pleasure is one currency in which differences are marked in a phallocentric economy, women's pleasures, in so far as they differ from men's, are relegated to a marginal position as that which cannot or may not be represented or circulated, and thereby enfranchised. Phallocentric hegemony is thereby maintained by an absence of cultural forms which allow women to represent ourselves to ourselves and others as agents, rather than as mere objects of desire.

The absence of discursive forms capable of representing women's pleasures in their differences has obvious benefits for a patriarchal social order. Since differences in erotic economies and desires are primary markers of sexual difference, failure to represent women's desire amounts to an annihilation of difference. In the absence of a female-identified voice, or for that matter the recognition by women of this absence and the conditions that produce and normalize it, self-interested male dominated discourse is free to construct women's desires in their absence, and to construct us in ways which both mark our subjugation and reproduce it, by investing us with forms of desire that facilitate their domination, like the pleasures of surrender, self-sacrifice, and service to others. More useful still to existing social arrangements are women who do not know what they want, since we will thereby be incapable of demanding it or acting to secure it. As long as men are the only ones providing answers to the question of what women want, the answers offered will continue to reflect and solidify male interests and male privilege. Because the silencing of women has been a tactic used to keep women in their place, Cixous believes that women's breaking silence by writing can work to disrupt and subvert the existing order.

> (W)riting has been run by a libidinal and cultural—hence political, typically masculine—economy, that this is a locus where the repression of women has been perpetuated, over and over more or less consciously, and in a manner that's frightening since it's often hidden or adorned with the mystifying charms of fiction; that this locus has grossly exaggerated all the signs of sexual opposition (and not sexual difference), where woman has never *her* turn to speak—this being all the more serious and unpardonable in that writing is precisely *the very possibility of change.*[5]

In this passage, Cixous shows what is at stake for women in writing their bodies. Given the relatively monolithic history of masculine hegemony over the sexual, despite variations in the apparatus which secure it, woman's sexuality has been represented either as lack, or as a series of self-interested masculine projections. This has allowed men to construct women in their absence, constructing and re-constructing sexual difference in a way that perpetuates men's position of dominance. By resisting this repressive dynamic through writing, women's discourse can disrupt or subvert a sexual order that has historically depended on our silence.

When as women we articulate what we want and what gives us pleasure, such writing carries with it the force both of a demand that these desires be fulfilled, and a self-validating statement of entitlement to gratification and satisfaction. Insofar as such demands are formulated in heterosexual terms, men can now be held accountable for refusing to cooperate, since they can no longer appeal to the traditional excuse that they do not know what it is that women want from them. To the extent that women's desires are addressed to other women, men are displaced from their position of centrality, and heterosexist hegemony, and all that follows from it, is subjected to challenge, critique, and ultimately denial. But beyond the effects such discourse will have in forcing a reconsideration of male-dominated assumptions about sexuality and desire, such discourse is also empowering to women, both because it legitimates our needs by making them public, and because expression allows for a contagious expansion of women's sphere of entitlement. Rather than having to settle for the options available through phallocentric discourse, women are also authorized to construct, elaborate, and celebrate differences, as well as having the occasion to have our desires recognized and validated by other women who read the work, and are prompted to contribute to an intertextual fabric by producing texts which support and proliferate a female-identified system of pleasure and desire.

In contrast to Cixous's analysis which stresses the stability and centrality of sexual difference as a constitutive principle, Foucault's analysis emphasizes the flexibility and diversity of power deployments with respect to constructing sexuality as a site for intervention into the lives of bodies and populations. Because power deployments always aim to organize social energies in the name of some contextually specific goal or utility, power is neither unitary nor uniform in its character or in its operations. It is certainly not limited to a dynamic of repression.

Foucault engages in an extended questioning of "the repressive hypothesis" which, he says, has been the dominant way of conceptualizing the relationship between sex and power. The repressive hypothesis assumes a negative relationship between sex and power, deployed as a dynamic of repression, control, and the demand for the conformity of sex to law. Foucault challenges this "juridical model" of power, which represents power as a figure of absolute authority. The figure of power is the figure of the King. What this repressive model of power with its emphasis on negative operations fails to capture, according to Foucault, is the proliferative dimension of power, which operates through a network of variable and context-specific social relations, each of which results in the creation of local authorities and points of resistance to them. Since "power is everywhere,"[6] there is no possibility of getting outside of power or of occupying a position untainted by its operations. There is also no discourse which cannot be contained by existing political deployments.

> (W)e must not imagine a world of discourse divided between accepted discourse and excluded discourse, or between the dominant discourse and the dominated one—but as a multiplicity of discursive elements that can come into play in various strategies. . . . Discourses are not once and for all subservient to power or raised up against it any more than silences are.[7]

Because power does not operate on the basis of some uniform repressive apparatus, one can no longer speak of some "liberatory discourse" opposed, through its productivity, to the negative operations of power. One can also no longer assume that by rallying energies in the name of "sex" that one occupies a position from which the deployment of power can be resisted. Consequently, the assumption that sexual discourse will function as a liberatory movement which counters the repressive function of power becomes problematic. Sexuality is not so much opposed to power as it is a product of a power deployment. "We must not think that by saying yes to sex, one says no to power; on the contrary, one tracks along the course laid out by the general deployment of sexuality."[8]

Foucault's reservations about the liberating potential of sexual discourse stem from his analysis of sexuality as a political construction, rather than as some natural or instinctual zone that can be isolated independently of the mechanisms by which it is aroused and regulated. Power in the modern era has functioned to circulate the demand for sexual discourse in the form of confessions which position subjects as sites for disclosure of truth and knowledge of sex. Foucault traces the proliferation of confessional discourse from its origins in a religious context to its further manifestations in medical, literary, and psychoanalytic discourse, each of which contributed specific mechanisms for facilitating the transformation of sex into discourse. The discursive structure of the confessional apparatus is revealing of how modern power deployments achieve their effects. First, the proliferation of confessional discourse results in a proliferation of local authorities who are empowered to hear, analyze, and judge the discourses of others and to act, therapeutically, punitively, managerially, on the basis of the discourse produced. It also produces specific subjects for these discourses, individuals whose bodies become subject to the rulings produced by these disciplinary discourses. As a consequence, power produces multiple points of access to the body, access gained through the discursive participation of its potential targets. Participation is not usually elicited through force, but through the production of context specific pleasures, pleasures attached to the production of sex as disclosive discourse. We have become a "singularly confessing society," according to Foucault, because our erotic economies have been inscribed by the politics of the confession. We take pleasure in reproducing ourselves as sexual subjects, and in sustaining the demand for the production of sexual discourse. As a consequence of its alliance with and construction of the sexual as that which must be represented and repeated, modern power works primarily through an apparatus of incitement rather than through the threat of repression. "Pleasure and power do not cancel or turn back against one another; they seek out, overlap, and reinforce one another. They are linked together by complex mechanisms of excitation and incitement."[9]

The privileging of sex as a theme of confessional discourse is therefore not a consequence of some instinctual impetus, but must rather be understood as the result of its strategic utility. Because sexuality serves as a link between individuals and the social body, power gained access to the body by being "organized around the management of life rather than the menace of death." In a post-scarcity economy, power intervenes in the lives of socially individuated and differentiated bodies not through an economy of deprivation but by organizing energies through the force of what it produces. As a society becomes more modern, i.e., more complex and functionally differentiated, the need for coordinating the activities of bodies becomes more necessary and harder to achieve. Thus sexuality, far from being censored, must be relentlessly circulated and reproduced. Sex is fundamentally allied with, rather than opposed by, modern methods of deploying power. Foucault challenges the idea of a struggle for sexual liberation through the production of sexual discourse, because he believes that the demand for such production is entirely compatible with the logic of hegemonic formations. If power does not operate primarily as repression, liberation of sex can no longer be conceived of as the disclosure of sex through discourse.

The connection between liberation and sexual disclosure is based on the assumption that sexuality has been concealed, a position Foucault refers to as "the repressive hypothesis." This hypothesis, which has dominated discussions of sexuality, needs to be challenged because it misrepresents the relationship between sex and discourse, and because it results in a series of erroneous expectations about the possibilities of liberation through the disclosure of sex. The repressive hypothesis assumes that power operates on sexuality in an essentially negative way, as a force which denies, conceals, or otherwise suppresses or limits sexual energies and expressions of sexual interest. According to Foucault, this hypothesis overlooks the ways in which power, far from working to restrict or limit the effects of a sexuality that exists separate and apart from it, actually serves to produce and intensify sexuality as a way of focusing and mobilizing bodies and populations. The function of power is not to limit or repress sexuality, but is rather to produce and proliferate sexuality and the demand for its disclosure through discourse.

By displacing the repressive hypothesis with a proliferative model of power, Foucault effects a *gestalt* shift which alters the way we think about power and the tactical and strategic options available for resisting it. Foucault is concerned that our concepts of power absolutize its operations, investing authority with force produced by the subjects constituted and ordered by it. Our concepts have not kept pace with historical transformations in the way power is deployed. The symbols and mechanisms of power have changed, but our concepts and language for representing it have not. Although we have abandoned the institutions and practices of monarchy, our understanding of power is still lodged in that anachronistic form. "In political thought and analysis we have not yet cut off the head of the king."[10]

Much of what Foucault writes about sex and power can be read as a challenge to the basis upon which a feminist like Cixous identifies the political problems and the strategies for addressing them. Most specifically,

Foucault challenges the claims for the historical stability of sexual difference as the fundamental structure linking patriarchal deployments which differ in tactics, but not in their intent. If deployments of power are always local, variable, and unstable, as Foucault argues, we can no longer conduct political analysis in terms of an oppositional logic between classes, genders, and included and excluded groups. Following Foucault, strategic analysis must remain local and resist reifying the terms of its own discourse by investing them with a discursive stability. Foucault instead recommends that we attend to the historically specific mechanisms through which power is capable of transforming its operations so as to appear capable of satisfying the needs of the subjects it generates.

> We must not look for who has the power in the order of sexuality (men, adults, parents, doctors) and who is deprived of it (women, adolescents, children, patients); nor who has the right to know and who is forced to remain ignorant. We must seek rather the pattern of the modifications which the relationships of force imply by the very nature of their process. . . . Relations of power-knowledge are not static forms of distribution, they are "matrices of transformations."[11]

This strategic recommendation has potentially serious consequences for the course assumed by feminist theory. Following this line of reasoning, it becomes problematic to talk, as Cixous does, of "feminine writing" as such or to advocate its proliferation on the basis of its having been repressed or excluded. Cixous's claim that feminine writing would function counter-hegemonically is also questionable from the point of view of Foucault, because feminine writing would be as subject to conditions of overdetermination and hence differentiation as is masculine writing. If the repressive hypothesis is displaced, feminist discourse can no longer mobilize women's energies in the name of retrieving a sexuality that was never ours to begin with.

If Cixous is right about the centrality of sexual difference, however, then Foucault's position can be read less as a contestation than as a prolongation of a patriarchal logic which constructs sexual difference and then selectively ignores it in a way that allows men to take control over the meanings attached to each of the poles of the sexual difference system. Considered within Cixous's context, Foucault can be regarded as extending "the chain of fathers" which has historically deployed sexual difference tactically, attenuating or intensifying differences as circumstances demanded. Because Cixous writes from a position explicitly identified with the feminine, she is more sensitive to the repressive dynamics of power, and better positioned to recognize that the elasticity of power has operated to advantage the masculine position which retains control over how and when the feminine is spoken. Cixous might very well argue that Foucault finds himself in a position where he can afford to displace the repressive dimension of sexual difference in a way that those identified as women cannot. In a phallocentric economy which has persisted by using sexual difference to deny or displace the feminine, women cannot afford to ignore the structures that have produced the feminine position, or the conditions that mandate writing. Rather than effacing the conditions of their own productions, Cixous urges women to seize them as the conditions and motive for writing, precisely because they are not essential but political, and hence subject to reconstitution.

> If woman has always functioned "within" the discourse of man, a signifier that always referred back to its opposite signifier which annihilates its specific energy and diminishes or stifles its very different sound, it is time for her to dislocate this "within," to explode it and turn it around and seize it and make it hers.[12]

From the language of this passage, it is clear that when Cixous speaks in terms of "man" and "woman," "masculine" and "feminine," she is referring to signs situated in a symbolic system of sexual difference which are opposed not on the basis of biology or for some other essential reason, but for purposes of maintaining male dominance. Because there are no essential invariable features in which to ground this difference, "man works very actively to produce "his woman'."[13] Woman must be continually reinvented both for reasons of maximum deployment capability, and because these projective fictions cannot be sustained without the continuing demand for their actualization.

Because sexual difference is a product of a political deployment, woman's silence must be regarded as a tactical construction, and not as some case of collective congenital aphasia. Because women's silence has been produced politically, it can also be contested, most forcefully by women's refusal of that position in writing. Writing is a particularly forceful gesture because it is public and because it has the potential to incite and provoke more writing. Unlike speaking, which is restricted in its effects to the situation that occasions it, writing allows for a wider sphere of circulation, and thus offers the potential for a far broader, and more enduring sphere of influence. In addition, writing is a cultural practice already invested with a certain authority, the authority to elicit a readership and hence establish and mobilize a community. For women whose field of expression has largely been restricted to the private domestic sphere, writing offers a way to take up a position in the public sphere of social constructions, as well as to reappropriate what has largely been a male-dominated space. Such writing also works to subvert the language which has stabilized sexual difference as an asymmetrical opposition, by giving voice to the feminine pole, which has historically been relegated to silence.

Cixous is decidedly non-utopian in her recognition of the obstacles women will have to confront in engaging the representational apparatus. The first is a condition of self-censorship, which allows power to efface its operations by enlisting women as self-stifling agents. Closely allied to this is a system of language and thought inadequate to the representation of a woman's economy, i.e., the system which produces, circulates, and re-produces the currency of women's desires and the modes by which they are satisfied.

> This opposition to woman cuts endlessly across all the oppositions that order culture. It's the classic opposition, dualist and hierarchical man/woman au-tomatically means great/small, superior/inferior. . . means high or low, means nature/history, means transformation/inertia. In fact, every theory of culture, every theory of society, the whole conglomeration of symbolic sys-tems—everything, that is, that's spoken, that's organized as discourse, art, religion, the family, language, everything that acts upon us—it is all ordered around hierarchical oppositions that come back to the man/woman oppo-sition, an opposition that can only be sustained by means of a difference posed by cultural discourse as "natural," the difference between activity and passivity.[14]

Because language and discursive practices are structured by a hierarchical arrangement of sexual difference, women writers will be faced with con-tradictions when trying to articulate their power in the language that has thus far produced a repertoire of self-interested masculine constructions of femininity. That is why women cannot resort to the utopian move of writing as though women have always written, denying the very denials that have historically defined their position. As a strategy, Cixous rec-ommends that women writers engage these male constructions with the intent of reappropriating and ultimately subverting that history. "In telling it, in developing it, even in plotting it, I seek to undo it, to overturn it, to reveal it, to expose it."[15]

Much of Cixous's work is devoted to examining the proliferation and circulation of feminine types. She analyzes classic narratives and symbols of femininity which have constructed women variously as Sleeping Beauty, Little Red Riding Hood, sphinx, vamp, and hysteric, and traces their cir-culation through the discourses of literature, philosophy, and psychoa-nalysis. In many respects the tactics operating in these re-readings are the opposite of what Foucault would recommend. Rather than focusing on their specificities, Cixous's analysis aims to show that although its forms and fashions may change, male dominance of the processes by which femininity is constructed and exchanged have not. The effect of this sustained strategy is not what Foucault's analysis would lead us to expect, because feminine writing is not simply a consequence of the existing power deployment, but is precisely that which cannot be anticipated or realized within its operative logic.[16] Rather than further empowering these constructions, the effect of women's writing is to demystify these images, empowering women in relation to them. But such empowerment depends on our recognizing that we are differentially placed in a way that disadvantages us. Because feminine writing is differentially positioned it must also avail itself of different strategies and ought not subject itself to the conventions of legitimation that dominate phallocentric discourse and which have been responsible for stifling the articulation of the feminine in its difference.

Given that sexual difference is always a political determination, and not a biological one, feminine writing differs not by virtue of the gender of the author, but on the basis of the textual strategies it employs, strategies that reconstitute the relationship between reader and writer, this text and others. Because feminine texts differ in the ways that they construct and circulate authority, they also work to reconfigure the patriarchal power-knowledge alliance, calling attention to its operations by subverting them. The subversive power of feminine writing is thus not a function of its occupying an ahistorical position of opposition, but is rather a function of a strategic determination, i.e., a context specific judgment about how the power that comes from our writing may be maximized in this impact and effect. Feminine writing is therefore always already political.

Comparative Textual Politics

Now I will return to the questions Foucault raises about sexual discourse and address them, as he would recommend, strategically. I will compare Cixous's and Foucault's respective textual strategies to indicate how they produce and circulate authority, who they empower and how. The crucial factor will be the differential treatment given to sexual difference as it affects writing. Analysis of this difference shows that Foucault's textual strategies often appear to be at odds with his stated purpose, recirculating the very forms of authority he aims to displace. Because he does not adequately thematize the effects of sexual difference as it operates in reading and writing, Foucault's analysis remains unhappily complicitous with the self-effacing dynamics of phallocentrism. Conversely, if the task is to decapitate the king, Cixous's strategies seem far more promising as a means of undermining the self-concealing operations of power, because they articulate and authorize a power economy that does not enact domination. If as feminists we want to behead the king, we cannot forget, as Foucault sometimes seems to, that the king is also a man.

Faced with the prospect of defining a "feminist text" in a way that is not simply reducible to biological or sexual difference, Cixous focuses on two textual strategies that, to use Foucault's language, function as "matrices of transformation" which establish a different relationship between reader and text, this text and others. The first is a strategy she calls the "affirmation of difference."[17] This strategy, which parallels and complements the re-readings of feminine tropes, works to transform the meaning of the feminine, from a site of subjugation to a source of power. By playing with the dominant constructions of sexual differences in a way that problematizes contempt for the feminine, Cixous's texts produce a space and rhetoric for revaluing the feminine, while inciting women readers to do the same. Where women have been debased by their association with the body, Cixous valorizes that connection. Against a background which has exploited maternity and used it as a ground for radically circumscribing women's sphere, Cixous reinterprets pregnancy as a metaphor for women's boundless life-giving capacities. Although women's alienation from a phallocentric economy has been used to discredit their discursive practices, this alienation reemerges in Cixous's texts as an emblem of their strength and subversive potency.

This strategy is directed toward women readers whom Cixous addresses frequently in her texts, with the hope that "in writing from woman and toward woman . . . woman will affirm woman somewhere other than in silence."[18] This tactic has the effect of calling attention to the male readership assumed by most texts, while displacing its centrality. Such a transgression of usual textual etiquette induces a kind of reversal which allows women readers a moment of identification with a rarely held position of primacy. Although Cixous is aware that women cannot simply rewrite the history of subjugation, her invocation of women as readers is intended to incite us to write so as to continue the process by which we will come to recognize and exercise our powers. As a polemical moment of the discourse, the affirmation of difference begins with constructions of the hegemonic feminine in order to begin the process of exploding it from within. Although it is offered to women readers in a rhetoric which elicits recognition and identification, it is not a discourse that demands or seeks agreement or allegiance. Because she considers essentialism to be a male construct, Cixous recognizes that affirmation of difference applies to her chosen readership, i.e., women, as well. Affirming women somewhere other than in silence means affirming the voicing of differences, including differences with the discourse offered by the author for recognition.

Foucault, by contrast, presumes rather than produces a position of identification with the readership, addressing them with a rather unself-conscious use of the royal and sexually undifferentiated "we" as when he speaks of "we other Victorians."[19] Because Foucault does not examine the operations of sexual difference in reconstructing the Victorian sexual economy, his analysis leaves the reader with the impression that men and women occupied comparable positions within the Victorian family, i.e., both were comparably victimized and gratified by it, and both were comparably culpable for its perpetuation. At the very least Foucault leaves women readers with the sense that differences in gender roles are not relevant to understanding how this particular deployment of power operated. Foucault's discussion of Victorian hypocrisy also suffers from the failure to make such distinctions between the positions women and men occupied in the illicit sexualities, like rape, prostitution, and adultery, that were also produced by the Victorian organization of sex.

Foucault's rhetorical strategy parallels the analytic one, with the combined effect of displacing women readers, while claiming to speak for and to them. In so doing, Foucault assumes a traditional discursive perogative of failing to address women directly, rhetorically, or substantively, while assuming a right to position them in a place comparable to that of a male reader. By failing to leave a place for a discourse of women's difference, the effect of Foucault's textual strategies is to reconstitute self-effacing masculinity as a unitary voice of authority. If part of Foucault's intention is to articulate a decentralized and proliferative model of power, his textual strategies work against this by consolidating authority in a form that denies difference and impedes access and authorization for women readers. This displacement is particularly problematic in the context of a genetic analysis of sexual power and is disappointing in a theorist as attuned to specificities as is Foucault. From the standpoint of his own project, if the point is to displace a repressive model of power with a proliferative one, a strategy which suppresses recognition of difference is not the most appropriate.

Foucault's textual strategies work to sustain a traditional economy associated with masculine texts which, to use Cixous's expression are "closed" by contrast with feminine texts which are "open."[20] The difference between open and closed texts is not primarily a difference of form or style. Certainly no text, masculine or feminine can be closed in the sense of being self-suturing, immune to polyvalence and intervention. The "open-closed" metaphor can best be understood as describing the text's relationship to authority, its readership, and other texts. Masculine texts are closed to the extent that their textual strategies limit access and intervention from readers and other texts by consolidating authority in the form of authorial privilege. They establish privilege at the expense, in part, of other texts which the masculine textual economy seeks to eliminate through mechanisms of subsumption, consumption, or conscription. Cixous attributes such strategies to the death wish that underlies phallocentrism.[21] As a consequence, discourse is organized on a model of combat which seeks to eliminate texts and positions by "herding contradictions into a single battlefield."[22] By marshalling evidence and accumulating knowledge that can be exchanged for authority, the masculine textual economy proceeds with a strategy of bibliocide geared toward eliminating other texts on the basis of their lack. In a death-ridden economy it is more important to know which texts to close than which to open.

Foucault is not above employing such combative tactics with respect to the other theories he addresses, most notably the repressive hypothesis which he seeks to replace. He is also not above appealing to a legalistic language of "rules" in articulating his meta-theory of power,[23] a strategy that is ironic in light of his critique of the juridical model. Foucault attempts to establish his authority with respect to these issues in fairly traditional ways, most notably on the basis of an accumulation of knowledge, in the form of readings of historical texts which are intended to certify the writer's expertise. The effect of this is to consolidate knowledge and hence authority in the voice of a unitary author who stands in a privileged relationship to the evidence presented, because Foucault is often reading documents to which he has relatively privileged access by comparison with his readers. His tactics reflect allegiance to and complicity with traditional codes of legitimation and authority.

Ironically, these tactics of condensation work against the direction mapped out by the language of proliferation. The relatively closed character of Foucault's text emerges more clearly in comparison with the way Cixous's texts work. To establish her differences from hegemonic forms of authority, Cixous dispenses with or conspicuously transgresses much of the textual etiquette and many of the conventions of academic discourse. Her texts are constructed eclectically, juxtaposing a discussion of Freud with a Chinese fable, the history of philosophy with fairy tales. By transgressing disciplinary and paradigmatic boundaries, Cixous positions her work within a different economy of legitimation. Dispensing with conventional footnotes and attributions, she constructs her authority as separate and apart from validation through the chain of fathers. This latter tactic also helps to minimize the distance between author and reader that is usually established on the basis of privileged access and expertise. When Cixous re-reads texts, she almost always chooses examples that are part of a general cultural repertoire with which her readers are likely to be familiar. Rather than attempting to establish her authority on the basis of superiority to her readers, Cixous seeks the identification and recognition of women readers as the source of an authority that is always mobile, moving in an open-ended circuitry between reader and text.

Cixous's texts resist closure through a strategy of multiplying voices and positions in ways which circumvent hegemonic exclusivities and oppositions, even as it invokes them. Rejecting a linear logic that culminates in some definitive position, Cixous's texts work against the reader's tendencies to stabilize meanings and consolidate textual power in the figure of a knowing author. This practice has two kinds of strategic value. On the one hand, this tactic results in texts that cannot be fully contained by a patriarchal logic because these movements confound its ossifications. Like a loop which ties up a computer in an endless but circular repetition of its own logic, Cixous texts move cyclically in a way that resists a phallocentric logic of closure. The other merit of this tactic is to transfer authority to women readers who are moved not to repeat a linear narrative of explanation, but rather to produce texts, and texts which are different.

With respect to the project of decapitation, the affirmation of difference and transvaluation of the feminine allows Cixous to operate from a relatively privileged position, since decapitation has traditionally been the fate of women in an economy dominated by masculine anxiety. "If man operates under the threat of castration, if masculinity is culturally ordered by the castration complex, it might be said that the backlash, the return of this castration anxiety is its displacement as decapitation, execution of woman as loss of her head."[24] Cixous's juxtaposition of these mutilatory practices is both ironic and ambiguous in its demonstration of the perverse oppositions produced from a hierarchical logic of sexual difference. The choices and contradictions generated by this opposition cannot be resolved or closed, nor, if these are the only choices, should they be.

Writing New Sexual Stories

To reopen the discourse of decapitation, Cixous retells "a little Chinese story" which provides a lesson in the strategies of decapitation. It is also a "perfect example of a particular relationship between two economies, a masculine economy and a feminine economy."[25] Because Cixous says "(e)very detail of this story counts," I include the entire tale.

> The king commanded General Sun Tse: "You who are a great strategist and claim to be able to train anybody in the arts of war . . . take my wives (all 180 of them!) and make soldiers out of them." We don't know why the king conceived this desire—it's the one thing we don't know . . . it remains precisely "un(re)countable" or unaccountable in the story. But it is a king's

wish after all. So Sun Tse had the women arranged in two rows each headed
by one of the two favorite wives, and then taught them the language of the
drumbeat. It was very simple: two beats—right, three beats—left, four
beats—turn or backward march. But instead of learning the code very
quickly, the ladies started laughing, chattering and paying no attention to
the lesson, and Sun Tse, the master, repeated the lesson several times over.
But the more he spoke, the more the women fell about laughing, upon
which Sun Tse put his code to the test. It is said in the code that should
women fall about laughing, instead of becoming soldiers, their actions might
be deemed mutinous and the code has ordained that cases of mutiny call
for the death penalty. So the women were condemned to death. This both-
ered the king somewhat: a hundred and eighty wives are a lot to lose: He
didn't want his wives put to death. But Sun Tse replied that since he was
put in charge of making soldiers out of the women, he would carry out
the order. Sun Tse was a man of absolute principle. And in any case there's
an order even more "royal" than of the king himself: the Absolute
Law. . . . One does not go back on an order. He therefore acted according
to the code and with his saber, beheaded the women commanders. They
were replaced and the exercise started again; and as if they had never done
anything except practice the art of war, the women turned right, left and
about in silence and with never a single mistake.

One could read this as a cautionary tale about the price women have to
pay when we step out of line. Read this way, the connection between
silence and survival for women is but a part of the fallout of a system whose
absolute law is death. What remains unaccountable, however, is the desire
which sets this system in motion and sustains it, because it is a king's
desire after all. Remaining unaccountable, it offers no account of itself
beyond demonstrating its proliferative capabilities on the women who will
continue to swell the ranks. Remaining within this unrecountable logic,
there is no way to valorize women's position. But Cixous offers the prospect
of rewriting that story in ways where women are not forced to repeat old
endings. It also makes it possible to tell stories about how to decapitate
the king. Spurred by Cixous's invitation to produce new texts from reading
hers, I offer the following as one possibility.

The King wants an army and has enlisted the master of discipline Sun Tse
to whip his wives into shape. Luckily the king has been prolific enough in
dispensing his phallus to have collected sufficient female capital for such a
project. But women being women, they do not respond as the disciplinary
logic would dictate. They still walk like women and not like soldiers. They
talk during drills, often so loudly that Sun Tse can barely make himself
heard. Frustrated, he goes to the king seeking reinforcements. Rather than
appear himself, the king sends Sun Tse back to the training ground armed
with the royal sword and permission to use it. As Sun Tse enters, the women
rapidly break rank, deploying themselves in different positions, surround-

ing and confounding him. Startled, his hands sweat, loosening his grip on the sword. He is disarmed. Swallowing up the master in the network of their bodies, the women fill the corridors of power with the echo of their footsteps as they approach the king's quarters carrying the sword above their heads. They each know the way. They have been this route before, at least once, but each one alone. The road feels different when it is walked with other women. Entering the king's chambers uninvited, they give back the king his henchman. The silence is broken by a woman at the back of the room, "What made you think to send a man to do a king's job?" whereupon the women begin to laugh. The laughter builds, vibrating with such force that it shatters the sword, splintering it into a thousand pieces at the sovereign's feet. In the face of such occurrences, the king, stunned, loses his voice, and begins to whimper like the child he has been. Having lost his sword, he has also lost his head.

What place do stories and laughter have in a sexual economy progressively dominated by the anxiety of epidemic? If as feminists we no longer ought to invest ourselves in the belief that liberating sex will set us free, especially in an erotic economy of diminishing returns, what can, or should we expect from the process which transforms sex into discourse, and from a society committed to proliferating this talking sex? Are we condemned to continue to produce confessions even without the barest prospect of salvation through them?

Although their tactics and strategies differ, Foucault and Cixous have each devoted considerable effort to alerting us to the need to generate some new stories, stories that do not mourn an irretrievable sexuality but that begin the process of formulating feminist images and symbols, so as to be able to invest our power and energies in an eroticism no longer ruled by a royal triumvirate of death, domination, and desire. At the conclusion of the first volume of *The History of Sexuality*, Foucault offers the following provocative suggestion. "The rallying point for the counterattack against the deployment of sexuality ought not be sex-desire, but bodies and pleasures."[26]

Cixous, in another ironic twist on the tactics of castration urges women to take up the task of subverting the masculine economy through insistence on a different *jouissance*. "(D)ephallocentrize the body, relieve man of his phallus, return him to an erogenous field and a libido that isn't stupidly organized round that monument, but appears shifting, diffused, taking on all the others of oneself."[27] In one of her more visionary moments, Cixous imagines the outcome of such a process as not some new self-stabilizing script, but as an emerging narrative which would allow for "a transformation of each one's relationship to his or her body and to the other body. . . . Difference would be a bunch of new differences."[28]

Current circumstances are forcing all of us, albeit for different reasons, to reconsider our investments in sexuality and to confront the historically specific alignment between sex and death in our age. In this context, Cixous's claims about phallocentrism being deadly take on a whole new meaning. In the end, I think that Foucault and Cixous are both right. We do talk about sex more than anything else, and we still need to talk about it. If such talk is to be capable of transforming our relations to our bodies and our pleasures, such talk must work to incite as well as to represent those pleasures. That possibility will depend, as both Cixous and Foucault suggest, on developing a discourse capable of instigating proliferative and imaginative powers, including the power of laughter, which, at least in my story, is sometimes powerful enough to cut off the head of the king.

NOTES

1. Hélène Cixous, "The Laugh of the Medusa," trans. Keith Cohen and Paula Cohen, *Signs* 1, no. 4(1976):875–93.

2. Michel Foucault, *The History of Sexuality, Volume I, An Introduction*, trans. Robert Huxley (New York: Vintage Books, 1980), 33.

3. Ibid., 159.

4. For a discussion of the polyvalency of "*jouissance*" as it operates in Cixous's text, see Betsy Wing's discussion in her translation of Hélène Cixous and Catherine Clement, *The Newly Born Woman* (Minneapolis: University of Minnesota Press, 1986), 165.

5. Cixous, "The Laugh of the Medusa," 879. The context is a discussion of liberating "the New Woman."

6. Foucault, *The History of Sexuality, Volume I*, 93.

7. Ibid., 100.

8. Ibid., 157.

9. Ibid., 48.

10. Ibid., 88.

11. Ibid., 99. The context for these remarks is Foucault's discussion of "the rule of continual variations" one of four "cautionary prescriptions" he offers for future analyses of sex and power.

12. Cixous, "The Laugh of the Medusa," 887.

13. Hélène Cixous, "Castration or Decapitation?" trans. Annette Kuhn, *Signs* 7(1981):46.

14. Ibid., 44.

15. Cixous and Clement, *The Newly Born Woman*, 6.

16. For Cixous, the consequence of this is that feminine texts are not predictable, because they are engaged in an emergence for which patriarchal logic has no room. See: "Castration or Decapitation?" 53.

17. Ibid., 52.

18. Cixous, "The Laugh of the Medusa," 881.

19. This is the title of part one of Foucault, *The History of Sexuality, Volume I*.

20. For a fuller discussion of the difference, see Cixous, *The Newly Born Woman*, 83–100.

21. See Cixous, "Castration or Decapitation?" 48–50, and *The Newly Born Woman*, 70–78.

22. Cixous, "The Laugh of the Medusa," 882.
23. See Foucault, *The History of Sexuality, Volume I*, pt. four.
24. Cixous, "Castration or Decapitation?" 43.
25. Ibid., 42.
26. Foucault, 157.
27. Cixous, "Castration or Decapitation?" 51.
28. Cixous, *The Newly Born Woman*, 83.

DIFFERENCE ON TRIAL
A CRITIQUE OF THE MATERNAL METAPHOR IN CIXOUS, IRIGARAY, AND KRISTEVA

Domna C. Stanton

> When the infinite bondage of woman will
> be broken, when she will live for herself
> and by herself, man—abominable until
> now—having discharged her, she too will
> be a poet! Woman will discover the un-
> known! Will her world of ideas differ from
> ours? She will discover strange things, un-
> fathomable, repulsive, delicious; we will
> take them, we will understand them.
>
> —Arthur Rimbaud

> Woman becomes the possibility of a "dif-
> ferent" idea.
>
> —Luce Irigaray

The future perfect that Rimbaud envisioned a century ago remains un-
realized in our present imperfect: woman is still in(de)finitely in bondage,
she exists in the real and the symbolic neither by nor for herself. And yet,
during the past decade, most notably in France, female critics and theorists
have used poetic modes of speech to explore *la différence féminine* and thus
to subvert a phallocratic system predicated on the perpetuation of the same.
For Hélène Cixous, Luce Irigaray, and Julia Kristeva—whom I consider
emblematic of this tendency, notwithstanding undeniable dissimilarities in
their work—the exploration of that sexual difference constitutes "the fe-
cund horizon" of the future which will herald the birth of "a new era of

thought . . . the creation of a new *poïetic*."[1] In their "maternal" pursuit of this poetic quest, the three exponents of difference, who are the subject of this essay, have privileged metaphor, the trope upheld from classical to modernist times as the optimal tool for transporting meaning beyond the known (*meta-phorein*).[2] Metaphor, says Kristeva, creates "a surplus of meaning," which "manages to open the surface of signs toward the un-representable."[3] Through this transporting metaphor, Cixous, Irigaray and Kristeva strive to articulate the unrepresented, the female unknown re-pulsed by Rimbaud's abominable man.

According to Rimbaud's visionary scenario, "we" would expect man to take and understand the difference woman is discovering. However, some-thing far more ambiguous has occurred. First, the emphasis on female difference is part and parcel of the philosophy of difference that pervades contemporary thought since Heidegger and dominates theories of moder-nity. Accordingly, the idea of female difference or the female as principal metaphor for difference has marked the work of Neumann and Marcuse, for instance, on this side of the Atlantic, Deleuze, Derrida, Lacan, and Lyotard on the other. As Alice Jardine has remarked, modernist masters in France have consistently coded as feminine that which exceeds the grasp of the Cartesian subject—be it called nonknowledge or nontruth, unde-cidability or supplementarity, even writing or the unconscious.[4] It is pos-sible, then, that the feminization of difference and its articulations involve a replaying of that age-old scene in which, and in contrast to Rimbaud's scenario, the male discloses, the female disposes. In effect, female-authored inscriptions of *la différence féminine* seem decisively, but often unavowedly, influenced by the texts of contemporary masters.[5] At the very least, these women's explorations represent a complex give and take with modernist discourse, a writing-between or re-writing, which comprises significant continuity and varying degrees of oppositional discontinuity. As Barthes reminds us in *Writing Degree Zero*, all writing, even the most intentionally subversive, is confined by the parameters of discourse at a particular mo-ment, which is always an imperfect present.

Leaving aside the troubling relation between modernism and *le féminin*, which warrants its own extended analysis, the "quest for the Unknown Woman"—"la quête vers l'Inconnue"[6]—pursued by these three female critics should be examined to determine whether and how it involves a transportation of meaning beyond the known. Despite or, in fact, because of its inspiring, empowering value for women, their challenging discourse should be probed for the traces of the same it contains—what Irigaray, with Heidegger, calls indifference.[7] It can be scrutinized, in other words, for the extent to which phallocentric scenes and semes are re-present-ed, despite the desire to subvert, eliminate, and replace them. In that process, metaphor itself must be interrogated to see whether it provides the best means for exploring the many aspects of the female unknown; or, then, whether other rhetorical strategies may be more propitious and productive. And finally, since this metaphorical discourse constitutes "a trial of difference"—"une épreuve de la différence"[8]—difference as teleology must be put on trial. Such an undertaking is critical to a dynamic feminist method(ide)ology, in my view. It seems crucial at a moment when American feminist critics are affirming *The Future of Difference* beyond earlier claims to equal value with men and to fundamental similarities among all women. It is particularly pertinent at a time when we are emphasizing the importance of *Writing and Sexual Difference* under the growing influence of French theories on the feminine. A partial investigation, of necessity both fragmentary and subjective, this essay extracts and examines, in certain texts by Cixous, Irigaray, and Kristeva, the strands of an extended metaphor—woman as/is mother[9]—for its special relevance to the contemporary preoccupation with female difference, and beyond, the problematics of difference itself.

I

> As mother of the virgin woman, in her
> comings and goings, in her search, she
> turns all the scenes of representation
> upside down, deconstructs the old cities
> and the new old cities, the whole
> imaginary and symbolic universe of the
> ancient men, with a merciless step renders
> obsolete the imperfect present.
>
> —Hélène Cixous

In her radical re-writing of Rimbaud's scenario, Cixous delineates the metaphorically maternal role that she, like Irigaray and Kristeva, assumes to give birth to the unsaid feminine, "the virgin woman." In turn, the vehicle for this exploration of difference is essentially maternal, what Irigaray terms "the maternal-feminine."[10] Just as Cixous locates the "essence of femininity" in the womb, and hails the feminine as "the maternal sex,"[11] so too does Irigaray affirm that "when we are women, we are always mothers."[12] And from *Revolution in Poetic Language* on, Kristeva depicts the feminine "function" as the maternal, and unrepresented feminine sexuality as maternal *jouissance.*[13] So saying, Cixous, Irigaray, and Kristeva take as their point of departure the primordial definition of woman in the phallocratic order, what could be viewed as the concrete agent of (its) re-production.

Now this valorization of the maternal marks a decisive break with the existentialism of *The Second Sex,* wherein de Beauvoir stressed the oppressiveness of motherhood as an institution and rejected maternity as a solution to the problem of female transcendence *(le pour-soi).* By contrast, Cixous considers feminist denunciations of the patriarchal trap of maternity a perpetuation of the taboo of the pregnant woman, and a new form of repression, the denial of the "passionate," "delicious" experiences of women's bodies.[14] Likewise, Kristeva interprets the rejection of maternity as a feminist incapacity to transcend the phallocratic attitude of "idealized contempt,"[15] and to see in the maternal the ultimate love for another.[16] Although the views of Kristeva and Cixous are not necessarily incompatible with those of de Beauvoir, their analyses are basically unconcerned with "the real" or the historical, despite occasional references to the "radical transformations in socio-political structures (which) would create a radically different inscription of difference."[17] Instead, their notion of the maternal difference centers exclusively on the symbolic and the imaginary. According to Kristeva, "only a full elaboration of maternity, and its relation to creation" can lead to "a true feminine innovation (in every single field)."[18] More radically, Irigaray argues that such an elaboration predicates "another 'syntax,' another 'grammar' of culture."[19] In *Le Corps-à-corps avec la mère* and *Amante marine,* and in direct opposition to Freud, she declares the murder of the mother to be the foundation of Western culture and society.[20] Thus to "think of the mother in every woman, of the woman in every mother" is a forbidden act, she claims, that will undermine the patriarchal edifice,[21] and bring about a revolutionary ethic of sexual difference.[22]

In this symbolic context, it becomes clear that "the Mother" is, as Cixous states, "a metaphor."[23] Accordingly, quotation marks often frame the "mother" in Cixousian texts: in *La Jeune Née,* "woman is never far from the 'mother' "[24]; in *La venue à l'écriture,* "Woman is always in a certain way, 'mother' to herself and the other."[25] That Cixous upholds metaphor as desirable and efficacious[26] presupposes faith in its capacity to transform existing meanings, ultimately, the system of significance. In effect, Irigaray maintains that similitude or analogy, in contrast to the rigor/rigidity of male geometricity "entails a reworking of meaning,"[27] especially when it involves "symbolism created among women."[28] And for Kristeva, the maternal, coupled with the paternal, represents a "theoretical bisexuality . . . a metaphor designating the possibility of exploring all aspects of signification."[29]

This venerated and idealistic conception of metaphor, however, ignores the problematic implications of metaphoricity. As the trope of similitude, metaphor affirms the verb to be—A is (like) B—or the notion of "being as," and thus has an ontological function, what Derrida describes as a hidden essence: "Metaphor is able to display properties, to relate to each other properties on the basis of their resemblance, without ever directly, fully or properly stating the essence, without itself making visible the truth of the thing itself."[30] Going further, Derrida concurs with Heidegger that the metaphorical exists within the metaphysical and represents a religious construct.[31] By that token, the maternal *sein* (breast) would partake of the ontotheological *Sein*, and already be caught up in the structures of phallogopresence. In fact, the trope of similitude itself could be regarded as a metonymy for the philosophy of sameness which, as Irigaray has convincingly shown in *Speculum, de l'autre femme*, dominates Western thought from Plato to Freud. Not surprisingly, then, Kristeva subsumes metaphoricity under the paternal function.[32]

The hidden ontotheology of the maternal metaphor is ignored and implicitly denied by these exponents of *la différence féminine*, even though they oppose essentialist and religious thinking.[33] Kristeva's work, in particular, strives to undermine identity in favor of a subject always in process, on trial, or what she calls "a process without subject."[34] She contrasts the Christian conception of the mother, which sustains the symbolic order and supports the dominant notion of the subject, with an-other, un-symbolic conception that can subvert phallogopresence, since "then every speaker would be led to conceive of its Being in relation to some void, a nothingness asymmetrically opposed to this Being, a permanent threat against first, its mastery, and ultimately its stability."[35] For Kristeva, the difference between the two conceptions of the maternal, which parallels the two conceptions of metaphor, is exemplified, on the one hand, by Leonardo's paintings of the madonna, a *père-version*[36] and, on the other, by certain Bellini madonnas, which suggest to her "the luminous serenity of the unrepresentable."[37] The same dichotomy appears in "Héréthique de l'amour": the right, the doxic side of the text exposes the ontotheological vision of maternity, while the left (the left out), inscribes in fragmented, elliptical images the female speaker's maternal experience. Concurrently, Kristeva cautions feminists against the "naively romantic" belief in identity, since "woman cannot *be*, is even that which does not go into *being*."[38] The feminist assertion of being, she states, is theological: "women must stop making feminism a religion . . . or a sect."[39]

Although Irigaray does not censure feminism as yet another man-ism, she too warns women against trying to "rival [man] by constructing a logic of the feminine which would still take for its model the ontotheologic."[40] But that warning is addressed only to other women, while the speaking self urges women to substitute for god the Father "a goddess mother or woman, both mother and woman," and heralds in the future feminine a new *parousia*.[41] Like Kristeva, Irigaray does not put her own metaphorization of the maternal into question to probe and counteract its ontotheological traces. Even Irigaray's *Ce Sexe qui n'en est pas un*, which struggles self-consciously, haltingly to move beyond existing scenes of representation—"how can I say in another way?"; "how can I say it?," asks the speaker repeatedly[42]—ends with the moment "when our lips speak together," finally free of the male-imposed fear of speaking properly, but also impervious to the implications of speaking metaphorically.

The tensions between a conscious repulsion of the ontotheologic and its enduring lures or traps are dramatized in Cixous's works. Although she states, like Irigaray, that there is no feminine essence, nature, or destiny,[43] her desire to create an empowering mythology or "magic without gods"[44] leads to the affirmation of "a universal woman subject," "the New Woman,"[45] who would represent Adam in the feminine "if God had been a woman."[46] To be sure, the Cixousian "I" occasionally recognizes and criticizes her "religious writing."[47] More important, the weight of the old phallosystem and the problematics of speaking in the new feminine are extensively inscribed. Typically, lyrically, the Cixousian text evokes the difficult rite of passage from the old order to the tentative, slippery moment of birth of that yonder feminine, which the Latin *illa* denotes, and which Aura (the future of the Latin, to have) symbolizes.[48] This strategy would seem to bypass the notion of presence/essence, but it transpires through the textual delineation of "the maternal sex" whose pervasive metaphoricity is never questioned. And it becomes particularly visible in the evocation of Clarice Lispector, the maternal Muse or Angela ("Ange-est-là"), who exemplifies feminine writing in a "present interior" in which "all women [speak] the same music.[49] Self and other become a presence; so do things— "she has a way of pronouncing the essence of things, and things are there"[50]—so do "their presence-names . . . their names full of presence, their living, heavy, audible names."[51] For the most Derridean of the exponents of feminine difference, as Gayatri Spivak has described Cixous,[52] this emphatic presence marks a break with the symbolic father. But it remains a lyrical gesture that paradoxically reaffirms the phallophilosophy of presence which the maternal feminine is designed to efface.

As such examples suggest, *la différence féminine*, defined as absence, becomes present in the maternal text through the ontological maternal metaphor. To be sure, the very function of metaphor is to provide for a missing term, to say what lacks, is absent. As the metaphor is elaborated semantically, the unrepresented/unrepresentable feminine is recuperated into the scenes of representation that this maternal discourse aims to shatter.[53] Now it could be argued that far from constituting the critical difference, the unrepresentable has always been part of the discursive system. Indeed, in examining the principles of catachresis, "a foundation for our entire tropological system," the venerable Fontanier notes that this forced or abusive metaphor predicates the existence of "a new idea . . . having no sign at all or no other proper sign within the language."[54] By extension, the unrepresented may be the very sign in our discursive system that sustains the illusion of its capacity to speak difference. Clearly, then, the problematic of the unrepresented is not peculiar to the maternal metaphor. It is endemic to any practice that tries to name the unnamed; it is embedded in the bind that all affirmation of difference creates. For either we name and become entrapped in the structures of the already named; or else we do not name and remain trapped in passivity, powerlessness, and a perpetuation of the same. Either way, to paraphrase Cixous, "we still flounder in the ancient order."[55]

II

> But is there an elsewhere? . . . If it's not yet "here," it's already there—in that other place . . . where desire makes fiction exist.
>
> —Hélène Cixous

Given the constraints of a global discursive bind, Cixous's question has particularly relevant, but more relative, implications for the maternal metaphor. To what extent does the metaphor, as a desirable fiction, bespeak an elsewhere, an-other place? Although philosophers of language, Derrida most recently, rightly insist that no thought is ever free of old metaphors, instances of extended metaphorization can represent varying degrees of "innovation," to use Kristeva's term, if not of difference in an absolute sense, which can effect a movement (*mouvance*) beyond sameness to some reworking of meaning.[56] In the instance of the maternal, a more detailed analysis of the conceptual bases of the metaphor, and its constituent semes and scenes can help determine whether and in what specific ways inscriptions of the "new" feminine represent an elsewhere, a re-writing otherwise from the stereotypology of woman as mother.

At the outset, the elaboration of the maternal metaphor is grounded in the patriarchal Freudian text, for what it both says and silences. Refuting the oedipal version of maternity and girlhood, Cixous, Irigaray, and Kristeva focus instead on the pre-oedipal, that shadowy sphere "almost impossible to revivify," which Freud discovered through his female disciples, that "prehistory of women" which, he claimed, accounts "almost entirely" for the substance of their ulterior relations to father and husband.[57] An absent presence, the pre-oedipal attracts maternal exponents of difference as a gynocentric space, even though, as the word implies, it remains bound up with the oedipal Weltanschauung. Still, the pre-oedipal can be rewritten to eliminate its pejorations in Freudian texts, suggests Irigaray.[58] For Cixous, it can serve as an originary point for the future feminine: "As if there were, buried alive, between the breasts, under the clay curtains, in the chest, behind the fertile lungs, a woman in the cradle, hardly conceived, already perfectly formed, a living presence . . . daughter of woman, a female engendered without father . . . fruit of mother love, the kind that can be conceived *naturally* only in the regions of pre-oedipal culture" (italics mine).[59] This naturalization of a pre-historical, purely hypothetical construct points to the desire for an archaic past before the advent of the symbolic. Abducted and buried alive by man, like Persephone,[60] that past can be recaptured as a "rebeginning,"[61] insists Cixous, through the derepression of unconscious or archaic memories: "the gods have lost their divinity but memories, which replace them, keep their divine viscosity."[62] But the quest for the lost trace, for the origin that coincides with the telos, is, once again, religious in impulse. In fact, Irigaray unearths in "this ignorance . . . of woman's relation to her primordial desires, this nonelaboration of her relation to her origins"[63] a primal plot based on man's and god's fear of the power of the archaic Mother (*Amante marine*). Its undoing would presumably be marked by a re-writing of John in the feminine. "In the beginning there was Woman," we read in Cixous's *With ou l'art de l'innocence*, "and the beginning was woman."[64]

In Kristeva's work, more than Irigaray's or Cixous's, the pre-oedipal is the cornerstone of a theory of subversive production. She names the "revival of archaic pre-oedipal modes of operation" the *semiotic*, a notion that is admittedly "only a theoretical supposition justified by the need for description."[65] Logically and chronologically anterior to the imposition of the symbolic (or paternal) order, the semiotic is conceptualized as the preverbal moment when the child is bound up with, and dependent on, the mother's body, when instinctual drives are organized, and rhythmic models developed. This semiotic relation to the maternal body must undergo repression for the acquisition of language, a phenomenon that pervades the entire structure of the symbolic order.[66] By that token, the semiotic is part of the dialectical process of *signifiance* through which all subjects constitute themselves. And yet, while remaining "inherent in the symbolic," the semiotic "also [goes] beyond it and [threatens] its position."[67] In effect, only the reactivation, the irruption of the semiotic/maternal can fracture and remodel the symbolic to produce the heterogeneous, which is the mark of the poetic.[68] Poetic language, art in general, is, then, "the semiotization of the symbolic."[69]

In more precise terms, however, the delineation of the subversive semiotic apparatus relies on a series of traditional images. Among these, the topos of the child at the breast. "The superego and its linear language," writes Kristeva, " . . . are combatted by a return of the oral glottic pleasure" of suction and expulsion, fusion, and, above all, rejection (rejet).[70] Aside from the breast, the semiotic privileges the archetypal maternal voice and rhythms: "with a material support like the voice, this semiotic network gives 'music' to literature"; "melody, harmony, rhythm, 'gentle' and 'pleasing' sounds."[71] By extension the semiotic produces alliterations, anaphoric constructions, lexical repetitions or lapses which, for Kristeva, perturb the logic of the signifying chain. Such effects ultimately serve to "overturn the normativity of the language of communication: its semantics, its syntax, its contextual relations, its subjective instances."[72] The radical quality of the poetic/semiotic text does not merely predicate a return of the repressed, but what Kristeva depicts as metaphorical incest: the artist/child commits the paternally forbidden act of "appropriating the archaic, instinctual and maternal territory."[73] By emphasizing the subject's desire to destroy the father and to (re)possess the mother, Kristeva's model for engendering the poetic does not then deviate fundamentally from the patriarchal oedipal script.

In a further echo of Freudian phallocentrism, Kristeva's encoding of the artist/child privileges the male to the detriment of the female. "Son permanently at war with the father," he allies with the parent of the opposite sex, and commits the "son's incest . . . a meeting with . . . the first other, the mother."[74] The daughter, for whom the mother is not the other but the same,[75] forms a principal alliance with the father which makes her conform more rigidly to symbolic authority, and renders her implicitly less subversive/creative than semiotic man. Woman attains her creative limits "(and in our society especially) through the strange form of split symbolization (threshold of language and instinctual drive), of the 'symbolic' and the 'semiotic' [that] the act of giving birth" represents.[76] Accordingly, she has the artistic function of articulating the repressed maternal experience. And yet, in Kristeva's work, the only articulate mother is the "I" in "Héréthique de l'amour," who recurs in the "Stabat Mater" of Histoires d'amour.[77] Although the maternal/semiotic is crucial to the Kristevan theory of art as the exemplary subversive practice, the mother remains, as the phallotext defines her, a passive instinctual force that does not speak, but is spoken by the male: "the artist speaks from a place where she is not, where she knows not. He delineates what in her is a body rejoicing (un corps jouissant)."[78]

By contrast, Cixous's work centers on the mother/daughter bond as the privileged metaphor for "femininity in writing."[79] She uses topoi of the maternal voice and breast far more extensively than Kristeva, although the voice represents, yet again, "[the] song before the law, before . . . the symbolic," which can "make the text gasp or fill it with suspense or silences, anaphorize it or tear it apart with cries."[80] But Cixous opposes (masculine) "writing by the written" to (feminine) "writing by the voice,"[81] because of an essential connection to the voice that man lacks and maternal woman has. "The voice is the uterus," states the speaker in *Illa*,[82] who internalizes the "woman-voice" of the maternal muse in her song for other women. Extending the metaphor for birthing and nourishing, the maternal poetic voice merges with the breast: "Voice. Inexhaustible milk. Is rediscovered. The lost mother. Eternity: voice mixed with milk."[83] More typical and exclusive, however, is the Cixousian assertion that "there is always in [woman] at least a little of the mother's good milk. She writes in white ink."[84] Transmuted into *le languelait* and the unique "knowledge of the breast,"[85] maternal milk emerges as the predominant metaphorical vehicle for Cixousian writing in the feminine.

Voice and milk also serve to revisualize the traditional maternal trait of giving (as) love. "There are voices that . . . give birth to the gift," says the speaker in *Illa*,[86] acknowledging the women who gave her life in/as writing: "there is a Gabrielle who gave me the bottle long after the end of the milk, beyond the law, in the absence of the first Mother."[87] Like "the Mother goddess,"[88] woman gives/loves in ways that are radically different from proprietary man: "To love, to watch-think-seek the other in the other, to despecularize, to unhoard . . . a love that has no commerce with the apprehensive desire that provides against the lack and stultifies the strange, a love that rejoices in the exchange that multiplies."[89] This essential capacity to give life/love to another in an-other way is concretized through the metaphor of the pregnant body. Indeed, the delights and mysteries of interiority unknown to man, the pleasures of an expansive waiting fertile with possibilities, and the uniquely maternal experience of arrival, issue (*sortie*), and separation number among the elements of a *jouiscience*[90] metaphorically mined in Cixous's *With* to delineate the feminine elsewhere.

Aside from exploring the umbilical ties between mother and other, daughter or woman, the Cixousian vision of the *elledorador*[91] invokes a maternal reconnection with the material things of nature. Just as Demeter's world is bereft of all vegetation when she grieves for her lost daughter, the return of flowers, "emitted maternally by the earth," and of the lost fruits—Eve's apple, Clarice's orange—requires an obstetric act of deliverance, as the German *obst* (fruit) suggests. With "delicate attentions . . . which wait patiently, patiently, and surrender to inspiration . . . the things which have always been present mute, make themselves heard," the speaker in *Illa* affirms: "There is no silence. The music of things always resounds, waiting for us to hear it faithfully." Emulating the experiences of Proust's Marcel with hawthorne flowers, the female "I" rediscovers the "rose being" (*la rose en soi*). Even more significant, she resurrects the bond between word and thing, guided by Clarice Lispector, whose voice "passes gently behind things and lifts them, gently bathes them, and [takes] the words in [her] hands." The maternal muse bestows this transcendent gift to Illa, the third-person feminine beyond Demeter and Persephone, who reestablishes the Ariadnean thread of communication among women and things and brings on/back the *Primeverbe*.[92]

In her verbal rhapsody of traditional feminine symbols, Cixous does not merely valorize the *materrenelle*, woman as Mother Earth or earth mother.[93] Like Irigaray, she consistently exploits the age-old association of mother and water, capitalizing on the homophony between *mère/mer:* "it's my mother! The sea floats her, ripples her, flows together with her daughter, in all our ways. Then unseparated they sweep along their changing waters, without fear of their bodies, without bony stiffness, without a shell. . . . And sea for mother (*mer pour mère*) gives herself up to pleasure in her bath of writing."[94] While Cixous may favor topoi of the continuity and variety of the rhythms and songs of "our women's waters,"[95] both she and Irigaray uphold the unceasing movement (*mouvance*) of the sea as the very symbol of the feminine elsewhere.[96] Notwithstanding Irigaray's extended critique of Plato's identification of women and water in *Speculum, de l'autre femme*, the terrifying storminess of the sea which eludes mastery, even destroys identity, and its enchanting mysteries, which connote unfathomable alterity, are enlisted in her apotheosis of the liquid mother as the ultimate source of difference.[97]

Going beyond the global implications of the sea, Irigaray highlights an essential fluidity in/among women. Rejecting the notion of self and other as part of binary phalloeconomy, she depicts the feminine body/bodies in "When Our Lips Speak Together" as "always one and the other at the same time," open and shared, wall-less and boundless in multiplicity.[98] Women's capacity for an (over)flowing diffusiveness that is "alien to unity"[99] is opposed to the phallocentric mentality fixated on "the privilege, domination, and sollipsism of the One."[100] And the rigid hardness or "the solid that the penis represents"[101] is contrasted to an intrauterine, amniotically fluid sexuality, which Irigaray identifies as specifically feminine: "the sea (*marin*) element, as an attempt to mark a difference, is both the amniotic waters . . . and also . . . the movement of the sea, the coming and going, the continual flux. [It] seems to me quite close to my *jouissance* as a woman, completely foreign to an economy of erection and tumescence."[102] Not surprisingly, then, "When Our Lips Speak Together" constitutes a paean to the female as *amante marine:*

> How can I speak you, who remain in a flux that never congeals or solidifies? How can this current pass into words? It is multiple . . . ; yet it is not decomposable. . . . These streams don't flow into one, definitive sea; these rivers have no permanent banks; this body no fixed borders. This unceasing mobility, this life. Which they might describe as our restlessness, whims, pretenses or lies. For all this seems so strange to those who claim "solidity" as their foundation. Speak, nevertheless. Between us, "hardness" is not the rule. . . . Our density can do without the sharp edges of rigidity. We are not attracted to dead bodies.[103]

In this evocation of fluidity, softness, movement, life, antithetical to masculine solidity, hardness, rigidity, and death, the feminine, the devalued term in phallologic, becomes the superior value, but the system of binary oppositions remains the same. Indeed, in their maternal metaphorizations, Irigaray, Cixous, and Kristeva countervalorize the traditional antithesis that identifies man with culture and confines woman to instinctual nature, "always childlike, always savage."[104] And they reproduce the dichotomy between male rationality and female materiality, corporeality, and sexuality, which Irigaray has traced to Plato and Plotinus.[105] The noncultural, nonintellectual, feminine elsewhere also suggests a return to Plato's cave redefined as a uterine symbol.[106] Rejected by classical thinkers in favor of external reality, that shadowy, nocturnal, oneiric domain[107] is extolled by Romantics and exponents of difference as the interior locus of mystery and creativity. "I want to remain nocturnal and find again . . . my softly luminous night," intones Irigaray's "Lips."[108] Ultimately, the maternal-feminine is the mysterious black continent, which Freud, symbol of protophallic man, feared, colonized, and debased as *la contrée du con.*[109] By contrast, the Cixousian "I" instructs the future feminine explorers:

> To enter the domain where you can reclaim your nursling you will . . . have split the eardrums of resignation's preachers, punctured the crust of death's throes, threading your way into its entrails, into the black continent where women don't kill their dead. They relodge them in their flesh by bits scrupulously tasted . . . woman proceeds black in the black/feminine. . . . We who know that love illuminates and who have heard the psalms of the black continent and made them reverberate . . . we can affirm that black radiates, that the country of femininity reserves for us the most dazzling revelations.[110]

In this critical passage, the maternal-feminine voice moves from the future perfect to a present that proclaims "dazzling revelations." Judging from the present texts that explore *la différence féminine*, however, the maternal metaphor does not produce revelations so much as revalorizations or re-lodgings of topoi, images, and myths embedded in binary phallologic. Do these make an elsewhere reverberate? Do they signal movement *(mouvance)* to another place when inscribed by maternal women, and just because they are inscribed by women? Or is this a utopian vision that denies the bind of the present imperfect?

In more circumspect terms, Cixous has suggested that while we strive to "puncture the system of couples and oppositions,"[111] *l'écriture féminine* must first steal *(voler)* male discourse in order to explode and fly *(voler)* beyond it:

> If woman has always functioned "within" the discourse of man . . . it is time for her to dislocate this "within," to explode it, turn it around, and seize it; to make it hers, containing it, taking it into her own mouth, biting that tongue with her very own teeth to invent for herself a language to get inside of. And you'll see with what ease she will spring from that "within"—the "within" where once she so drowsily crouched.[112]

Undeniably, the maternal metaphor exemplifies women "getting within," seizing, powerfully manipulating male discourse on women. Through ex-tended play with signifiers and signifieds, the traditional conception of the maternal is expanded, swollen with meanings that move to the limits of the same. That feat alone should not be minimized in a system that equates femininity with passivity and silence; at the very least, then, these expo-nents of the feminine give voice to woman as a potently poetical/theoretical speaking subject. But the maternal metaphor, in my view, does not herald the invention of a different poetic or conceptual idiom. Indeed, it under-scores not "the ease" but the unease of "springing from within" to a radical elsewhere.

Like Cixous, Irigaray has emphasized the necessity, even the desirability of reappropriating the feminine "within" binary phalloeconomy:

> In the first stage, there is, perhaps, only a single "way," that which has historically been assigned the feminine: *mimeticism*. It's a matter of assuming this role deliberately, which is already to transform subordination into af-firmation, and thereby to start spoiling the game. . . . To play at mimesis is, then, for a woman, to try to rediscover the locus of her exploitation by discourse, without being simply reduced to it. It is to resubmit herself . . . to "ideas" about her, elaborated in/by a masculine logic, but in order to "mani-fest" by ludic repetition what was to remain hidden: the recovery of a pos-sible operation of the feminine in language. It is also to "unveil" the fact that if women mime so well it's because they cannot simply be reabsorbed in that function. *They also remain elsewhere.*[113]

Despite the seductiveness of Irigaray's logic, the repetition of masculinist notions and images of the feminine does not necessarily have a ludic or subversive impact that points to an elsewhere. The adoption of the mimetic function, traditionally assigned to woman, may freeze and fixate the feminine at the mirror stage, rather than lead to a difference beyond the same old binary plays. As Irigaray herself recognizes, a revalorization that is "a simple reversal," a displacement of positive/negative value from one term to another in binary structures, "finally comes back to the same. To phallocratism."[114] While *l'écriture au maternel* is anything but "simple," Irigaray's awareness does not preclude internalization, what Cixous terms "the risk of identification,"[115] and thus an enduring confinement within the parameters of the dominant discourse. In fact, since it depicts the maternal-feminine as voice, breast, giving, loving, plurality, fluidity, sea, nature, and body—this metaphorical body of work may be viewed, somewhat perversely perhaps, not as an elaboration of the unrepresented/unrepresentable, but rather—to use a metaphor—as an offspring delivered by/from the father; an appealing, empowering reproduction, not a different production. The assertion that the maternal constitutes the crucial difference even evokes the stance of the phallic mother, who lays down the Law of the father, rather than lays waste to it; who keeps, in so many words, both the symbolic baby and the bathwater.

III

> . . . "that's not it" . . . "that's still not it" . . .
>
> —Julia Kristeva

That the maternal-feminine remains within sameness is, of course, no reason to bathe in despair or banish poetic women to silence. More usefully, this corpus underscores the need to confront the inescapable fact that any inscription of difference is (over)determined by the indifferent dominant discourse. As Derrida suggests in "The Law of Genre," the symbolic order needs transgressions to sustain it; transgressions need the order to define their specificity; and thus, order and dis-order are inextricably bound one with the other. In this respect, Irigaray's "And the One Doesn't Stir Without the Other," a text that describes the daughter's attempts and failures to free herself from the mother, may be read as a metaphor for the inability to achieve freedom from the body of law, and that includes the maternal and the metaphorical.[116]

Metaphoricity and binarism may be our (present) destiny. But the aware-ness that sameness permeates all efforts to speak difference, and further, that every alternative practice tends to erect itself as ultimate authority can instill the imperative of unceasing vigilance and self-interrogation. This "permanent analytical attitude," which Kristeva defines as dissidence it-self,[117] is elaborated in her essay, "Semiology: A Critical Science and/or a Critique of Science":

> semiology is, each time, a reevaluation of its object and/or its models, a critique of its models (and thus the sciences from which they are taken) and of itself (as system of constant truths). An intersection of sciences and of a theoretical process always in progress, semiology cannot constitute itself as one science, even less as *the* science: it is an open path of research, a constant critique that turns back on itself, in other words, an autocritique.[118]

Although it represents a demanding ideal, which semiology itself has failed to realize, autocriticism needs to be interwoven in the fabric of *l'écriture au maternel*. It is not enough to proclaim a future feminine born "in the light of questions," the possessor of "a Gay ignorance,"[119] which is contradicted by essentialist propositions on woman-as-mother. Instead, there should be a critical negation of the negation, not toward some imperial, Hegelian pinnacle, but as an ongoing process with (a) telos. Thus the symbolic func-tion that Kristeva ascribes to woman—"negative, in opposition to what exists, in order to say, 'that's not it,' and 'that's still not it' "[120]—should be inherent in explorations of *la différence féminine* and directed at the ma-ternal metaphor.

This is not to deny the importance of an initial counter-valorization of the maternal-feminine as a negation/subversion of paternal hierarchies, a heuristic tool for reworking images and meanings, above all, an enabling mythology.[121] But the moment the maternal emerges as a new dominance, it must be put into question before it congeals as feminine essence, as unchanging in-difference. In my view, inscriptions of the maternal meta-phor have reached the symbolic point outlined in Monique Wittig's epic *Les Guérillères*, when the women recognize that their feminaries, which are filled with images and symbols, "have fulfilled their function"[122]: "They say that at the point they have reached they must examine the principle that has guided them. They say it is not for them to exhaust their strength in symbols."[123] Closer to home, that critical voice has been assumed by trans-Atlantic feminists weighing *The Future of Difference*. "Do we want to continue reorganizing the relationship of difference to sameness through the dialectics of valorization," asks Alice Jardine, "or is there a way to break down the overdetermined metaphors which continue to organize our perceptions of reality?"[124] More specifically, Christiane Makward warns that "the [French] theory of femininity is dangerously close to recreating in 'deconstructive' language the traditional assumptions on femininity and female creativity,"[125] while Josette Féral cautions against neofeminine values becoming "newly imposed norms, thereby reinstituting an antisystem that would be just as repressive . . . a new dictatorship."[126]

Assuming the role of vigilant/dissident same/other, the trans-Atlantic feminist could also propose that the maternal as metaphor for *la différence féminine* undergo a symbolic renomination. In this tentative scheme, "feminine," a signifier that seems to serve, in retrospect, to activate patriarchal scenes and topoi, would be replaced by "female," and, more important, the status of the "maternal" would be displaced from metaphor to metonymy.[127] For the maternal, which is metaphorized as total being to substantiate a notion that can combat the paternal, represents only one aspect of potential female difference. To be sure, this displacement onto the metonymic is not innocent. It promotes a shift from the principal, indeed obsessive, preoccupation with the "difference from" man, which underlies the maternal-feminine, to "differences within" (a) woman, and "among" women; for if all women are maternal, where's the difference(s)? At the same time, this proposed displacement does not imply the (re)discovery of a virgin space free of phallocratic modes of thinking, much less of outworn metaphors. The conventional opposition between metaphor and metonymy, like Irigaray's distinction between metaphoric solidity and metonymic fluidity,[128] still partakes of binary thinking.

Because of that discursive bind, I put "metonymy" into question, under erasure, even as I argue, after Lacan, that this figure evokes the more numerous elements that are missing and thus, in contrast to metaphor, suggests lack of being.[129] Because it does not cross the bar to truth, according to the French Freud, metonymy underscores the desire for the other, for something/somewhere else, a desire extended along an indefinite chain of signifiers by substitution, by a displacement that wanders off the subject.[130] By that token, a reconception of the maternal as a metonymy can help generate indefinite explorations of other desirable known and unknown female functions and effects. In traditional rhetorical terms that should appeal to modernist exponents of difference, metonymy represents the trope that cannot be defined; as Hugh Bredin observes, it is composed of a "raggle-taggle collection of those tropes for which we can find no other name."[131] The left-over,[132] the supplement that is multiple, metonymization can create propitious conditions within the present imperfect for speaking women in the plural, over and beyond the trinitarian mother, child, and the holy ghost of *illa*.

No less critical for my purpose is the possibility that the metonymic process would favor more concrete, contextual inscriptions of differences within/among women. Because of its association with contiguity, metonymy is context-bound, says Bredin, thus it exposes specific cultural values, prejudices, and limitations.[133] By analogy and extension, metonymization would promote the recognition that the mother cannot symbolize an untainted origin, isolated in a virgin black continent, and as such, an unbounded source or force of subversion; but rather, that this idea(l) is always/ already inhabited by, and accomplice to, the workings of contextual phallogocentric structures. After all, even Demeter's daughter lives half the year in the masculine, Hadean realm. So saying, I endorse for the moment Jakobson's decidedly arbitrary claim that the metonymic pole characterizes realistic narratives.[134] I do so not simply to reemphasize a needed awareness of the essentialist traps of Romantic fictions and poetic symbols. I do so primarily to promote female practices grounded in contextual, sociohistorical discourses. A metonymic practice should/would displace focus from the utopian arche or future to the imperfect past/present in which all processes of exploration are located and all discoveries must begin.

It would also be utopian, however, to uphold the more metonymic studies of American feminist scholars as models for undoing the fixation on the metaphorical process among French exponents of *la différence maternelle*. Although the American work on the maternal, which has proliferated since 1975, has concentrated on sociohistorical critiques of institutions, it still contains distinctly metaphorical tendencies and traits, which are nonetheless denied in the name of a political criticism rooted in the real.[135] Even more, this discourse on the maternal has undeniable traces of essentialism, which can be detected in the influential texts of Adrienne Rich and Nancy Chodorow, but are most dramatically revealed in Sara Ruddick's "Maternal Thinking."[136] These multidisciplinary studies repeatedly extol pre-oedipal unboundedness, relatedness, plurality, fluidity, tenderness, and nurturance in the name of the difference of female identity. Indeed, in what appears to be a repetition, compulsion or contagion, today those "different" traits are being reproduced far more extensively and intensively in America than in France.

That women in two cultures with distinct philosophical and methodological traditions have hypostasized the maternal in the same decade leads the trans-Atlantic feminist to ask what exigencies their discourses fulfill. In what can only be a partial and ambiguous answer, this body of work surely marks, on one level, the explosive return of the repression of maternity in postwar feminist thought until the late 1960s. Moreover, by exposing the suppressed mother/daughter bond, the work has served to validate and cultivate gynocentric connections and lineages. In fact, the metaphorization of the mother/daughter relation has provided an important vehicle for depicting lesbian love and dramatizing a lesbian continuum in opposition to homophobic, hegemonic discourse. At the same time, the maternal may also satisfy conservative and fundamentalist imperatives allied with the (re)assertion of "traditional values," and right-wing politics, even the irruption of militant religiosity. And from yet another perspective, the life-engendering, future-oriented vision of the maternal may be a compensatory response to a world imperiled by nuclear extinction. Whatever other global or partial factors may obtain,[137] the overdetermination of the maternal militates against our overcoming the conceptual impasse it represents. To displace/replace the maternal as the metaphor for female difference, and to conceive more compelling metonymic visions, may not be feasible at present, but must become the possibility of the future.[138]

There is no final analysis, no solution, nor should there be. Inevitably, however, predictably perhaps, the problematics of the maternal metaphor makes it imperative to question difference itself as the privileged construct of modernist masters. As Nancy Chodorow argues in *The Future of Difference*, "men have a psychological investment in difference that women do not have"; and, going further, Jessica Benjamin insists that "in theory and practice, our culture," even "Western rationality . . . knows only one form of individuality: the male stance of overdifferentiation."[139] While those ideas are still binary-bound—but then, what idea is not?—they reinforce the possibility that difference as teleology is part of the phallocentric design. Thus they underscore the importance of deferring any affirmation of essential difference between male and female subjects bound within the same discursive order. But even that idea is not different, as Derrideans will confirm; nor is it phallogo-free. For metonymic deferral, postponement, or putting off ironically represents the traditional feminine posture whenever a question of inter(dis)course arises. Nevertheless, in the present imperfect, that putting off is the more desirable course for diverse female explorations than excessive, tumescent metaforeplay.

NOTES

1. Luce Irigaray, *Éthique de la différence sexuelle* (Paris: Éditions de Minuit, 1984), 13 (hereafter cited as *Éthique*).

This essay is, in some ways, a continuation of my "Language and Revolution: The Franco-American Dis-Connection," wherein I focused on the same three writers and interpreted their theories on the revolutionary force of the feminine as poetic discourse. See Stanton, "Language and Revolution: The Franco-American Dis-Connection," in *The Future of Difference*, ed. Hester Eisenstein and Alice Jardine (Boston: G. K. Hall, 1980), 75, 80–82. However, whereas I then urged American feminist critics to be receptive to the challenge of this body of work, the present essay, written five years after the first, expresses in much stronger terms a concern about a mystification of the feminine and, more generally, about the difficulties of getting "outside" phallogocentrism. In retrospect, I regard the two essays as complementary; they assume a different oppositional stance in response to what I perceive(d) as emerging or dominant tendencies or blindspots within American feminist criticism. An earlier version of this essay was read at the universities of Michigan and Montreal in 1982. Unless otherwise indicated, the translations are mine.

2. According to Ricoeur, for instance, "metaphorical utterance brings an unknown referential field toward language, and within the ambit of this field, the semantic aim functions and unfolds." And for Lacan, metaphor represents a "crossing of the bar" of repression that allows meaning to emerge "as a poetic or creative effect." See Paul Ricoeur, *The Rule of Metaphor*, trans. Robert Czerny (Toronto University Press, 1977), 299; and Jacques Lacan, *Ecrits* (Paris: Éditions du Seuil, 1966), 515.

3. Julia Kristeva, *Histoires d'amour* (Paris: Denoël, 1983), 254, 344 (hereafter cited as *Histoires*).

4. Alice Jardine, "Gynesis," *Diacritics*, Special Issue: "Cherchez la femme," (Summer 1982), 54–63.

5. Discrete references to this influence appear in Josette Féral, "The Powers of Difference," in *The Future of Difference*, ed. Hester Eisenstein and Alice Jardine; in Christiane Makward, "To Be or Not to Be . . . A Feminist Speaker," in *The Future of Difference*; in Gayatri Chakravorty Spivak, "French Feminism in an International Frame," *Yale French Studies*, Issue on "Feminist Readings: French Texts/American Contexts" 62(1981):170–73; and more extensively in relation to Lacan, in Jane Gallop's *The Daughter's Seduction: Feminism and Psychoanalysis* (Ithaca: Cornell University Press, 1982).

6. Hélène Cixous, *La* (Paris: Gallimard, 1976), 80.

7. Luce Irigaray, *Ce Sexe qui n'en est pas un* (Paris: Éditions de Minuit, 1977), 67ff. (hereafter cited as *Sexe*).

8. Hélène Cixous, *Illa* (Paris: Éditions des Femmes, 1980), 65.

9. It must be emphasized that this is not a systematic analysis of the maternal metaphor in contemporary French women's writing, which would have to include, for example, texts by Chantal Chawaf, Marguerite Duras, Sarah Kofman, Eugénie Lemoine-Luccioni, Marcelle Marini, and Michèle Montrelay. Nor is this a systematic study of the work of Cixous, Irigaray, and Kristeva, but rather a symptomatic reading of some texts published in the last decade. It goes without saying that their dense and demanding texts cannot be reduced to an inscription of the maternal metaphor.

10. Irigaray, *Éthique*, passim.

11. Cixous, *Illa*, 122, 204.

12. Irigaray, *Éthique*, 27.

13. Julia Kristeva, *La Révolution du langage poétique* (Paris: Éditions du Seuil, 1974), 499–500 (hereafter cited as *Révolution*).

14. Hélène Cixous, *La Jeune Née* (Paris: Union Générale d'Éditions [10/18], 1975), 166 (hereafter cited as *Jeune*).

15. Julia Kristeva, "Héréthique de l'amour," *Tel Quel*, Special Issue: "Recherches féminines" (Winter 1977), 74(30–49):30 (hereafter cited as "Héréthique," *Quel*).

16. Julia Kristeva, "Un nouveau type d'intellectuel," *Tel Quel*, Special Issue: "Re-

cherches féminines" (Winter 1977), 74(3–8):6–7 (hereafter cited as "Un nouveau," *Quel*).

17. Cixous, *Jeune*, 152–53. See also Irigaray, *Ce Sexe*, 123–25. However, as I argued in "Language and Revolution," these exponents of difference regard their work as profoundly political, or at least, as Cixous puts it, "poetically political, politically poetic" (Verena Andermatt Conley, *Hélène Cixous: Writing in the Feminine* [Lincoln: University of Nebraska Press, 1984], 139ff.).

18. Kristeva, "Un nouveau," *Quel*, 6–7.

19. Irigaray, *Sexe*, 140.

20. In Luce Irigaray, *L'Oubli de l'air* (Paris: Éditions de Minuit, 1983), which could be entitled *L'Oubli de la mère*, the repression or forgetting of the mother is considered by Irigaray the foundation of the Western conception of Being.

21. Luce Irigaray, *Le Corps-à-corps avec la mère* (Ottawa: Éditions de la pleine lune, 1981), 25, 27, 86 (hereafter cited as *Corps*).

22. Irigaray, *Éthique*, 70, 71, 143.

23. Hélène Cixous, "The Laugh of the Medusa," trans. Keith Cohen and Paula Cohen, *Signs: Journal of Women in Culture and Society* 1:4(Summer 1976):875–93 (hereafter cited as "Laugh," *Signs*).

24. Cixous, *Jeune*, 173.

25. Hélène Cixous, "La Venue à l'écriture," In Cixous, Madeleine Gagnon, and Annie Leclerc, *La Venue à l'écriture* (Paris: Union Générale d'Éditions [10/18], 1977), 56 (hereafter cited as *Venue*).

26. Cixous, "Laugh," *Signs*, 882; Cixous, *Jeune*, 271.

27. Irigaray, *Sexe*, 108.

28. Irigaray, *Éthique*, 103.

29. Quoted in Carolyn Burke, "Rethinking the Maternal," in *The Future of Difference*, 112.

30. Jacques Derrida, "White Mythology: Metaphor in the Text of Philosophy," trans. F. C. T. Moore, *New Literary History* 6:1(Autumn 1974):50.

31. Opposition to the Derridean/Heideggerian view of metaphor has been voiced by Ricoeur, *The Rule of Metaphor*, 257–311, among others.

32. Julia Kristeva, *Powers of Horror*, trans. Leon Roudiez (New York: Columbia University Press, 1982), 53.

33. In *Histoires d'amour*, Kristeva confronts the metaphysical implications of metaphor and attempts to circumvent the problem posed by Derrida by relocating the production of metaphor to the transference between analysand and analyst and, by analogy, the transference of affect between two lovers.

34. Kristeva, *Révolution*, 489.

35. Julia Kristeva, *Desire in Language: A Semiotic Approach to Literature and Art*, ed. Leon Roudiez, trans. Tom Gora, Alice Jardine, and Leon Roudiez (New York: Columbia University Press, 1980), 238 (hereafter cited as *Desire*).

36. Kristeva, "Héréthique," *Quel*, 47.

37. Kristeva, *Desire*, 243.

38. Julia Kristeva, *Polylogue* (Paris: Éditions du Seuil, 1977), 519.

39. Kristeva, "Un nouveau," *Quel*, 7.

40. Irigaray, *Sexe*, 75.

41. Irigaray, *Éthique*, 71, 139.

42. Irigaray, *Sexe*, 74, 77.

43. Cixous, *Jeune*, 152; Luce Irigaray, *Amante marine: de Friedrich Nietzsche* (Paris: Éditions de Minuit, 1980), 91 (hereafter cited as *Amante*).

44. Hélène Cixous, *With ou l'art de 1'innocence* (Paris: Éditions des Femmes, 1981), 185 (hereafter cited as *With*).

45. Cixous, "Laugh," *Signs*, 878.

46. Cixous, *With*, 89.

47. Hélèn Cixous, *Vivre l'orange* (Paris: Éditions des Femmes, 1979), 13 (hereafter cited as *Vivre*).

48. Cixous, *With*, 90.

49. Cixous, *Illa*, 99, 129, 183.

50. Ibid., 148.

51. Cixous, *Vivre*, 72, 74.

52. Gayatri Chakravorty Spivak, "French Feminism in an International Frame," 170–73.

53. Mary Jacobus has argued that *l'écriture au féminin* is not essentialistic, but that it is constrained by the conditions of representability (Jacobus, "Is There a Woman in This Text?" *New Literary History* (1982):139). Elizabeth L. Berg, however, shares my concern for the essentialism of the maternal and the metaphysics of presence it sustains (Berg, "The Third Woman," *Diacritics* (Summer 1982):11–20).

54. Pierre Fontanier, *Les Figures du discours*, ed. Gérard Genette (Paris: Flammarion, 1968), 213. On catachresis, see also Derrida, "White Mythology," 57, and Ricoeur, *The Rule of Metaphor*,62ff.

55. Cixous, *Jeune*, 153.

56. Kristeva, *Histoires*, 258.

57. Sigmund Freud, *The Standard Edition of the Complete Pyschological Works*, 25 vols. (London: The Hogarth Press, 1975), 21:226; 22:119, 130.

58. Irigaray, *Sexe*, 46, 136.

59. Cixous, *Illa*, 37.

60. Ibid., 203–9.

61. Ibid., 205.

62. Ibid., 121.

63. Irigaray, *Sexe*, 61.

64. Cixous, *With*, 201. In *With*, which implies "to be with child," the origin and telos of the feminine is conceived as a "pre-legal childhood" (67) of freedom, joy, and especially of "innocence beyond ignorance" (139), which is personified by Aura. The same pre-oedipal qualities are ascribed to the unbound, "delivered" female lover in *Le Livre de Promethea*.

65. Julia Kristeva, *On Chinese Women*, trans. Anita Barros (New York: Urizen Press, 1976), 58; Julia Kristeva, *Revolution in Poetic Language*, ed. Leon Roudiez, trans. Margaret Waller (New York: Columbia University Press, 1984), 68 (hereafter cited as *Revolution*, trans. Waller).

66. Kristeva, *Desire*, 136.

67. Kristeva, *Revolution*, trans. Waller, 81.

68. Ibid., 62ff.

69. Ibid., p. 79.

70. Kristeva, *Polylogue*, 74.

71. Kristeva, *Revolution*, trans. Waller, 63; Kristeva, *Polylogue*, 73.

72. Kristeva, *Révolution*, 612.

73. Kristeva, *Desire*, 136.

74. Kristeva, *Polylogue*, 86; Kristeva, *Desire*, 138, 191.

75. Kristeva, *Polylogue*, 475.

76. Kristeva, *Desire*, 240.

77. The only female writer discussed in Kristeva's work is the seventeenth-century mystic, Jeanne Guyon (*Histoires*, 277–96). With one or two exceptions, notably in *Histoires*, Kristeva's texts deal solely with avant-garde male writers from Mallarmé to Sollers.

78. Kristeva, *Desire*, 242.

79. Cixous, *Jeune*, 170.

80. Ibid., 170, 172.

81. Cixous, *Illa*, 208.

82. Ibid., 168.

83. Cixous, *Jeune*, 173.

84. Ibid.

85. Cixous, *With*, 120, 202.

86. Cixous, *Illa*, 129–30.

87. Ibid., 104.

88. Ibid., 196.

89. Cixous, "Laugh," *Signs*, 893.

90. Cixous, *With*, 219.

91. Cixous, *Illa*, 32.

92. Ibid., 140, 187, 194–95, 155, 159, 133, 74, 141.

93. Cixous, *With*, 201.

94. Cixous, *La*, 143.

95. Cixous *Venue*, 62.

96. Irigaray, *Amante*, 19.

97. Even air, the irreducible, but forgotten, element explored in *L'Oubli de l'air* is consistently liquefied and maternalized as "the first fluid along with blood given freely and unconditionally in the mother" (Éthique, 122). See also *L'Oubli*, 16, 31, 34–38, 77–78.

98. Luce Irigaray, "When Our Lips Speak Together," trans. Carolyn Burke, *Signs: Journal of Women in Culture and Society* 6:1(Autumn 1980):72–73 (hereafter cited as "Lips," *Signs*).

99. Irigaray, *Amante*, 92. The capacty to overflow has led Irigaray and Cixous to idealize feminine hysteria, even madness (*Corps*, 82; *Jeune*, 161–68), and Kristeva to probe the abject that lacks ego boundaries (*Powers of Horror*). Moreover, an element like the mucous, which eludes both numerical order and fixity, and which "always [becomes] the fluid, merges boundaries" (*Passions élémentaires* [Paris: Éditions de Minuit, 1982], 18) is, in Irigaray's view, imperative for "thought of or in the feminine" (*Éthique*, 107–8).

100. Irigary, *Sexe*, 270.

101. Ibid., 112.

102. Irigaray, *Corps*, 49.

103. Irigary, "Lips," *Signs*, 76–77.

104. Cixous, *Jeune*, 57.

105. Luce Irigaray, *Speculum, de l'autre femme* (Paris: Éditions de Minuit, 1974), 210–25, 375.

106. Ibid., 347.

107. Ibid., 386.

108. Irigaray, "Lips," *Signs*, 78. See the opposition between mother/night and male/day in *L'Oubli de l'air*, 50, 90, 99; see also *Passions élémentaires*, 46ff.; *Éthique*, 144–45.

109. Cixous, "Laugh," *Signs*, 879.

110. Hélène Cixous, *Souffles* (Paris: Éditions des Femmes, 1975), 147–48.

111. Cixous, *Jeune*, 179.

112. Cixous, "Laugh," *Signs*, 887.

113. Irigaray, *Sexe*, 73–74.

114. Ibid., 32, 78.

115. Cixous, "Laugh," *Signs*, 887.

116. See Jacques Derrida, "The Law of Genre," trans. Avital Ronell, *Glyph* 7(1980):205; and Luce Irigaray, "And the One Doesn't Stir Without the Other," trans. Hélène Vivienne Wenzil, *Signs: Journal of Women in Culture and Society* 7:1(Autumn 1981):60–67.

117. Kristeva, "Un nouveau," *Quel*, 7.

118. Julia Kristeva, "La Sémiotique, science critique et/ou critique de la science," *Semeiotiké: Recherches pour une sémanalyse* (Paris: Éditions du Seuil, 1969), 30.

119. Cixous, *Illa*, 208, 211.

120. Kristeva, *Polyloque*, 519.

121. See Elizabeth Abel, ed., *Writing and Sexual Difference* (Chicago: University of Chicago Press, 1982), Preface, 6.

122. Monique Wittig, *Les Guérillères*, trans. David Le Vay (New York: Avon, 1973), 49.

123. Ibid., 72. It is possible that some such examination of their *modus operandi* informs the most recent texts of Cixous and Kristeva. As Conley observes, Cixous's "desire to write *with* presence"—indeed, as *Le Livre de Promethea* indicates, to depict the "real," "true" female other accurately and faithfully—may represent, notwithstanding the impossible nature of this goal, "a writing-out of a certain guilt for . . . taking the metaphoric vehicle" (*Hélène Cixous: Writing in the Feminine*, 124). Although Kristeva's *Histoires* upholds the idealistic conception of metaphor, her analyses of literary texts and psychoanalytic cases are not markedly metaphoric. Irigaray's *modus scribandi* has not changed, although her focus of concern in *Éthique* is the ethics of relations between the sexes founded on acceptance of sexual (maternal) difference.

124. Alice Jardine, "Prelude: The Future of Difference," in *The Future of Difference*, xxvi.

125. Christiane Makward, "To Be or Not to Be . . . A Feminist Speaker," 96.

126. Josette Féral, "The Powers Of Difference," 92.

127. In keeping with recent practice (e.g., Jakobson and Lacan), I take metonymy to include synecdoche, although the two were considered different tropes in traditional rhetoric (e.g., Quintilian, Ramus, Fontanier); see Hugh Bredin, "Metonymy," *Poetics Today* 5:1(1984):45–58 (hereafter cited as *Poetics*). However, Naomi Schor has privileged synecdoche in elaborating what she calls a "clitoral theory" of writing; see "Female Paranoia: The Case for Psychoanalytic Feminist Criticism," *Yale French Studies* 62(1981):219.

128. Irigaray, *Sexe*, 108ff.

129. Jacques Lacan, *Ecrits* (Paris: Éditions du Seuil, 1966), 515, 528.

130. Ibid., 515, 528.

131. Bredin, *Poetics*, 47.

132. Ibid., 50.

133. Ibid., 57–58.

134. Roman Jakobson, "Two Aspects of Language and Two Types of Aphasic Disturbances," in *Fundamentals of Language* (The Hague: Mouton, 1956), 76–82. Jakobson's often-cited polarization and characterization of the metaphoric and the metonymic have been criticized by Ricoeur (*The Rule of Metaphor*, 178ff.) and Maria Ruegg, "Metaphor and Metonymy: The Logic of Structuralist Rhetoric," *Glyph* 6(1977):141–57, among others.

135. Because of the dimensions of this body of work, I refer the reader to Marianne Hirsch's very useful review essay, "Mothers and Daughters," in *Signs: Journal of Women in Culture and Society* 7(Autumn 1981):200–222. See also Jane Gallop's critique of this work, "The Difference Within," in *Writing and Sexual Difference*, Elizabeth Abel, ed. (Chicago: University of Chicago Press, 1982).

136. Adrienne Rich, *Of Woman Born* (New York: Norton, 1976); Nancy Chodorow, *The Reproduction of Mothering* (Berkeley: University of California Press, 1978); and Sara Ruddick, "Maternal Thinking," *Feminist Studies* 6(Summer 1980):342–67.

137. For instance, the timing of the maternal fixation could be related to the ticking of the biological clock for a generation of female/feminist critics who "came of age" during the last decade and, more paradoxically perhaps, to the legalization of abortion in France (1974) and America (1973).

138. I note that Cixous's *Le Livre de Promethea*, Irigaray's *Éthique*, and Kristeva's *Histoires* all privilege women as lover in her relation to man or, in Cixous's case, to women. Although its inscriptions do not seem nearly as rich or powerful as the maternal, this notion may signal a new departure or more of the same; only time and texts will tell.

139. Nancy Chodorow, "Gender, Relation, and Difference in Psychoanalytic Practice," in *The Future of Difference*, 14; Jessica Benjamin, "The Bonds of Love: Rational Violence and Erotic Domination," *The Future of Difference*, 45–46.

QUESTIONS FOR JULIA KRISTEVA'S ETHICS OF LINGUISTICS

Eléanor H. Kuykendall

What is knowledge of language? For Ferdinand de Saussure, it is the speaker's use of signs, accepted by social consensus to constitute language, or *la langue*. For Noam Chomsky, it is the speaker's understanding grammar and word meaning, or linguistic competence. For Jacques Lacan, it is the speaker's accepting symbolic meaning, or renouncing forbidden unconscious desires and becoming a separate subject. But in "The Ethics of Linguistics"[1] Julia Kristeva proposes expanding conceptions of language and its knowledge to include rhythmic and tonal—prosodic—interventions in uses of signs, syntax, and symbols. The speaker or writer alternates between syntactic and symbolic, and prosodic communication, perpetually recreating a decentered, divided subjectivity in process. Kristeva proposes that linguistics and its allied disciplines be obligated to disclose the unconscious origins of this divided subjectivity to speakers and writers.

In that which follows I want to show that Julia Kristeva's conceptions of language and its knowledge—which extend the Saussurian conception of the sign, reject the Chomskyan conception of the rational speaker, and revise the Lacanian conception of the separate speaking subject—clash with her conception of ethics itself, an ethics which leaves a Lacanian conception of subjectivity in place. First, I offer a brief account of what Kristeva takes an ethics of linguistics to be and why, for her, psychoanalysis has a positive role in it. Second, I ask whether the "speaking subject" of Kristeva's argument is masculine, gender-neutral, or possibly feminine. I do this by comparing interpretations of Freud's famous example of language acquisition—a child's game with a spool while uttering the words "fort" ("gone") and "da" (here)—by Lacan, by Kristeva herself, and by Jacques

Derrida and Luce Irigaray. Third, I conclude that Kristeva's conception of ethics, which characterizes the feminine as "outlaw" or "heretical" and thus outside ethics entirely, renders a conception of "female subjectivity," at best, problematic[2] and at worst, a contradiction in terms. Despite the apparent centrality of the feminine in her writings on maternity, Kristeva's ethics of linguistics is not, finally, feminist, in a sense of the term that Americans would accept,[3] in that it is avowedly Freudian and leaves no place for a feminine conception of agency.

I

What does Kristeva take an ethics of linguistics to be? And why, for her, does psychoanalysis have a positive role in it? Kristeva both rejects Chomskyan rationality and revises a narrowly conceived Freudian and Lacanian conception of symbolic meaning. She also proposes a positive program to expand the Saussurian conception of the linguistic sign. Psychoanalysis plays a positive role in her ethics of linguistics by helping to describe interventions in symbolic meaning "admitting of upheaval, dissolution, and transformation," in which the "social constraint" perpetuated by descriptions of language as "signified structure" is also disrupted, "with the speaking subject leaving its imprint on the dialectic between the articulation and its process."[4]

Kristeva's ethics of linguistics rejects Chomskyan rationality and revises Lacanian subjectivity. Her "Ethics of Linguistics" rejects Chomsky (whom she does not name in that essay though she does elsewhere[5]), by rejecting Chomsky's conception of the primary object of inquiry—the sentence—as well as Chomsky's conception of what the speaker knows—syntax and conventional meaning which conform to the law of contradiction. For Kristeva, Chomskyan linguistics err by imposing an adult generative model of knowledge of language both on the utterances of infants, whose communication precedes conventional language use, and also on adult poetic discourse and its semiotic interventions, which evince and recreate the unconscious desires of infants before they learn conventional syntax and symbols.[6]

Kristeva's ethics of linguistics not only rejects Chomskyan rationality, but also revises Lacanian subjectivity which repeats an error by Freud. Kristeva argues that Freud erred by attributing to the pre-speaking infant a relationship to the father and to discourse that can occur only after the child learns conventional meaning. Yet Kristeva also contends that Freud's error has not affected the structure of linguistics, which need only be expanded to include semiotics.[7] By extension, Lacan also erred, conflating the structure of semiotic communication during the pre-Oedipal mother-infant bond, with symbolic communication, which the (male) child must learn in and by separating from the mother and identifying with the father. Lacan's reinterpretation of Freud's account of the child's resolution of the Oedipus complex by learning the symbolic discourse of the father,[8] it follows, has not affected linguistics either.

Thus in presenting her positive proposal for an ethics of linguistics Kristeva leaves in place a Lacanian conception of the acquisition of symbols. This account does not differ structurally from Freud's account of the resolution of the Oedipus complex, in that both Freud and Lacan tie their accounts of language learning to a male child's identification with the father, acquisition of a superego or moral sense, and renunciation of forbidden erotic desires for his mother. Kristeva's proposal does, though, supplement a conception of the symbolic in which Freudian and Lacanian psychoanalysis continues to play a positive role, with her own conception of the semiotic, which she criticizes Freud and Lacan for overlooking.

Kristeva has repeatedly presented and reaffirmed a distinction between semiotic and symbolic meaning tied to Freudian and Lacanian psychoanalysis. For example, in her 1974 *Revolution in Poetic Language*, she offers the following definition of "semiotic," which is tied to Freud:

> We understand the term "semiotic" in its Greek sense: sémiotiké = distinctive mark, trace, index, precursory sign, proof, engraved or written sign, imprint, trace, figuration. . . . This modality is the one Freudian psychoanalysis points to in postulating not only the *facilitation* and the structuring *disposition* of drives, but also the so-called *primary processes* which displace and condense both energies and their inscription. Discrete quantities of energy move through the body of the subject who is not yet constituted as such and, in the course of his development, they are arranged according to the various constraints imposed on this body—always already involved in a semiotic process—by family and social structures. In this way the drives, which are "energy" charges as well as "psychical" marks, articulate what we call a *chora*: a nonexpressive totality formed by the drives and their stases in a motility that is full of movement as it is regulated. . . . [9]

Kristeva also offers the following definition of the symbolic, which is tied to Lacan:

> We shall distinguish the semiotic (drives and their articulations) from the realm of signification, which is always that of a proposition or judgment, in other words, a realm of *positions*. This positionality, which Husserlian phenomenology orchestrates through the concepts of *doxa, position*, and *thesis*, is structured as a break in the signifying process, establishing the *identification* of the subject and its object as preconditions of propositionality. We shall call this break, which produces the positing of signification, a *thetic* phase. All enunciation, whether of a word or of a sentence, is thetic. It

requires an identification; in other words, the subject must separate from and through his image, from and through his objects. This image and objects must first be posited in a space that becomes symbolic because it connects the two separated positions, recording them or redistributing them in an open combinatorial system.[10]

Despite many turns in Kristeva's work,[11] a constant theme remains her distinction between the semiotic and the symbolic, a theme which she argues in "The Ethics of Linguistics" as well as in other works. For example, she reaffirms it explicitly in her 1985 *Au commencement était l'amour*[12] and again in *Soleil Noir*, from 1987, where she writes: "The 'semiotic' and the 'symbolic' become the communicable marks of a present affective reality, perceptible to the reader (I like this book because it communicates sadness, anguish, or joy to me), and nevertheless dominated, separated, conquered . . . "[13]

Kristeva's method of countering the symbolic with the semiotic, as well as her conceptions of them, also holds constant. For example, in 1970 she described her inquiry into a subjectivity in process as a "logic of dialogism," in which there appears, first, a "logic of distance and of relation between different terms of a sentence or narrative structure" and, second, a "logic of analogy and of nonexclusive opposition, in opposition to the level of causality and of identifying determination." In the second stage of this process, a Chomskyan identification of syntax with logic and rationality is turned against itself.[14] In 1975 Kristeva wrote that the Freudian anti-logic of the first stage, with its opposition between separation and desire for merger, is perpetually recreated through the interventions of the semiotic into conventional syntax and sense.[15] The process is continual, dynamic, diachronic—it is a historical process taking place over time, so that the writer of the literary text, through the disintegrated perception of a subjectivity wrought by that text, is thereby transformed with the reader together as subject origins of an unconscious knowledge of language.[16]

Consequently Kristeva's ethics of linguistics, which is a negative rejection of Chomskyan rationality and a revised and elaborated version of Lacanian subjectivity, continues to embrace Freudian and Lacanian psychoanalysis. But, critical as she is of narrower Freudian and Lacanian conceptions of symbolic meaning, Kristeva leaves untouched their conception of ethics, which is tied to their account of (symbolic) language acquisition.

II

Is the "speaking subject"—revealed, for Kristeva, through interventions by the semiotic into symbolic meaning—masculine, gender-neutral, feminine, or simply absent? I want to consider alternative answers to this question given by Freud (in a famous example), by Lacan, by Kristeva herself, by Jacques Derrida, and by Luce Irigaray. Freud's and Lacan's accounts, of course, are "symbolic," in Kristeva's sense of the term. Kristeva's, in which, as we have seen, she postulates a perpetually dislocated and moving subject, I shall characterize as "adverbial;" and Derrida's and Irigaray's, as "performative."

Kristeva states both that Freud was wrong in supposing that language learning begins with learning symbolic meaning, and that his error has not affected linguistics. Compounding this apparent contradiction, Kristeva repeatedly cites as authoritative Freud's conception of symbolic language acquisition, which he ties to an account of the acquisition of the superego or moral sense. And she also endorses Lacan's interpretation of Freud's conception of language acquisition.[17]

Kristeva has reaffirmed these endorsements in her most recent writings. In *Au commencement était l'amour*, for example, she states: "The sadness of young children, their renunciation of maternal paradise and of the immediate satisfaction of their demands, which precedes the appearance of language, has frequently been observed. It is necessary to abandon the mother and to be abandoned by her in order that the father take me up and that I speak."[18] In *Soleil Noir* she writes,

> This identification which one might call phallic or symbolic assures the entrance of the subject into the universe of signs and of creation. The father-support of this symbolic triumph is not the Oedipal father, but rather this "imaginary father," "father of individual prehistory," according to Freud, who guarantees primary identification. However, it is imperative that this father of individual prehistory be able to assure his role of Oedipal father in symbolic Law, for it is on the basis of this harmonious alliance of the two faces of paternity that the abstract and arbitrary signs of communication can to be connected to the affective sense of prehistoric identities.[19]

According to both Freud and Lacan, the child learns conventional word meaning simultaneously with becoming a separate subject, learning to substitute words for an absent and desired object—the mother. The child in question is a boy, the identification with the symbolic is with the father, and so the Freudian or Lacanian "speaking subject" is masculine.

In Freud's example, an eighteen-month-old boy named Ernst—Freud's own grandson, a child of Freud's daughter, Jacques Derrida tells us in *La carte postale*[20]—invents a game with a cotton-reel or spool tied to a piece of string. Throwing the spool over the edge of his curtained crib with a drawn-out "oooh," and recovering it with an elated "ah," the child, according to Freud, comes to accept his mother's absence by learning to substitute the spool for his mother and to control the spool by pulling on the string. Moreover, the child's utterance, wrote Freud, is semantically meaningful: the "oooh" and "ah" are the boy's first attempts at the German words "fort" and "da," which mean "gone" and "here." The child thus learns to control not only the spool, but also the words. Freud drew from this example the child's attempt to master a (temporary) loss of his primary object of satisfaction—the mother—as the child's mastery of language. The child perceives that his action of throwing the spool places the object out of view—destroys it—but that he can cause it to reappear or disappear again at will by manipulating the string to which it is tied. In the same way, the child learns that by uttering words he, too, can magically banish or reevoke the desired object. It was the "fort . . . da" game that led Freud to postulate the pleasure principle, the death drive, and the acquisition of language, since the child's use of words in this game is a sadistic destruction of the objects referred to, then a symbolic and omnipotent resurrection of them.[21]

Both Freud and Lacan also argue that the child learns to reject the mother and accept, under threat of castration, the words representing the rule of the father; but Lacan's account of the "fort . . . da" example is more radical still, in that for Lacan the words themselves stand for the spool, which in turn stands for the mother symbolically and sadistically thrown away, so that the game "demonstrates in its radical features the determinacy which the human animal receives from the symbolic order."[22] Anika Lemaire adds that the game illustrates Lacan's theory of anchoring points, in that the symbol—the spool—is substituted for the child's experience of the mother's absence, and the spool as symbol is replaced, in turn, by the linguistic symbol—the words:

> This mechanism of access to language simultaneously constitutes both the unconscious and conscious language. But it is followed by the separation of the unconscious from conscious language, as the phonemes substituted for the child's imaginary lived experience have the universal meaning of the concepts 'gone' and 'present' as well as their subjective reference. . . . To sum up: language re-produces reality.[23]

Although critical of Freud's and Lacan's neglect of semiotic meaning, Kristeva endorses both Freudian and Lacanian interpretations of the "fort . . . da" example, adding that the Freudian fort-da is the origin of the drive to rejection, or negativity.

> This negativity—this expenditure—posits an object as separate from the body proper, and, at the very moment of separation, fixes it in place as *absent*, as a *sign*. In this way, rejection establishes the object as real and, at

the same time, as signifiable (which is to say, already taken on as an object within the signifying system and as subordinate to the subject who poses it through the sign). . . . Negativity—rejection—is thus only a *functioning* that is discernible through the *positions* that absorb and camouflage it: the real, the sign, and the predicate appear as differential moments, steps in the process of rejection.[24]

Since Kristeva's conception of semiotic meaning turns on contradictory and shifting references and significations, the point of her own argument is that the semiotic meaning is originally not referential, but adverbial: "The well-known "reel game" with its *fort-da*, observed around the age of eighteen months, finds, over a period of time, its linguistic realization first in demonstrative or localizing utterances and finally in personal and negative utterances."[25] Even according to Freud's interpretation of his grandson's utterances of "oooh" and "ah," the German words "fort" and "da" or "gone" and "here" are not, of course, nouns at all, but adverbs; for they have no definite reference. Nor, according to Kristeva's reading of the example, does the speaker have a stable self-reference either. The "speaking subject" of Freud and Lacan is thus transformed into Kristeva's "subject in process." For her this subject is gender-neutral, alternating between a masculine identification with the symbolic and a feminine identification with the semiotic, in fusion with the mother. But Kristeva's adverbial account of the example does not question—indeed, it repeatedly reaffirms, as we saw at the beginning of this section—the Freud-Lacan conception of the child learning conventional word meaning in separating from his mother under threat of castration. Thus Kristeva's portrayal of the "speaking subject" as gender-neutral is problematic. But other readings of the same Freud-Lacan "fort . . . da" anecdote support an alternative to Kristeva's own expanded conception of the "speaking subject."

For example, both Jacques Derrida and Luce Irigaray have argued, with differing conclusions, that the child's game with the spool is not simply an acquisition of symbols mastering the absence of a forbidden yet still-desired mother, as in Freud and Lacan, nor even an adverbial dislocation both of the desired object and of the subject himself, as Kristeva proposes. Rather, the child's game with the spool is a performance. By uttering words suitable to the deed the child does not, of course, make the object disappear and reappear simply by uttering the words. Rather, the child utters the words repeatedly to evoke the action—making the object disappear and reappear at will.

The child's performance is not a simple matter of exercising the pleasure principle in alternation with a sadistic drive, Derrida suggests, but rather, perhaps, of Freud's own autobiography:

> We observe that something repeats itself. And (has this ever been done?) the repetitive process is to be identified not only in the content, and the material described and analyzed by Freud but already, or again, in Freud's writing, in the *démarche* of his text, in what he does as much as in what he says, in his "acts" if you will, no less than in his "objects". . . . [26]

The performance in the "fort.. .da" example, as Derrida here observes, is not only ritual but also rhythm—the rhythm of Kierkegaardian repetition, of Nietzschean eternal return. Perhaps it is a ritual for Freud himself, as well as a rhythm of generations and of the transmission of power from one generation to another through the intermediary of the mother. Derrida notes that Freud's daughter Sophie, mother of the little boy who played with the spool and of a second child of whom the first was extremely jealous, died when her first-born was five years old, leaving an inconsolable husband. Although Derrida acknowledges Freud's indication that he finished *Beyond the Pleasure Principle*, which includes the "fort . . . da" anecdote, before the child's mother fell sick, Freud's story can also be interpreted as the father's adjustment to the loss of his daughter, forbidden to him as the son is to his mother by the incest taboo.[27] Thus as rhythm, the utterance of "fort . . . da" ritually invokes Freud's own contact between the generations, dispelling the separation of death.

The Freudian "fort-da" is a performance or a ritual for the mastery and control of absences other than the mother's, Derrida suggests: of truth, veiled like the child's cot or like the forbidden mother; of eros, which, as in Aristophanes's speech in Plato's *Symposium*, arises in a desire to overcome separation from the object of desire; and finally of power itself, transformed from a reflective quest for control to an ecstatic search for fusion with another. Though for Derrida this quest is mediated through an archetypal woman, he also acknowledges that the infantile castration fantasy, which Freud (followed by Lacan and Kristeva) attributes to little boys, does not exist for women.[28] Hence Freudian and Lacanian interpretations of the origins of morality and of the power of discourse do not exist for women either, if castration does not. If the driving force toward fusion characterized by both Freud and Lacan is beyond morality, it is also beyond morality in its derivative erotic, which equates fusion with death.[29] But the little boy's attempt to control his mother's absence, reinterpreted in a Derridean erotic, then becomes a three-stage process through which she never becomes fully visible to the beholder.

In the first stage the woman appears as truth, though veiled, much as the infant's cot was veiled so that the spool thrown over its edge disappeared from view. In the second stage the woman appears as untruth, the unlawful object of the erotic desire of a son who can enter into intimacy with her only by violating her, thus, destroying the father's morality. In the third stage, Derrida proposes, "Woman is recognized and affirmed as an affirmative power, a dissimulatress, an artist, a dionysiac. And no longer is it man who affirms her. She affirms herself, in and of herself, in man."[30] But in presenting woman as "dissimulatress," though a specifically feminine presence, Derrida perpetuates a conception of the male child's fantasy of control, since the mother still does not act directly. Thus Derrida perpetuates the Freudian and Lacanian assumption, which Kristeva tacitly accepts, of the masculinity of the speaking subject.

The conception of an animating belief or faith in the return of what was absent ("la croyance") supporting the child's performance with the spool or the words can be regarded apart from Derrida's mythic interpretation of it. For example, according to Luce Irigaray, it is not the mother's absence merely, but the mother herself, who is the object of the male child's search for mastery and control. But for Irigaray it is rather the mother's experience of fusion with the child, preceding the child's separation from her, that provides the basis for faith in a return after separation. Then the power to speak is not a matter of a male child's control or mastery over his mother's absence but rather of a mother's exercising a power having nothing to do with the threatened intervention of a punishing father. Consequently, for Irigaray, there is no question of a further retelling of the story of the absent spool, for "In this peek-a-boo game the son plays only with himself: with himself in her, her in him, above all face-to-face between them."[31] It is instead a question of altogether abandoning the game, with its symbolism and its conception of symbolic meaning, as imposing a nonreciprocal power on the mother.

For Irigaray, the belief that the child supposedly exercises in uttering the ritual "fort . . . da" is a belief in sexual difference, which reaffirms the mother's absence. But that belief has nothing to do with the mother's experience, or with a little girl's experience of learning language either. It is, indeed, another kind of doctrine: "Belief is not safe except in not knowing in what one communes or communicates. If one knows it, no need to believe, at least according to a certain mode of adherence. But truth, all truth, has always depended on a belief which mines and undermines it. Whether that belief announces itself or veils itself in myths, dogmas, figures, or religious rites, does that not also reveal what metaphysics holds in its crypt?"[32] Confidence or "croyance" in a community which makes communication possible undermines both Derrida's proposal to shift the focus of speaking subjectivity to an inaccessible feminine figure, and the Freud-Lacan analysis of masculine language acquisition which Kristeva endorses.

Further, for Irigaray, both the Freud-Lacan "fort . . . da" and Derrida's revision of it tell of a banishment of the mother, and by extension of the feminine, from speaking subjectivity. This banishment creates an ethical problem for Irigaray which is no problem at all for Kristeva: Kristeva's conception of the feminine is, by definition, and in consequence of the Freudian and Lacanian conception of the "speaking subject" which she endorses, outside ethics entirely.

III

In several essays on the maternal Kristeva depicts an absent, hysterical, or wounded mother as a heroine. She is a two-faced being, an object of horror.[33] She is the Virgin present at the crucifixion of Christ: the goddess-mother whom the Judeo-Christian tradition supplanted with the father-son.[34] She is, then, a mystical being, dwelling in the semiotic, pre-Oedipal preconsciousness, beyond the reach of a punishing father who compels accession to the symbolic order of discourse and thereby to the order of phallic Law. Yet for Kristeva this mother is phallic—powerful—in the Freudian sense of the term.

Rather than reject the mystification of the mother, as Simone de Beauvoir did—too quickly, Kristeva says[35]—and rather than respect the glorification of a subordinate mother, in accordance with conventional belief, Kristeva calls for an ethics of the "second" sex. This ethics, Kristeva says, does not exclude women, as Freud and Lacan do, or place her in a deferential position, as conventional religious belief does, but resolutely separates women from morality altogether:

> Now, if a contemporary ethics is no longer seen as being the same as morality; if ethics amounts to not avoiding the embarrassing and inevitable problematics of the law but giving it flesh, language, and jouissance—in that case its reformulation demands the contribution of women. Of women who harbor the desire to reproduction (to have stability). Of women who are available so that our speaking species, which knows it is mortal, might withstand death. Of mothers. For an heretical ethics separated from morality, an *herethics*, is perhaps no more than that which in life makes bonds, thoughts, and therefore the thought of death, bearable: herethic is undeath, love.[36]

This conception of a "heretical" or outlaw ethics appears to give value to the feminine by resurrecting the pre-Oedipal, prerational part of the unconscious while reviving, as we have seen, the lost area of semiotic meaning evoked in poetry and *avant-garde* writing. But, by her own account, Kristeva's conception of a heretical ethics of the feminine leaves in place

Freudian and Lacanian conceptions of ethics itself, which tie the acquisition of symbolic meaning to a male child's acquisition, under threat of castration, of a superego, identifying himself with the father and more generally with the Law of the Fathers. Ethics itself, for both Freud and Lacan and, as we now see, for Kristeva too, is masculine, as is consciousness, the symbolic, and the superego or what Kant called "the moral sense"—that is, rationality. Indeed, Kristeva considers that subjectivity can only be masculine; "feminine subjectivity" is, at best, problematic.

An ethics of linguistics, it follows, obligates linguists, psychoanalysts, and literary critics to disclose the hidden resources of the unconscious for the benefit of *male* writers—and it is with male writers and artists, and their portrayals of the feminine, that Kristeva is concerned. The one exception is Kristeva's discussion of the erotic works of Marguerite Duras, some of which seem to concern women primarily. But even here Kristeva concludes that Duras "recounts the psychic underground anterior to our conquest of the other sex," so that Kristeva interprets even an author's exploration of this "quasi-uterine space"[37] in terms of a subsequent engagement with the male, or of the depression accompanying the failure of such an engagement.

And so, for Kristeva, "Belief in the mother is rooted in the fear—fascinated with a weakness—the weakness of language. If language is powerless to locate myself and state me for the other, I assume—I want to believe—that there is someone who makes up for that weakness. . . . In that sense any belief, anguished by definition, is upheld by the fascinated fear of language's impotence."[38] Kristeva's maternal, heretical, outlaw ethics argues for the mystery or unknowability of the mother while at the same time rejecting the subordinate mother assumed by conventional morality, appearing to make the feminine primary in all experience. But the return to the mother which Kristeva celebrates in calling for a recognition of the semiotic is necessary for the creativity and even the psychic survival of the male. Of the mother's own experience—which, as Luce Irigaray pointed out and as we have seen, Freudian (and Lacanian) and Derridean tellings of the "fort . . . da" episode overlooked—Kristeva's ethics of linguistics has little to say.

Even in her most recent work, *Soleil Noir*, in which Kristeva gives numerous examples from her (primarily but not exclusively) female psychoanalytic patients, she accepts uncritically a Freudian conception of the "castration complex" and accounts for her patients' depressions by invoking a Lacanian equation between phallic power and the power to speak. Accepting a Freudian and Lacanian conception of ethics as well, Kristeva attempts to carve out a place for maternal communication within that system, and ends by placing maternal communication—indeed all communication that she identifies as feminine—outside the phallic power system entirely. Kristeva's maternal ethics of linguistics ends where rationality, cognitive knowledge, and the social order imposed by paternal law begins.

Thus, Kristeva says that the mother's body is the locus of the confrontation between nature and culture—the symbolic, the "phallic" mother who makes discourse possible—and further places the mother between the "symbolic paternal facet" and the "homosexual feminine facet" that precedes discourse.[39] Denoting the mother's body, and more generally maternal communication, as the reference point for the male speaker's ambivalence, Kristeva adopts a patriarchal system whose structure she does not question. The mother is always there, but there is no place for her. In that Kristeva's "ethics of linguistics," here elaborated as a maternal ethics, makes no place for the mother, or, more generally, for the feminine, it is an ethics of male sexuality, male ambivalence. Subjectivity in the process of traversing and retraversing the boundary between unconscious and irrational communication and that which is cognitive and rational is primarily a male concern.

The question remaining for Kristeva's ethics of linguistics is whether its call for a recognition of the value of semiotic communication could ever be separated from the Lacanian and phallocentric conception of ethics it also espouses. If it cannot, then no conception of feminine, conscious agency is possible for it either. In "Stabat Mater" Kristeva writes in two parallel columns; the citations above have been taken from both. In that the one column can be taken to represent the mother's own voice, commenting on cultural mystifications of the maternal, Kristeva can be taken as offering at least one example of feminine agency. But Kristeva is not concerned with establishing a theoretical conception of feminine agency. She has written ironically of support she received from feminist women in public lectures in the United States, has mocked American feminist publications she found ("One finds that weak, naive, and ugly"),[40] and has otherwise distanced herself from the American women's movement. She cannot, then, be considered a feminist, as Americans understand the term. And she has distanced herself from all factions of the French women's movement as well, writing, "Are women subject to ethics? . . . The answer . . . can be considered affirmative only at the cost of considering feminism as but a *moment* in the thought of that anthropomorphic identity which currently blocks the horizon of the discursive and scientific adventure of our species."[41] In that Kristeva remains resolutely identified with Lacan, and, above all, with Freud, even in her most recent writings, and in that, in particular, she endorses an ethics resolutely located in an irrational, pre-Oedipal preconscious, her conception of "feminine subjectivity" is, in the end, a contradiction in terms.[42]

NOTES

1. Julia Kristeva, *Desire in Language*, ed. Leon Roudiez (New York: Columbia University Press, 1980), 23–35. Julia Kristeva, "L'Ethique de Linguistique," in *Polylogue* (Paris: Les Éditions du Seuil, 1977), 357–72.

2. For Kristeva's own discussion, see her "Women's Time," trans. Alice Jardine and Harry Blake, *Signs* 7(Autumn 1981):16–18.

3. For example, see Alice Jardine, "Introduction to Julia Kristeva's 'Women's Time,' " *Signs* 7(Autumn 1981):12; Gayatri Chakravorty Spivak, "The Politics of Interpretations," *Critical Inquiry* 9(September 1982):259–78; Domna C. Stanton, "Difference on Trial," this volume; Toril Moi, *Sexual/Textual Politics* (London: Methuen, 1985), 172; Ann Rosalind Jones, "Julia Kristeva on Femininity: The Limits of a Semiotic Politics," *Feminist Review* 18(November 1984). See also, however, Jaqueline Rose's reply to Jones, "Julia Kristeva-Take Two" in her *Sexuality in the Field of Vision* (London: Verso, 1986), 141–64; and Susan Rubin Suleiman's more sympathetic view of Kristeva in "Writing and Motherhood," in Shirley Nelson Garner, Claire Kahane, and Madelon Sprengnether, *The (M)other Tongue: Essays in Feminist Psychoanalytic Interpretation* (Ithaca: Cornell University Press, 1985), 367–69.

4. Kristeva, "Ethics of Linguistics," 24–25.

5. Kristeva, *Revolution in Poetic Language*, trans. Margaret Waller (New York: Columbia University Press, 1984), 21, 37, 237–238n. Cf. *La Révolution du langage poétique* (Paris: Les Éditions du Seuil, 1974), 36–37. Also "Du sujet en linguistique," *Polylogue*, 308–20.

6. Kristeva, "Du sujet en linguistique," *Polylogue*, 308–20. For a recent account of his own position, see Noam Chomsky, *Knowledge of Language* (New York: Praeger Publishers, 1986), especially 3–4 and 251.

7. Kristeva, "Place Names," *Desire in Language*, 277. Cf."Noms de Lieu," *Polylogue*, 473.

8. For his own account see Jacques Lacan, "The Meaning of the Phallus," trans. Jacqueline Rose, ed. Juliet Mitchell and Jacqueline Rose, *Feminine Sexuality: Jacques Lacan and the École Freudienne* (New York: W. W. Norton, 1985), 74–85.

9. Kristeva, *Revolution in Poetic Language*, 25; *La révolution du langage poétique*, 22–23.

10. Kristeva, *Revolution in Poetic Language*, 43; *La révolution du langage poétique*, 41–42.

11. See Alice Jardine, "Opaque Texts and Transparent Contexts: The Political Difference of Julia Kristeva," in Miller, 96–116.

12. Julia Kristeva, *Au commencement était l'amour: Psychanalyse et foi* (Paris: Hachette, 1985), 13–14.

13. Julia Kristeva, *Soleil Noir: Dépression et Melancholie* (Paris: Gallimard, 1987), 33: "Le 'semiotique' et le 'symbolique' deviennent les marques communicables d'une réalité affective présente, sensible au lecteur (j'aime ce livre parce qu'il me communique la tristesse, l'angoisse ou la joie), et néanmoins dominée, écartée, vaincue." This and other translations not otherwise credited are mine.

14. Julia Kristeva, *Le texte du roman: Approche sémiologique d'une structure discursive transformationnelle* (The Hague: Mouton, 1970), 93.

15. "Practique signifiante et mode de production," in Julia Kristeva *et al.*, eds., *La Traversée des signes* (Paris: Les Éditions du Seuil, 1975), 17n.

16. Kristeva, "La sujet en procès," *Polylogue*, 55–106.

17. For example, in Kristeva, "The Mirror and Castration: Positing the Subject as Absent from the Signifier," *Revolution in Poetic Language*, 46–51; cf. *La révolution du langage poétique*, 43–49.

18. Kristeva, *Au commencement était l'amour*, 56: "On a observé en effet la tristesse des jeunes enfants, leur rénoncement au paradis maternel et à la satisfaction im-

médiate de la demande, que précede l'apparition du langage. Il faut abandonner la mere et être abandonné par elle pour que le père me recueille et que je parle. . . . "

19. Kristeva, *Soleil Noir*, 34: "Cette identification qu'on peut appeler phallique ou symbolique assure l'entrée du sujet dans l'univers des signes et de la création. Le père-appui de ce triomphe symbolique n'est pas le père oedipien, mais bien ce 'père imaginaire', 'père de la pre-histoire individuelle' selon Freud, qui garantit l'identification primaire. Cependant, il est imperatif que ce père de la préhistoire individuelle puisse assurer son role de père oedipien dans la Loi symbolique, car c'est sur la base de cet alliage harmonieux des deux faces de la paternité que les signes abstraits et arbitraires de la communication peuvent avoir la chance de se lier au sens affectif des identifications préhistoriques. . . . "

20. Jacques Derrida, *Post Card*, trans. Alan Bass (Chicago: University of Chicago Press, 1987), 298ff. Cf. *La Carte Postale* (Paris: Aubier-Flammarion, 1980), 319ff.

21. Sigmund Freud, *Beyond the Pleasure Principle* (London: Hogarth Press and Institute of Psychoanalysis, 1951), *Standard Edition* (1955), 18, chap. 2.

22. Jacques Lacan, *Écrits: A Selection*, trans. Alan Sheridan (New York: W. W. Norton, 1977), 103–104; Rosalind Coward and John Ellis, *Language and Materialism* (London: Routledge & Kegan Paul, 1977), 141ff.

23. Anika Lemaire, *Jacques Lacan*, trans. David Macey (London: Routledge & Kegan Paul, 1977), 52.

24. Kristeva, *Revolution in Poetic Language*, 123; *La Révolution du langage poetique*, 114.

25. Kristeva, "Place Names," *Desire in Language*, 290–91. Cf. "Noms de lieu," *Polylogue*, 489.

26. Derrida, *Post Card*, 294–95; *La Carte Postale*, 314–15

27. Derrida, *Post Card*, 301ff.; *La Carte Postale*, 319ff.

28. Derrida, *Spurs/Éperons*, trans. Barbara Harlow (Chicago: University of Chicago Press, 1979), 58ff.

29. Derrida, *Post Card*, 404–405; *La Carte Postale*, 431–32.

30. Derrida, *Spurs/Éperons*, 97.

31. Luce Irigaray "La croyance même," *Les fins de l'homme; A partir du travail de Jacques Derrida*, Philippe Lacoue-Labarthe et Jean-Luc Nancy (Paris: Éditions Galilée, 1981), 375: "Dans ce jeu cache-cache, le fils ne joue qu'avec lui-même: avec lui en elle, elle en lui, avant tout face-à-face entre eux." Also published separately as *La croyance même* (Paris: Éditions Galilée, 1983). Reprinted in Luce Irigaray, *Sexes et parentés* (Paris: Les Éditions de Minuit, 1987).

32. Irigaray, "La croyance même," 369: "La croyance n'est sauve qu'à ne pas savoir en qui on communie ou communique. Si on le sait, pas besoin de le croire, du moins selon un certain mode d'adhérance. Mais la vérité, toute vérité, a toujours reposé sur une croyance qui la mine. Que cette croyance s'affirme ou se dévoile en mythes, dogmes, figures ou rites religieux ne revelent-t-il pas aussi ce que le métaphysique garde en crypte?"

33. Julia Kristeva, "Those Females who can Wreck the Infinite, *Powers of Horror: An Essay on Abjection*, trans. Leon S. Roudiez (New York: Columbia University Press, 1982); *Pouvoirs de l'horreur* (Paris: Les Éditions du Seuil, 1980).

34. Julia Kristeva, "Stabat Mater," *Tales of Love*, trans. Leon S. Roudiez (New York: Columbia University Press, 1987); "Stabat Mater," *Histoires d'amour* (Paris: Denoel, 1983). First published as "Héréthique d'amour," *Tel Quel* 74(Hiver 1977):30–49.

35. Kristeva, "Stabat Mater," *Tales of Love*, 247; *Histoires d'amour*, 235.

36. Kristeva, "Stabat Mater," *Tales of Love*, 262–63; *Histoires d'amour*, 247.

37. Kristeva, *Soleil Noir*, 263: "Elle raconte le sous-sol psychique antérieur à nos conquètes de l'autre sexe, qui reste sous-jacent aux eventuelles et perilleuses rencontres des hommes et des femmes. On a l'habitude de ne pas faire attention à cet espace quasi uterin."

38. Kristeva, "Stabat Mater," *Tales of Love*, 251–52; *Histoires d'amour*, 239.

39. Kristeva, "Motherhood according to Giovanni Bellini," *Desire in Language*, 239; "Maternité selon Giovanni Bellini, *Polylogue*, 411.

40. Kristeva, "D'Ithaca a New York," *Polylogue*, 511: "On trouve ca faible, naif et laid."

41. Kristeva, "Women's Time," 35.

42. A version of this essay was presented at the Society for Women in Philosophy, Mount Holyoke College, and at the New York State Women's Studies Conference, SUNY Oswego, in April 1985.

DISPLACING THE PHALLIC SUBJECT
WITTIG'S LESBIAN WRITING

Namascar Shaktini

> Adieu continent noir de misère et de peine
> adieu villes anciennes nous nous
> embarquons pour les îles brillantes et
> radieuses pour les vertes Cythères pour les
> Lesbos noires et dorées.
>
> —Monique Wittig
>
> (Farewell black continent of misery and
> suffering farewell ancient cities we are
> embarking for the brilliant and radiant
> islands for the green Cytheras for the black
> and gilded Lesbian Islands.)

Though Monique Wittig's first two books, *L'opoponax (The Opoponax)* and *Les guérillères (Les Guérillères)*, have been the focus of considerable attention, her last two, which have the word "lesbian" in the title, have been relatively ignored. The present essay analyzes one of these neglected works, *Le corps lesbien*,[1] which I consider an important contribution to the epistemological revolution now being carried out by feminist thought, especially the aspect of the revolution that attacks the semiological problem of "phallogocentrism." Wittig's reorganization of metaphor around the lesbian body represents an epistemological shift from what seemed until recently the absolute, central metaphor—the phallus.[2]

Phallogocentrism may be described as the current tradition that constitutes a signifying system organized around gender. By "gender," I refer to a binary concept of relation that assumes such dichotomies as male presence/female absence, male word principle *(verbe)*/female verbal object, male center/female margin. I regard gender as the "logical" dichotomizing principle of phallogocentrism. This organizing principle regulates a set of systems that maintain the male-identified subject at the center of words. These signifying systems occur in all the arts and sciences, not just in "belles lettres." Thus the phallus may be regarded as the organizing principle for all standard systems including that of law, since at this time—though, we can hope, not forever—no legal communication can entirely ignore its referential order.[3]

Currently, when we use standard forms of communication, we default to the male-centered, heterosexual point of view. We do so even in the word used to name us as adult, human females: "women." The English word "woman" derives etymologically from the word for "wife"; even today the French word "femme" means both "woman" and "wife." The social idea of "wife" has thus become indistinguishable from the bodily idea of adult, human female, making it impossible for the word "woman" to represent us except as past, present, or future "wives" of men.

What, essentially, is the concept, "wife"? The structuralist answer to this question can be examined in Claude Lévi-Strauss's representation of women-wives as "ball of twine" or "liana." Men, in this view, just as they build a network of roads or thatch a roof from materials, create a communication-exchange network from the females they turn into wives in the act of wife-exchange. In the following passage Lévi-Strauss explains that women are exchanged like money, passing from hand to hand, establishing for the exchangers relations of reciprocity:

> It is the same with women as with the currency the name of which they often bear, and which, according to the admirable native saying, "depicts the action of the needle for sewing roofs, which, weaving in and out, leads backwards and forwards the same liana, holding the straw together."[4]

Note that the phallic subject (Lévi-Strauss's at least, and the subjectivity that presumably produced the "admirable native saying") depicts the "needle for sewing roofs" as leading the liana (a vine that grows in tropical rain forests), which is itself depicted as led. If we take a close look at this structuralist figuration we see that the action seems to reside in the needle (no doubt an image of the phallus), while the liana seems to be inert. The connecting function of the liana is like the reproductive function of a woman in the view of structuralism. And the straws that need to be united are like men (who, we may note, are distinguished here from the phallus). We may compare this functional image of woman-wife to another that Lévi-

Strauss takes from a Kachin myth of creation and uses in a headquote to make vivid his theory of masculine networking:

> The earth, it is true, is in good condition, but roads are yet wanting; Ning-kong is going to open them; he takes under his arm his sister, 'Ndin Lakong, a ball of twine, unwinds part of it on China, and re-enters his palace; hence-forth there is a fine road to China. He then goes towards the Shan countries, again unwinds his sister, and it is the Shan road. In the same way he opens the Kachin, Burmese, and Kala roads.[5]

Here the woman is figured as a ball of twine, as the matter itself from which her brother forms a webbing, a weaving, a network.

This concept of woman-as-wife, we see, is essential for the social contract assumed by structuralist theory, since this theory is developed exclusively from the male, heterosexual point of view. The two-sentence disclaimer on the penultimate page of *The Elementary Structures of Kinship* notwith-standing, Lévi-Strauss systematically reifies women as "signs," only once recognizing "woman . . . as a generator of signs."[6] Wittig dryly points to this contradiction when she says, "Since, as Lévi-Strauss said, we talk, let us say that we break off the heterosexual contract."[7] The result of this break is lesbian writing, an "illicit" poetic method that escapes the centralizing "presence" of wife-exchanging subjectivity. It escapes at the same time the dichotomizing organizational mode of sex-gender itself.[8]

Any pair of concepts, like masculine/feminine or male/female, that sig-nifies sex-gender automatically constitutes a distinction of "markedness." It was the "unmarked" status of the masculine that led Simone de Beauvoir in 1949 to identify it as both "neutral" and "positive," while the "marked" status of the feminine led her to identify it as "negative." Today, marked-ness is increasingly recognized as essential to the sex-gender distinction.[9] As the Harvard Linguistics Department has put it, "For people and pro-nouns in English the masculine is the unmarked and hence is used as a neutral or unspecified term."[10] The unmarked is assumed to be desirable, expected, familiar, while the marked is considered undesirable, unex-pected, unfamiliar. The unmarked form is usually shorter and therefore easier to say than the marked; for example, "male" is shorter than "female," and "man" is shorter than "woman." If a person crosses the sex-gender line in occupational roles, the unexpected situation must be "marked" by an additional signifier. Marking may be carried out by suffixes like the "-ess" in "poetess" or by qualifiers such as those in the expressions "woman doctor" and "male secretary." More obvious than the complicated sexism of "markedness" in language is the simple quantitative overrepresentation of male figures in books; according to the computerized study of Alma Graham, seven times as many men as women appeared in children's textbooks in the United States in 1973.[11] It is the trace of this all too ubiquitous masculine "presence" that must be erased from lesbian language. Lesbian metaphor must overwrite phallogocentric metaphor, just as, historically, phallogocentric metaphor had to overwrite an earlier symbolic system. Let us now examine the process of overwriting.

The phallus is not without a token "presence" in Wittig's lesbian book. Placed near the center of the collection of 110 poems, we find in poem 51 the ithyphallic god, Osiris. But he has been lesbianized. If we read the poem in the original French, we see that Osiris has been attributed grammatically feminine gender through the feminine modifiers, "m/a . . . cherie . . . m/a . . . affaiblie . . . m/a . . . belle . . . défaite . . . épuisée." The reader can see that this grammatical feminizing is lost in Le Vay's English translation of the French.

> m/oi Isis la très puissante j/e décrète que comme par le passé tu vis Osiris m/a très cherie m/a très affaiblie j/e dis que comme par le passé nous pourrons faire ensemble les petites filles qui viendront après nous, toi alors m/on Osiris m/a très belle tu m/e souris défaite épuisée. (*Lcl*, poem 51, lines 34–39, p. 87)[12]

> (*J* Isis the all-powerful *J* decree that you live as in the past Osiris m/y most cherished m/y most enfeebled *J* say that as in the past we shall succeed together in making the little girls who will come after us, then you m/y Osiris m/y most beautiful you smile at m/e undone exhausted.) (*TLB*, p. 80)

Powerful as a displacer of consciousness, Wittig relocates subjectivity outside the orbit of phallogocentrism. In the passage cited above, she has effeminized the ithyphallic figure, evoking an old tradition of the brother's castration of Osiris. A closer look at this myth, central to Wittig's treatment of death and rebirth, will make clearer the essentially metaphorical nature of the phallus, and the political nature of metaphor.

According to one version of the Isis-Osiris myth, recounted by Esther Harding, "Set . . . tore the body of Osiris to pieces. . . . Isis managed to collect thirteen of the pieces which she welded together by magic. But the phallus was missing. So she made an image of this part and 'consecrated the phallus.' Isis conceived by means of this image and bore a child."[13]

The phallus produced is a simulacrum, an artifact crafted by Isis who then attributes to it sacred meaning. Thus the "phallus" comes into existence according to the wish of the goddess Isis. Harding's research points to both the symbolic nature and social importance of the phallus: "Public rituals of Isis and Osiris were celebrated. . . . The festival culminated in a procession at the head of which was carried the huge image of the phallus, representing the lost organ of Osiris."[14]

Although Harding refers to the gender symbols "the bowl and the phallus" as "the eternal symbols of generation," the examples she cites show the nature of the phallus to be destructive, not generative, and historical rather than eternal: "We find [the 'eternal' symbols] in primitive rites— the fire stick, which is called the man, and the cup in which it bores, called the woman; the fundus in the earth in the center of the camp into which each Roman soldier threw his spear; the chalice of the Holy Grail into which a spear, perpetually dripping blood, was thrust; the holy font of baptism fertilized by plunging in the lighted candle."[15]

Harding, though contributing much useful research, remains metaphorically within a contradictory position, according to which fire (an agent of destruction) "signifies" fertility. This problematic metaphor may have a traditional root in the concept of the Old Testament god, both fire-god ("logos" as fire speaking out of the burning bush to Moses) and father-god.

Norman O. Brown, who on the penultimate page of *Love's Body* refers to the "Word" (Greek "logos") as "spermatic," has also contributed useful research on the phallus. His report of the "cult" of Hermes, like the myth retold by Harding, emphasizes the magical rather than biological nature of the phallic symbol: "The phallus is so closely identified with magic in Roman religion that the word *fascinum*, meaning 'enchantment,' 'witchcraft' (cf. fascinate), is one of the standard Latin terms for the phallus. . . . When Greek craftsmen [sic] hung images of ithyphallic demons over their workshops, it is clear that to them the phallus symbolized not fertility but magic skill at craftsmanship [sic]."[16] As is consistent with his phallogocentric view, Brown simply identifies the activity of "crafting" as phallic—crafters for him were "craftsmen," notwithstanding the ancient evidence of female crafters (e.g., Isis as welder in the myth cited above, or females in general identified with the "magic skill" of witchcraft). But most important for feminist thought is Brown's report that historically the phallus is not essentially a signifier of the penis but of craft itself. It alerts us to look for the origins of linguistic sexism in "crafty" and misogynist practices in the crafting of words. By comparing Wittig's recrafting of the phallic figure, Osiris, and Hesiod's recrafting of Pandora, we may better understand the political nature of metaphorical takeover.

The takeover of Pandora, a figure of womankind, is a prime example. She was, as Brown reports, "originally a figure of the earth-goddess type, the original meaning of the name being 'the all-giver.' "[17] But as Hesiod exercises his craft a remodeled Pandora figure emerges typifying woman as "gift," the object of gift-exchange by men.[18] She is brought into existence according to the wish of the Father, made "in the likeness of a decorous young girl, as the son of Kronos had wished it."[19] Like the phallus made by Isis or its extensions—the burning stick or the soldier's spear—she is an artifact, a product of craft. By textually redefining this figure of womankind, Hesiod strips her of subjectivity. Taking as his material the existent earth goddess figure, Pandora, he recrafts her into a man-made Pandora, "modeled . . . of earth."[20]

Transformed by Hesiod's text, the Pandora figure may be read as the product of a displacement of subjectivity, the displacing process itself figured by the author effecting it. Hesiod's text points to a prepatriarchal symbolic order, where the principle of intelligence is embodied in a female-identified figure, Metis, who "knew more than all the gods or mortal people."[21] Zeus, metaphorically described by Hesiod as swallowing Metis, appropriates to his own phallic body two of her subject-signifying attributes—the ability to think and the ability to reproduce parthenogenetically: "Zeus put her [Metis] away inside his own belly so that this goddess should think for him, for good and for evil. . . . Then from his head, by himself, he produced Athene. . . . The father of gods and men gave birth to her."[22] Athena's birth from the brow of the father figure repositions there the point of view of subjectivity, the standard for good and evil. This viewpoint, subsequently absolute, takes over the function of divinity as Roland Barthes has defined it: "Divinity's role is . . . to *mark* one of the two terms of the binary."[23]

According to Hesiod, Athena is born (or more precisely, rebirthed and renamed) "with her panoply of war upon her." As we see from the *Oxford English Dictionary*, Athena's symbol of power is but a "marked" version of the aegis of Zeus: the aegis is "a shield or breastplate emblematic of majesty that was originally associated chiefly with the god Zeus but later, bordered with serpents and set with a Gorgon's head, associated mainly with the goddess Athena."[24] The aegis or shield (and the weapon it implies), a militaristic means of social control, thus ultimately signifies the authority of the father-god.

This aegis figures importantly in the death of Pallas, whose name was to become the "extra name of Athena."[25] As we learn from Jeanette Foster's *Sex Variant Women in Literature*: "The conscientious chronicler Apollodorus reports . . . of Athene and her boon companion, Pallas . . . that in their girlhood they were so equally matched in the practice of arms that Zeus felt obliged one day to interpose his aegis between them lest his daughter be slain. As a result, Athena's thrust killed Pallas, whereupon, overcome by grief, Athene herself fashioned a wooden statue of her friend, wrapped it in the aegis [sometimes described as made of sheepskin], set it up beside that of Zeus, and honored it as she did his image. Hence her later epithet,

Pallas-Athene."[26] It is in relation to the father's brow—the epistemological center of Olympian metaphor—that Metis, Pallas, and Athene are related by Hesiod to each other. In one version of Hesiodic text, it was actually Metis who "conceived Pallas Athene, but the father of gods and men gave birth to her."[27] In this version "Metis herself, hidden away under the vitals of Zeus, stayed there; she was Athene's mother. . . . Metis made the armor of Athene, terror of armies, in which Athene was born with her panoply of war upon her."[28]

Athena emerges as the central figure while Metis and Pallas are marginalized. Metis, a figure of generation (the producer of Athena and of her armor), exists from the moment of the swallowing only for Zeus, not for herself. Pallas, a shadowy amazon-lesbian figure, is effectively killed by the authority of Zeus, ambiguously associated with that of Athena. Like Isis, Athena fabricates and consecrates an image of the beloved to replace what has disappeared. Thus only a trace remains of the existence of the amazon-lesbian figure.

Hesiod's story of Zeus' appropriation of Metis and suppression of Pallas figures the displacement and appropriation of a prepatriarchal form of subjectivity by a patriarchal one, the "brow" of the father thereby becoming the figurative center of consciousness for Greek myth. It is in this sense that the "Word" became "spermatic," in Norman O. Brown's phrase, or, as feminists more commonly say today, "male-identified."[29] The shift to the "brow" of Zeus is at once a shift to logocentrism (word centeredness) and phallogocentrism (male-centered word centeredness).

Athena, issuing directly from the divine "brow," may be seen as a figure of the male-identified feminine subject. She then acts as Zeus' agent in the Olympic fabrication of Pandora, male-defined feminine object. Athena thus mediates between absolute phallic subject and absolute feminine object. As bearer of the Gorgon-marked aegis, she represents herself as agent— half subject, half object. The mark on her aegis, the head of the Gorgon, may be read as another aspect of herself as goddess figure—that aspect slain and appropriated by Perseus. Identified with the head of Zeus, Athena is marked by a beheaded form of the goddess and effects the veiling (hiding) of the head of Pandora. The Athena figure is thus a triple denial of feminine subjectivity: Herself "born" from the father's brow, she may be considered an extension of it; "marked" by an appropriated image of the goddess, she may be considered an appropriated goddess figure; and finally, "veiling" (hiding) the head, the place of Pandora's logocentric subjectivity, she helps produce the Greek prototype of alienated woman—woman as gift, exchange-object, chattel.

"Woman," then, signifies "gift" for others to give-exchange. Understandably, in a profoundly lesbian gesture, Wittig puts under erasure the concept "woman." At the Simone de Beauvoir Conference of 1979 in New York, delivering a paper titled to echo de Beauvoir's own words, "One is not born a woman," Wittig defines, at least for herself, the concept "lesbian": "Lesbian is the only concept that I know of that is beyond the categories of sex (woman and man) . . . because the designated subject (lesbian) is *not* a woman either economically or politically or ideologically."[30] We see that as defined by Wittig, lesbianism is not just a matter of "sexual preference" but one of class. And it is as a trace of this lesbian class consciousness that we may examine Wittig's modification of the heterosexual metaphors that have provided her with writing material.

By comparing Wittig's recrafting of the phallic figure, Osiris, and Hesiod's recrafting of Pandora, we may see the significance of her transformation of myth for the history of consciousness. As she reidentifies the phallic figure as lesbian, Wittig operates a reversal in the signifying system and a displacement of subjectivity. By producing Olympian metaphor (specifically in metamorphosizing unalienated feminine figures into alienated ones), Hesiod also operates a reversal and displacement. Hesiod historically displaces a prepatriarchal order by emplacing the brow of Zeus (metaphorically the male-identified subject) at the absolute center of his signifying system. In *Le corps lesbien* Wittig displaces this phallic body and subject with the lesbian body and the lesbian subject. (See, for example, her ironic recrafting of Zeus as Zeyna in poem 43.) The reversal operated by both of these crafters of words signifies a shift of the biological body of reference for human consciousness.

By showing her own process of transformation of meaning from that of the current phallogocentric order, Wittig makes visible the earlier process of absorbing and transforming that took place when the idea of mothergoddess was superseded and appropriated (overwritten) by the idea of father-god. Taking the persona of the goddess Isis, "j/e" assumes the subjective posture of the female-identified subject before its illocutionary power became alienated by that of the phallic Word:

m/oi Isis la trés puissante j/e décrète . . . j/e dis . . . (*Lcl*, poem 51, lines 34–36, p. 87)

(*I* Isis the all-powerful *I* decree . . . *I* say . . .) (*TLB*, p. 80)

Isis, as we learn in the *Egyptian Book of the Dead*, possessed the power of the living Word: "I am Isis the goddess, lady of words of power, worker with words of mighty power, in utterance of speech."[31] Her power must have been greater than that of the divine sun-king, Ra, for she could "make Ra reveal to her his greatest and most secret name."[32] And, as we have noted, it was she who empowered the very phallus of Osiris.

The figure of Isis embodies the power of speech, the power of naming with which we may symbolically fragment and reassemble the world. Although the process of naming is largely unconscious for us, Wittig's frequent use of the word "nom" (name)—which appears twenty-seven times—heightens our consciousness of the power of the illocutionary process while also making us aware that naming implies the point of view of the namer.

It is the displacing process itself that is figured in poem 106 of *Le corps lesbien* on "Archimedea." That is, this poem may be read as a reflection or figuration of "j/e" in its aspect as displacing subject. The first-person singular, present-tense narrator, "j/e," displaces us as readers from the mainland to an island, which serves as image of both the central and marginal position. Central from the point of view of its own center, the island is marginal from the point of view of the body of water that surrounds it. The displacing lesbian subject, "j/e," addresses the beloved as "Archimedea," whose name may be associated with the historical Greek figure credited with the discovery of the principle of displacement. Archimedes, the author of *On Floating Bodies*, a text on hydrostatics, is credited with discovering that "the solid will, when weighed in the fluid, be lighter than its weight in air by the weight of the fluid displaced."[33]

> N'y a-t-il pas Archimedea d'autre endroit pour se rencontrer que les bains si parfumés d'eau de Chypre soient-ils? Jamais j/e ne te vois dans les pinèdes fraîches bleues sombres qui bordent la côte de l'île, là pourtant dans l'obscurité m/es yeux se reposent de l'éclat du jour le poids de m/es bras de m/es jambes ne m//embarrasse plus quand j/e les appuie sur les aiguilles de pin, l'odeur de la résine chaude de la mer mêlées m/e porte à te chercher toute couchée à côté de m/oi. Mais c'est un fait tu es aux bains, c'est là que j/e te rejoins, tu es occupée à flotter tout à plat sur l'eau chaude, j/e te regarde, ton corps se détache au-dessus des mosaïques orange et violettes. (*Lcl*, poem 106, lines 1–13, p. 181)

> ([However perfumed with Cyprus water they may be is there no place to meet other than the baths, Archimedea?[34]] *I* never see you in the cool dark-blue pine groves which flank the island shore, but there in the gloom m/y eyes relax from the daylight's dazzle the weight of m/y arms m/y legs burdens m/e no longer when *I* rest them on the pine needles, the mingled odours of the warm resin and the sea lead m/e to seek you lying beside m/e. But in fact you are at the baths, it's there that *I* join you, you are engaged in floating flat on the warm water, *I* look at you, your body stands out against the orange and violet mosaics.) (*TLB*, p. 159)

In the first sentence of this playful passage, the speaker questions whether the only meeting place for the lovers is that place of displacement, the baths. The next two sentences, an interesting example of Wittig's method of displacement, situate the lover and the beloved outside the centristic organizational mode of the phallic subject by placing them outside of the presence/absence and center/margin dichotomies. In the second sentence, an image of absence and marginality is juxtaposed to the image of central presence constituted by the third sentence. The scene of the lover's absence is set on the margin of the island while the scene of the lover's presence is made to seem more central through heightening of the visual foreground/background effect. Yet Wittig gives as much textual development to the beloved's image as absent-marginal as she does to her image as present-central. This juxtaposition of absence with presence has the effect of making relative the otherwise absolute logocentric privilege of presence over absence. Wittig thus deconstructs her own word-centered positionality, situating herself now in the center, now in the margin, signifying now what is present, now what is absent.[35]

These Archimedean baths, perfumed with water from Cyprus, the island reputed to be the birthplace of Aphrodite, are situated on an island—the setting par excellence for lesbianism in *Le corps lesbien*, no doubt because of the historical association with Lesbos, the site of Sappho's lesbian community. "Ile" (island) occurs twenty-nine times in the text as compared with the word "continent" (continent), which occurs only three times.[36]

The epigraph of this essay, taken from the end of poem 11, contains one of these appearances:

> adieu continent noir de misère et de peine adieu villes anciennes nous nous embarquons pour les îles brillantes et radieuses pour les vertes Cythères pour les Lesbos noires et dorées.(*Lcl*, poem 11, lines 30–34, p. 20)

> (farewell black continent of misery and suffering farewell ancient cities we are embarking for the shining radiant isles for the green Cytheras for the dark and gilded Lesbos.)[37] (*TLB*, p. 26)

By setting the pluralized *Cythère* and the pluralized *Lesbos* in apposition, Wittig has lesbianized the idea of Watteau's famous painting, *Embarquement pour Cythère*, which portrays heterosexual couples of the French classical period presumably embarking for Cythera, a Greek island known for its magnificent temple of Aphrodite. This lesbian poet invokes Sappho—whose name appears twenty-four times. Wittig's poems situate lesbianism in relation to islands (on them, in the air above them, in the water around them) and contrast the islands to the "black continent."[38] She evokes the metaphor of embarkation as an image of displacement from the "dark continent of femininity which Freud never really penetrated."[39]

Wittig's semiological method does not aim at feminizing meaning, nor does it continue the default situation, which constitutes meaning for the male-identified subject. When, for example, she inserts the name "Medea," known as a figure of prepatriarchal myth, into the name "Archimedea" (and into the name "Ganymedea" in poem 23), Wittig is placing herself neither at the feminine nor at the masculine end of the gender polarity. By introducing a female name into these male names, Wittig mixes gender signifiers, confounding the dichotomizing principle of gender. She positions herself, her text, and her readers outside the system which makes female and male into polar opposites.

Even in reference to time, Wittig has succeeded in situating herself without having recourse to dichotomous, linear, phallogocentric methods. In the dominant, officially Christian society, time is measured in reference to a central metaphor and reference point: the supposed birth of the male Logos, Christ, which divides time absolutely into B.C. and A.D. But this linear, phallogocentric system can be easily displaced by an older, cyclical one, ready at hand.

In poem 36 Wittig marks time in relation to a metaphor that existed prior to words—"la lune" (the moon). The lunar cycle provides a point of reference for marking the months at the "vingt-huitième . . . jour" (twenty-eighth . . . day) (*Lcl*, poem 36, line 2, p. 60; *TLB*, p. 59). From this central point, the four-week month and lunar-centered system of representing time can be constructed. Concomitantly, the Logos-centered system of representing time is deconstructed. In *Le corps lesbien* there are fourteen references to the moon. The birth of Christ is thus displaced as the central reference point for the marking of time and replaced, at least in the context of poem 36, by a central lunar point of reference.

The male Christ, moreover, as a sacrificial figure, is replaced by "Christa la très crucifiée" (Christa the much-crucified) (*Lcl*, poem 17, line 24, p. 30; *TLB*, p. 35). "J/e," in poem 82, one of the most beautifully written in the book, assumes the lesbianized persona of Christ:

> J/e suis au Golgotha par vous toutes abandonée. (*Lcl*, poem 82, line 1, p. 138)

> (Abandoned by you all *J* am at Golgotha.)[40] *TLB*, p. 122)

Displaced by lesbian metaphor, Golgotha is stripped of its phallic signifiers. Wittig's telescoped scene of Gethsemene/Golgotha is peopled with lesbians. The indefinite "quelqu'une" (grammatically feminine "someone") in a universe with no occurrence of "quelqu'un" (grammatically masculine "someone") takes on a "generic" meaning (*Lcl*, poem 82, line 14, p. 138; *TLB*, p. 123).[41] And the subject addressed is generic feminine, both as the specific "tu" and in the more general context of the plural "vous."

"Tu" is compared to a female figure from a prepatriarchal order of divine power:

> tu ressembles à une des Gorgones terrible puissante rouge de rêve (*Lcl*, poem 82, lines 4–5, p. 138)

> (you resemble one of the Gorgons terrible powerful ruddy in dream) (*TLB*, p. 122)

Similarly, the "generic" use of "une" represents a shift from a phallic to a lesbian assumption concerning human subjectivity:

> pas une de vous ne sait rien de m/on angoisse (*Lcl*, poem 82, lines 8–9, p. 138)

> (not one of you knows anything of m/y anguish) (*TLB*, pp. 138–39)

And when the deity is addressed, it is as mother-goddess rather than as father-god:

> j//implore la grande déesse ma mère et j/e lui dis mère mère pourquoi m// as tu abandonnée (*Lcl*, poem 82, lines 9–11, p. 138)

> (*I* cry out in m/y distress mother mother why have you forsaken m/e) (*TLB*, p. 123)

By systematically displacing phallic with lesbian linguistic assumptions, Wittig changes meaning itself.

What happens if meaning is for the lesbian rather than the phallic subject? In poem 5, for example, Wittig rewrites a famous heterosexual love story from the lesbian perspective. Though the names "Orphée" and "Eurydice" are not uttered, this poem, in four sentences, appropriates the main structures of the well-known narrative of Orpheus' descent into the underworld to save his bride. Here, the speaker assumes the persona of Eurydice:

> J/e dirai seulement comment tu viens m/e chercher jusqu'au fond de l'enfer. . . . Tu chantes sans discontinuer. Les gardiennes des mortes attendries referment leurs gueules béantes. Tu obtiens d'elles de m/e ramener jusqu'à la lumière des vivantes à condition de ne pas te retourner sur m/oi pour m/e regarder. (*Lcl*, poem 5, lines 2–10, p. 11)

> (*I* shall recount only how you come to seek m/e in the very depths of hell. . . . You sing without pause. The female guardians of the dead mollified close their gaping mouths. You obtain their permission to bring m/e back as far as the light of the living on condition that you do not turn round to look at m/e.) (*TLB*, p. 19)

Wittig's lesbianized Orpheus figure, however, unlike the phallic one, triumphs over Eurydice's death through the force of lesbian love:

> Pas une fois tu ne te retournes, pas même quand j/e m/e mets à hurler de désespoir les larmes roulant sur m/es joues rongées à te supplier de m/e laisser dans m/a tombe à te décrire avec brutalité m/a décomposition les purulences de m/es yeux de mon nez de m/a vulve les caries de m/es dents les fermentations de m/es organes essentiels la couleur de m/es muscles blets. Tu m//interromps, tu chantes à voix stridente ta certitude de triompher de m/a mort, tu ne tiens pas compte de m/es sanglots, tu m// entraînes jusqu'à la surface de la terre où le soleil est visible. C'est là seule- ment là au débouché vers les arbres et la forêt que d'un bond tu m/e fais face et c'est vrai qu'en regardant tes yeux, j/e ressuscite à une vitesse prodigieuse. (*Lcl*, poem 5, lines 36–50, pp. 12–13)

> (Not once do you turn round, not even when *I* begin to howl with despair the tears trickling down m/y gnawed cheeks to beg you to leave m/e in m/ y tomb to brutally describe to you m/y decomposition the purulence of m/ y eyes m/y nose m/y vulva the caries of m/y teeth the fermentation of m/y vital organs the colour of m/y rotten-ripe muscles. You interrupt m/e, you sing with strident voice your certainty of triumph over m/y death, you do not heed m/y sobs, you drag m/e to the surface of the earth where the sun is visible. Only there at the exit towards the trees and the forest do you turn to face m/e with a bound and it is true that looking into your eyes *I* revive with prodigious speed.) (*TLB*, p. 20)

Wittig's translation of the myth into lesbian terms not only radically im- proves the outcome of the story for Eurydice—who, we may recall from the heterosexual version, dies on the day she is married—but also changes the meaning by recasting the roles from the traditional active male/passive female figures to active lesbian lovers.

Appropriating from the most central cultural contexts phallocentric, het- erosexual metaphor, Wittig has lesbianized it. In *Le corps lesbien* the default, or unmarked, phallic subject has been displaced by the lesbian subject. *Ecriture lesbienne* is a *coup d'écriture*.

NOTES

1. Monique Wittig, *Le Corps lesbien* (Paris: Minuit, 1973), hereafter cited as *Lcl*; the book appeared in the United States as *The Lesbian Body*, trans. David Le Vay (New York: Morrow, 1975), hereafter *TLB*; a paperback ed. was published by Avon- Bard in 1976. Also neglected is the book she coauthored with Sande Zeig, *Brouillon pour un dictionnaire des amantes* (Paris: Grasset & Fasquelle, 1976); a translation by the authors was entitled *Lesbian Peoples Material for a Dictionary* (New York: Avon, 1979).

2. See Jacques Derrida's usage of the term "phallogocentrisme" in "Le Facteur de la vérité," *Poétique* 21(1975):96–147. For a discussion of this term, see Namascar Shaktini, "The Problem of Gender and Subjectivity Posed by the New Subject Pronoun *j/e* in the Writing of Monique Wittig" (Ph.D. diss., University of California at Santa Cruz, 1981), 1–103.

3. The reader who doubts this might recall that legal contracts must be dated in reference to Christ's birth, the point of demarcation between B.C. and A.D. This point functions as absolute origin for our legal time system much as Greenwich, England, functions as absolute origin for our geographical system of longitude.

4. Claude Lévi-Strauss, *The Elementary Structures of Kinship* (Boston: Beacon, 1969), 479.

5. Ibid., 231.

6. Ibid., 496.

7. Monique Wittig, "The Straight Mind," *Feminist Issues* 1, no. 1(Summer 1980):103–11, esp. 110.

8. See Gayle Rubin's discussion of the term "sex-gender" in her excellent theoretical article, "The Traffic in Women," in *Toward an Anthropology of Women*, ed. Rayna [Rapp] Reiter (New York: Monthly Review Press, 1975), 157–210.

9. For a discussion of "markedness," see Herbert H. Clark and Eve V. Clark, *Psychology and Language* (New York: Harcourt Brace Jovanovich, 1977), 426–28, 455–56, 498–99, 513, 523–24, 533–36, 538–39.

10. Quotation of the Harvard Department of Linguistics in Casey Miller and Kate Swift, *Words and Women* (New York: Doubleday/Anchor, 1977), 69. For a linguist's analysis of the so-called generic masculine, see Julia Penelope Stanley, "Gender-Marking in American English: Usage and Reference," in *Sexism and Language*, ed. Alleen Pace Nilsen et al. (Urbana, Ill.: National Council of Teachers of English, 1977), 43–74. For a social psychological analysis of the so-called generic masculine, see Wendy Martyna, "Using and Understanding the Generic Masculine" (Ph.D. diss., Stanford University, 1978). For a comprehensive annotated bibliography of studies on gender and language and selected papers, see Barrie Thorne and Nancy Henley, eds., *Language and Sex: Difference and Dominance* (Rowley, Mass.: Newbury, 1975).

11. "The schoolbook world," according to a computerized study of 5 million words found in a thousand representative books used by children in grades three through nine throughout the United States, is "inhabited by twice as many boys as girls and seven times as many men as women" (Alma Graham, "The Making of a Nonsexist Dictionary," *Ms.* [December 1973], 12–14, 16; reprinted in Thorne and Henley, eds., 57–63).

12. Poem numbers refer to the first-line cross-reference index, E-2 and E-3, in the appendices of Shaktini "The Problem of Gender and Subjectivity" (n. 2 above). Page numbers are cross-referenced for the Minuit French edition and the Morrow (hardcover) and Avon (softcover) English editions (see n. 1 above). There is one error of publication in the English Morrow (hardcover) edition and two in the Avon (softcover) edition concerning the pagination and placement of poems. The Morrow edition prints poem 16 (pp. 32–33, p. 28 in the Minuit edition) as if it were two poems, when in reality the poem is just continued onto the next page in the original French edition. (A translator with full comprehension of the text would not have made this mistake.) This error is repeated in the Avon edition (pp. 30–32). In addition, the Avon edition on p. 77 of its text joins poems 49 and 50 of the original French. The third line from the top, "The bandage keeps m/y eyes closed. *J* am in darkness," is the beginning of poem 50 (p. 84 in the Minuit edition).

13. Esther Harding, *Woman's Mysteries* (San Francisco: Harper & Row, 1971),175.

14. Ibid., 190.

15. Ibid., 190.

16. Norman O. Brown, *Hermes the Thief* (New York: Vintage, 1969), 37. I use [*sic*] after certain quoted words to indicate their erroneous "generic" usage of the masculine gender.

17. Ibid., 60.

18. Richmond Lattimore, trans., *Hesiod* (Ann Arbor: University of Michigan Press, 1959), "Works and Days," lines 84–85, p. 27.

19. Ibid., lines 70–71, p. 27.

20. Ibid.

21. Ibid., "Theogony, line 887, p. 176.

22. Ibid., lines 892, 924, 929a, pp. 177, 179, 180.

23. Roland Barthes, *Sade/Fourier/Loyola* (Paris: Editions du Seuil, 1971), 76; the English edition is *Sade/Fourier/Loyola*, trans. Richard Miller (New York: Hill & Wang, 1976), 72.

24. *The Compact Edition of the Oxford English Dictionary* (1971), s.v. "aegis."

25. Lattimore, trans., 238.

26. Jeanette Foster, *Sex Variant Women in Literature* (1956; reprint ed., Baltimore, Md.: Diana Press, 1975), 25–26.

27. Lattimore, trans., "Theogony," line 929a, p. 180.

28. Ibid.

29. Norman O. Brown, *Love's Body* (New York: Vintage, 1966), 265.

30. Monique Wittig,"One Is Not Born a Woman," *Feminist Issues* 1(Winter 1981):47–54, esp. 53.

31. Cited in E. A. Wallis Budge, *The Gods of the Egyptians II* (1904; New York: Dover, 1969), 227.

32. Ibid., 214.

33. Marshall Clagett, *Greek Science in Antiquity* (New York: Collier, 1963), 97–98.

34. The translation of the first sentence is mine. Le Vay's translation is incomprehensible: "Is there no Archimedea to be encountered anywhere that the baths are so perfumed with *eau de Chypre*?"

35. For other examples of this type of displacement, see poems 83 and 110.

36. References to word frequency in this article are based on the "Concordance of *Le corps lesbien*" in the appendices of Shaktini, "The Problem of Subjectivity" (n. 2 above), Cl-E663. I wish to thank Sally Douglas for programming this concordance and for lending me her computer, as well as for reading and criticizing this article.

37. In the epigraph, for greater clarity, I have changed Le Vay's translation, which, however, I have cited unchanged above. He correctly renders "les . . . Cythères" as the pluralized "Cytheras," but incorrectly renders "les Lesbos" (also plural in French) as the singular "Lesbos." I have changed the English for "les Lesbos" to "the Lesbian Islands," using the more familiar word for "isle," "island."

38. Wittig has herself made a "journey" of self-definition. In 1970, she participated in the writing of the "Hymne" of the Mouvement de Liberation des Femmes, which begins: "Nous qui sommes sans passé, les femmes, / Nous qui n'avons pas d'histoire / Depuis la nuit des temps, les femmes, / Nous sommes le continent noir. / Levons nous femmes esclaves / Et brisons nos entraves, / Debout!" (We who are without past, women / We who have no history / Since the night of time, women / We are the black continent. / Let's rise up women slaves / And break our chains, / Arise!) [My personal recollection and translation]. Wittig, in composing this with other feminists, speaks as a woman-identified subject. At that time, Wittig and other French feminists said "nous les femmes" (we women) in an effort to avoid the contradictory problem from which Simone de Beauvoir had failed to extricate herself when she referred to "les femmes" (women) as "elles" (they) in her famous book, *Le deuxième sexe* (*The Second Sex*). By 1973, however, in *Le corps lesbien*, Wittig

identifies subjectivity as lesbian. And by 1979, in her paper "One Is Not Born a Woman," Wittig radically puts into question the idea of "woman."

39. See Jane Gallop's article on Lacan, "The Ladies' Man," *Diacritics* 6(Winter 1976):28–34, esp. 29.

40. My translation replaces Le Vay's erroneous: "*I* am at the Golgotha you have all abandoned."

41. In addition to systematically changing to generic feminine for human reference, Wittig's lesbian writing includes—in one instance at least—the generic feminine "elles" for grammatical reference to words of mixed gender, though in English, a language without grammatical gender, this is lost: "la terre les arbres les eaux les fleuves les rivières les mers les étoiles du ciel ne tremblent-elles pas" [the earth the trees the waters the rivers the torrents the seas the stars of the sky do they not tremble] (*Lcl*, poem 61, lines 9–11, p. 102; TBL, p. 93).

CONTRIBUTORS

Jeffner Allen is an Associate Professor of Philosophy at SUNY Binghamton. Her explorations of reflections and social change include publications in feminist philosophy and contemporary European philosophy. She is the editor of *Lesbian Philosophies and Cultures*.

Judith Butler is an Assistant Professor of Philosophy at George Washington University. She is the author of *Subjects of Desire: Hegelian Reflections in Twentieth-Century France* (Columbia University Press, 1987). She is currently working on a book of gender, identity, and desire to be published by Methuen in 1989.

Linda Kintz is an instructor in English at the University of Oregon. She has a Ph.D. in Comparative Literature and is affiliated with the Center for the Study of Women in Society at the University of Oregon. She has written on the construction of subjectivity in the plays of Adrienne Kennedy, Marsha Norman, and Rosario Castellanos.

Eléanor H. Kuykendall is Chair of the Philosophy Department and Co-ordinator of Linguistics at SUNY New Paltz. From 1979 to 1981 she was Director of SUNY's Paris Philosophy Program.

Julien S. Murphy is a Visiting Scholar at the Institute for Research on Gender and Women at Stanford University. She is on leave from the University of Southern Maine, where she is an Assistant Professor of Philosophy. Her publications include a continental approach to medicine, with works on the topics of abortion, AIDS, reproductive technology, and pregnancy that supplement her writings on Sartre and Schutz.

Jo-Ann Pilardi teaches philosophy and women's studies at Towson State University in Baltimore, Maryland. She has lived in Baltimore since 1969 and has been active there in various women's movement projects and organizations. Continuing her interest in Beauvoir and continental philosophy, she is currently writing a book on the notion of the self in Beauvoir's philosophical and autobiographical writings.

Namascar Shaktini, active in the early period of the Mouvement de Liberation des Femmes, was arrested on August 26, 1970, in the first feminist demonstration in France at the Arch of Triumph. She is currently an Assistant Professor of French at Florida Atlantic University.

Linda Singer is an Associate Professor of Philosophy and an Affiliate in Women's Studies at Miami University. She has published articles on Merleau-Ponty, Beauvoir, and a feminist critique of Nietzsche. Her recent work has been devoted to analyzing feminist literature on women and power, and to reconsidering the relationship between feminist theory and the philosophical canon.

Domna C. Stanton, Professor of French and Women's Studies at the University of Michigan, is the author of *The Aristocrat as Art: A Comparative Analysis of the 'Honnête Homme' and the Dandy*, and of articles on seventeenth-century French literature, women's writing, and contemporary critical theory. She has also edited *The Female Autograph*, a collection of essays on women's autobiographies, letters, and memoirs; and a bilingual anthology of French feminist poetry, part of the four-volume work, *The Defiant Muse*.

Iris Marion Young is an Associate Professor of Philosophy at Worcester Polytechnic Institute. A long time political activist, she has written articles on theory of justice, democratic theory, feminist social theory, and female body experience for numerous philosophy and women's studies publications.

INDEX